Political Economy of Islam

All Middle Eastern countries, with the exception of Israel and Lebanon, profess Islam as their state religion. Islam, whether simply in words or in fact, is woven into the fabric of these societies, affecting everything from the political system, to the social, financial and economic system. Islam is a rules-based system, with the collection of rules constituting its institutions in the quest to establish societies that are just. Allah commands mankind to behave in a fair and just manner to protect the rights of others, to be fair and just with people, to be just in business dealings, to honor agreements and contracts, to help and be fair with the needy and orphans, and to be just even in dealing with enemies. Allah Commands humans to establish just societies, rulers to be just and people to stand up for the oppressed against their oppressors. It is for these reasons that it said that justice is at the heart of Islam. In the same vein, the state (policies) must step in to restore justice whenever and wherever individuals fail to comply with divine rules; government intervention must enhance justice. This series brings together scholarship from around the world focusing on global implications of the intersections between Islam, government, and the economy in Islamic countries.

Asif Mohiuddin

Human Rights Law in Egypt and Malaysia: Freedom of Religion and Expression, Volume 1

palgrave
macmillan

Asif Mohiuddin
Sultan Idris Education University
Perak, Malaysia

ISSN 2945-6479 ISSN 2945-6487 (electronic)
Political Economy of Islam
ISBN 978-3-031-63858-9 ISBN 978-3-031-63859-6 (eBook)
https://doi.org/10.1007/978-3-031-63859-6

This Palgrave Macmillan imprint is published by the registered company Springer Nature Switzerland AG
The registered company address is: Gewerbestrasse 11, 6330 Cham, Switzerland

Foreword

The complex relationship between human rights, religion, and the state has always been a topic of great importance, attracting the interest of scholars, policymakers, and advocates worldwide. In a world that is becoming more interconnected, where the boundaries between culture, faith, and governance are constantly overlapping, there is a growing need for detailed and thorough analyses of these intricate interactions. Asif Mohiuddin's book, *Human Rights Law in Egypt and Malaysia: Freedom of Religion and Expression*, is a vital and relevant contribution to the topic, given the current circumstances. The meticulous craftsmanship and profound understanding of the challenges and opportunities that arise when the concepts of human rights intersect with the realities of varied socio-cultural situations distinguish Mohiuddin's work.

The book's emphasis on Egypt and Malaysia is particularly remarkable, as both countries serve as different and compelling examples that shed light on the intricacies of protecting fundamental rights in Muslim-majority cultures. By comparing these two countries, Mohiuddin urges readers to reflect on how historical legacies, constitutional frameworks, and societal norms influence the boundaries of religious freedom and expression. An outstanding attribute of this work is its thorough and all-encompassing approach to the subject matter. Mohiuddin adeptly traverses the complex terrain of international human rights legislation, utilising a diverse range of legal tools, philosophical traditions, and scholarly discussions. The author's thorough examination of the Universal

Declaration of Human Rights, the International Covenant on Civil and Political Rights, and other important texts offers a strong basis for comprehending the fundamental principles of religious freedom and freedom of speech.

However, Mohiuddin does not merely present a theoretical discourse on human rights. The book skillfully places these theoretical concepts within the specific contexts of Egyptian and Malaysian societies. The author thoroughly analyses constitutional provisions, legal precedents, and policy efforts to shed light on how these nations have dealt with the difficulties of incorporating religious plurality and promoting open dialogue. Mohiuddin examines Egypt's involvement with human rights, starting with the 1923 Constitution and continuing through the turbulent period following the Arab Spring. The author provides a detailed and sophisticated examination of how Islam functions as the official religion of the state, the treatment of religious minorities, and the boundaries of freedom of speech. This analysis presents a captivating depiction of a society that is working to find a harmonious equilibrium between religious beliefs, cultural identity, and democratic ideals.

Similarly, the book's analysis of Malaysia's legal and political environment uncovers a country struggling with the complexities of multiculturalism and the enduring impact of colonial governance. Mohiuddin's thorough examination of the nation's constitutional structure, which acknowledges Islam as the official religion and ensures religious freedom, offers an intriguing insight into the complexities of balancing political authority, religious beliefs, and individual liberties. Mohiuddin's work is notable for its seamless integration of legal analysis with a profound understanding of the social, cultural, and historical influences that impact people's lives. The author's astute analysis of the influence of religious identity on political engagement, the advocacy efforts of civil society in promoting change, and the obstacles encountered by marginalised communities provide a comprehensive and nuanced understanding of the practical aspects of human rights.

Furthermore, the book's comparative approach aims to emphasise the similarities and differences between Egypt and Malaysia, encouraging readers to reflect on how the experiences of these countries can contribute to broader conversations about the universal and contextspecific nature of human rights standards. Mohiuddin's analysis of the parallels and variations in the approaches to religious freedom and expression in the two countries is enlightening. To promote these fundamental rights,

Acknowledgements

Embarking on the journey of writing this book titled "Human Rights Law in Egypt and Malaysia: Freedom of Religion and Expression" (Vol I) has been a profound exploration into the complexities of safeguarding fundamental liberties in diverse cultural and legal landscapes. At the heart of this endeavour lies a deep-seated belief in the importance of understanding and advocating for human rights, particularly within the realms of freedom of religion and expression. These liberties are not only cornerstones of democratic societies but also intrinsic to the dignity and autonomy of every individual. Yet, their realisation is often fraught with challenges, shaped by a myriad of legal, cultural, and societal factors.

In this book, we have sought to delve into the complex dynamics of freedom of religion and expression, unraveling the multifaceted layers that underpin these fundamental rights. By focusing on the specific contexts of Egypt and Malaysia, we aim to provide a nuanced understanding of how these rights are both enshrined and practiced within diverse sociocultural landscapes. Throughout the writing process, we encountered both intellectual challenges and enriching discoveries, grappling with complex legal frameworks, navigating cultural sensitivities and uncovering the historical legacies that continue to shape contemporary realities. It is our hope that the insights gleaned from this journey will not only contribute to academic scholarship but also inform policy debates and advocacy efforts aimed at promoting and protecting human rights worldwide.

The generosity and support extended to me by numerous individuals and institutions have been instrumental in bringing this project to fruition. I am deeply appreciative of their unwavering commitment to the advancement of knowledge and understanding in the field of human rights. Their belief in the importance of fostering dialogue and critical inquiry has provided me with the encouragement and support needed to embark on this challenging endeavour. Their collective contributions have not only enriched the content of this book but have also contributed to the broader discourse surrounding the protection and promotion of human rights globally.

I extend my sincere gratitude to Prof Tahir Abbas, Prof Peter Matthews Wright, Prof Muhammad Hashim Kamali, Prof Jocelyn Cesari, Prof Daniel Brown, Prof Ronald Luckens Bull, Prof. Abd Hadi Bin Borham, Dr. Adis Duderija, Prof. Ramazan Bicer, Prof. Rajab Izadi, Dr. Rahman Dag and Prof. Mariusz Maslak for their insightful guidance, expertise, and unwavering support throughout the research and writing process. Their input has enriched the content of this book, providing profound insights into the complexities surrounding freedom of religion and expression in Egypt and Malaysia. Special thanks also go to Angie Merila, the commissioning editor at Palgrave, whose dedication and expertise have been instrumental in bringing this project to fruition. Her support and guidance have been invaluable throughout the publication process.

I am thankful to the Faculty of Human Sciences, Sultan Idris Education University, Malaysia, for their generous support, which laid the groundwork for this research endeavour. Their recognition of the importance of fostering understanding and dialogue in the field of human rights has played a crucial role in bringing this volume to fruition. I also wish to acknowledge and express my appreciation to Perpustakaan Tuanku Bainun, Universiti Pendidikan Sultan Idris and IAIS Malaysia for their assistance and resources, which were vital to the completion of this project. Their professionalism and dedication to advancing scholarship have been indispensable

Lastly, I dedicate this volume to all those who tirelessly advocate for human rights and justice in Egypt, Malaysia, and beyond. May this book contribute to a deeper comprehension of the challenges and opportunities in upholding freedom of religion and expression for all individuals.

Funding and Competing Interests This book has not received any external funding for its research, creation, or publication. The author confirms that there are no conflicting interests that might sway the content or conclusions presented in these pages. The author maintains no financial, personal, or professional associations that could compromise the impartiality or integrity of the information provided.

Praise for *Human Rights Law in Egypt and Malaysia: Freedom of Religion and Expression, Volume 1*

"Asif Mohiuddin's two-volume work titled Human Rights Law in Egypt and Malaysia with a focus on freedom of religion and expression is a tour de force coverage of significant legal, political, and ethical developments in two major Muslim societies. These volumes are veritable source books on these very modern topics. Egypt represents a major current in contemporary Arab thought, and Malaysia plays a pioneering role in Southeast Asia. Yet both nations contribute significantly to global Islamic thought. Therefore, these volumes are imperative for libraries, lawyers, experts, and anyone interested in human rights."

—Ebrahim Moosa, *Mirza Family Professor of Islamic Thought & Muslim Societies, Keough School of Global Affairs, University of Notre Dame, USA*

"Asif Mohiuddin's "Human Rights Law in Egypt and Malaysia: Freedom of Religion and Expression" offers a profound examination of the complex relationship between human rights, religion and governance in Egypt and Malaysia. Through detailed analysis of legal frameworks and societal dynamics, Mohiuddin navigates the complexities of safeguarding freedoms amidst diverse cultural contexts. His comparative approach sheds light on both shared challenges and distinct strategies, making this book essential reading for scholars, policymakers, and activists committed to advancing human rights globally."

—Ismail Fajrie Alatas, *Associate Professor, New York University, USA*

"This volume provides a deep and insightful examination of the complex challenges surrounding freedom of religion and expression within two Muslim-majority nations, Egypt and Malaysia. Mohiuddin delves into the multifaceted obstacles confronting diverse communities in their pursuit of these fundamental rights. He sheds light on the legal constraints and cultural barriers that impede the full realisation of religious freedom and expression in these contexts. Mohiuddin's work offers invaluable insights into the complexities of navigating religious freedom and expression within societies where the majority often wields significant influence over the direction of civilisational changes. He provides a nuanced understanding of the challenges faced by individuals and communities in practicing and expressing their beliefs openly. This volume serves as an indispensable resource for policymakers, scholars, activists and individuals alike who seek to understand and address the constraints on freedom of religion and expression. It inspires meaningful dialogue and action towards creating a more inclusive and rights-respecting society, where individuals of all backgrounds can freely exercise their religious beliefs and express themselves without fear of repression or discrimination."

—Mariusz Maslak, *Professor, Crackow University of Technology, Poland*

"This book offers a compelling analysis of human rights development in Egypt and Malaysia, focusing on the constitutional status of freedom of religion and expression. By examining the unique legal, cultural and historical contexts of these two nations, it reveals significant disparities in the practical implementation and enforcement of these universally acknowledged freedoms. The comparative analysis not only highlights the complexities of human rights laws within diverse cultural and legal landscapes but also provides invaluable insights for policymakers, NGOs and legal experts."

—Ramazan Bicer, *Professor, Sakarya University, Turkey*

"The profound and daring two-volume monograph by Asif Mohiuddin, dedicated to a cross-national analysis of challenges and advancements in safeguarding the fundamental freedoms, the constitutional status of religious freedom, and its role in achieving tolerance, diversity, and societal harmony from the Synergetic Historicism Perspective, cannot be overestimated by jurists, sociologists, and philosophers. This investigation, based on the Law of Self-organizing Ideals and the Method of Dual Oppositions, is one whose author has rethought human rights in

Muslim societies in respect of Islamic principles diversely interpreted and influenced by global geopolitical transformations—not as a concession to Western civilization with its social, cultural, and ethical values circulating predominantly through neo-colonialism and globalization, but as a path toward constructing self-organizing, globally developing Muslim societies. These societies are committed to upholding Islamic *sharī'ah* as a legislative foundation while reconsidering Islamism as part of the digital globalization process, resulting in Islamic movements intertwined with traditional religious authorities."

—Prof. Irina Gennadievna Mikailova, *Department of Philosophy of Science and Technologies, Saint-Petersburg Humanitarian Centre for Education and Development, Russia*

About This Book

This volume scrutinises the legal frameworks of both Egypt and Malaysia, conducting a comparative analysis of their methodologies for safeguarding and advancing fundamental freedoms. It explores the complex interplay between law, culture and politics, shedding light on the challenges and advancements in safeguarding freedom of religion and expression within these distinct contexts.In Egypt, the struggle for human rights has been deeply intertwined with its political evolution. The volume delves into Egypt's legal framework, examining the complexities surrounding religious freedoms amidst a predominantly Muslim society and a history of authoritarian rule. Meanwhile, Malaysia's unique blend of ethnic diversity and Islamic tradition presents its own set of legal and societal dynamics. The volume examines Malaysia's constitutional guarantees of freedom of religion and expression, navigating the complexities arising from its multicultural society and the tensions between secular governance and Islamic principles. Through a detailed examination of legislative changes, cultural dynamics and societal challenges, this volume contributes to encouraging further scholarly inquiry and policy discussions. It serves as a comprehensive resource for scholars, policymakers and activists seeking a deeper understanding of the legal frameworks and challenges surrounding freedom of religion and expression in Egypt and Malaysia.

Contents

About the Author

Asif Mohiuddin is a Lecturer in the Department of Moral Studies, Civics and Character Building at the Faculty of Human Sciences, Sultan Idris Education University, Malaysia. Previously, he worked as a Post-doctoral Academic Officer at the same institution. He is the author of the book "Navigating Religious Authority in Muslim Societies: Islamist Movements and the Challenge of Globalisation" (Palgrave Macmillan, 2023). From 2021 to 2022, he served as a Post-Doctoral Fellow in the Faculty of Theology at Sakarya University, Turkey. Before joining Sakarya University, he was a Lecturer in the Department of Higher Education, Government of Jammu and Kashmir, India. He earned his PhD from the University of Kashmir in 2018.His research interests include globalisation and Islam, intersection between politics and religion in the Middle East, human rights law, Islam and the West and Muslim minorities in multicultural societies (Europe and South Asia).

CHAPTER 1

Introduction: Divergent Trajectories of Human Rights in Egypt and Malaysia

1.1 Introduction

Human rights are commonly understood as a range of activities, conditions and freedoms considered intrinsic to each person, regardless of their position (Gutterman, 2023). These rights are universally acknowledged as complete and unable to be divided, surpassing distinctions of nationality, ethnicity and gender. They cover a wide array of civil, political, economic, social and cultural privileges, from basic rights like life, freedom and protection, to freedoms such as the right to express oneself, fairness in legal matters and access to education and employment, among other entitlements. Despite the apparent acceptance of human rights by many nations in principle, the practical execution and enforcement of these rights can significantly differ. In their specific constitutional setups, Egypt and Malaysia, two nations with unique historical, cultural and political backgrounds, showcase varying viewpoints concerning human rights. Egypt's constitution recognises several human rights, including the rights to life, personal freedom and privacy. The 2014 constitution in Egypt specifically underscores the protection of human rights in its initial declaration, emphasising principles such as equality, social equity and the primacy of the law. Despite this, practical obstacles have emerged, leading to concerns from international human rights organisations about restrictions on freedom of expression, assembly and association, as well

A. Mohiuddin, *Human Rights Law in Egypt and Malaysia: Freedom of Religion and Expression, Volume 1*, Political Economy of Islam, https://doi.org/10.1007/978-3-031-63859-6_1

as a reduction in the independence of the judiciary (Abdel-Latif, 2014). Incidents of mistreatment against dissidents in the political sphere and disadvantaged communities have also been documented, casting doubt on the government's dedication to preserving human rights.

In contrast, Malaysia's constitution ensures fundamental freedoms for its citizens, including the right to life, freedom of expression and equal treatment under the law. The Federal Constitution of Malaysia also acknowledges the rights of minority groups and native populations. However, persistent concerns have arisen regarding the enforcement of these rights, particularly concerning freedom of speech, the rights of religious minorities and the welfare of refugees and migrant laborers (Laws of Malaysia, 2009). Furthermore, specific legal measures, such as the Sedition Act, have faced criticism for restricting freedom of expression, prompting further discussions about the extent to which human rights are safeguarded and valued in the nation.

Selecting Egypt and Malaysia as focal points for a book on the human rights discourse and legislation reflects a deliberate and strategic choice based on the distinctive features of these two countries. The legal systems in both nations display a distinctive amalgamation of influences, encompassing elements from Islamic law (*sharīʿah*) and civil law traditions. An exhaustive exploration into how these legal frameworks interact with and influence principles of human rights is imperative for a nuanced comprehension. Moreover, delving into the cultural and historical milieus of Egypt and Malaysia assumes paramount importance. Both nations flaunt intricate histories that have played pivotal roles in shaping their perspectives on human rights. Scrutinising the ways in which historical events and cultural dynamics have molded the ongoing discourse on human rights in these countries furnishes a holistic backdrop for the research. The political landscapes of Egypt and Malaysia have undergone metamorphoses over the years, necessitating an analysis of the repercussions of political developments on human rights policies and practices. A comprehensive understanding of the human rights challenges confronting each country, spanning issues such as freedom of expression, religious freedom, minority rights, and women's rights, enriches the depth of the study.

Given the active involvement of Egypt and Malaysia in international organisations and treaties pertaining to human rights, an exploration of their participation and adherence to global standards introduces a critical international facet to the research. Engaging in a comparative analysis between these two nations facilitates a more profound comprehension of how unique cultural, legal and political contexts shape the interpretation and implementation of human rights. The research also harbors the potential to make substantial contributions to policy development. By pinpointing exemplary practices and areas in need of improvement, the study can furnish invaluable insights for policymakers, non-governmental organisations (NGOs) and advocates of human rights. Furthermore, the challenges faced by Egypt and Malaysia in the sphere of human rights carry implications that extend beyond their borders. This research contributes to the worldwide conversation on human rights, supplying insights that can inform international strategies aimed at promoting and safeguarding human rights across diverse contexts.

Throughout the world, countries grapple with the complexities of translating universal principles of human rights into effective legal structures that can cater to the unique challenges and ambitions of their societies. Countries like Egypt and Malaysia serve as interesting cases in point, each distinguished by a rich historical legacy, a diverse cultural fabric and a distinctive legal framework that shapes the form of their respective human rights laws. The importance of this examination lies in its exploration of the intricate connections between human rights laws and the socio-cultural dynamics within Egypt and Malaysia. While both nations have made notable progress in promoting human rights, their paths have been marked by specific hurdles, including political shifts, societal movements, the intricacies of legal diversity, and the coexistence of diverse religious and cultural customs. Through a comparative scrutiny of these two nations, this book endeavors to fill gaps in current scholarship, offering a comprehensive grasp of the intricacies involved in the formulation, execution and enforcement of human rights regulations within diverse cultural and legal milieus.

Through an exploration of the historical development, significant achievements and presentday obstacles, this research endeavors to uncover the complexities of human rights laws in Egypt and Malaysia, providing insights into the accomplishments, constraints, and potential pathways for advancement. This research seeks to add to the ongoing discussion on the universal relevance of human rights standards, the complexities associated with cultural particularities and the importance of cultivating a fairer and more inclusive society. By highlighting the insights drawn from the examples of Egypt and Malaysia, this book strives to influence discussions on policy, encourage additional scholarly inquiry, and foster a deeper comprehension of the complex interplay between human rights laws, cultural changes, and societal shifts in today's world.

1.2 Shaping Egypt's Legal Landscape: Political Shifts and Transformations

In the early 1880s, Egypt was officially under the governance of the Ottoman Empire and had a population of fewer than 7 million individuals. However, by the end of the twentieth century, it had evolved into a modern independent country with a population of 70 million, which has now grown to 100 million. Over this period, it experienced four significant phases of political instability. The first event was the British takeover in 1882, eventually resulting in its incorporation as a protectorate of the British Empire in 1914. The second notable event was the 1919 Revolution, a nationwide protest demanding an end to the occupation and the recognition of national independence, which subsequently reshaped Egypt's relationship with Britain and led to a form of autonomy. The third crucial event was the July 1952 Revolution, a military coup that removed an unpopular monarchy and an ineffective political ruling class in favor of a republican government with an ambitious agenda (Moustafa, 2021, p. 264).

Eventually, the January Revolution of 2011 led to the removal of a progressively weakened and discredited government, propelling the nation into yet another era of political uncertainty. Each of these tumultuous events was preceded by periods of political strife, during which the shortcomings of the existing regime became apparent and the popular desires for freedom and reforms in both politics and economics gained momentum. Following these transformations, the political struggle gave way to the emergence of authoritarian governance, as the new leadership aimed to tackle issues of political credibility, economic prosperity and national identity. In navigating this progression from an Ottoman territory to an independent nation, Egyptian authorities and society have engaged in a complex negotiation, sometimes productive and at other times detrimental, to establish not just an efficient political and economic structure but also to position the country within a historical context that spans from the time of the Pharaohs to the legacies of Ottoman and British colonialism, encompassing the diverse cultural dimensions of Arab, Christian and Muslim influences (Moustafa, 2021, p. 265).

The beginning of the modern era of Egyptian state formation can be traced back to the leadership of Muhammad Ali (r. 1805–1848), who initially served as an Ottoman governor before securing his position as a hereditary ruler in the first half of the nineteenth century. By the latter part of the nineteenth century, Egypt had established itself as a mostly autonomous region, even though it was still officially under the dominion of the Ottoman Empire, embarking on its unique trajectory of progress. In the 1870s, this local initiative faced a critical political and economic dilemma that led to the emergence of the Urabi movement, aiming to resist the growing external influence in the nation and the autocratic rule of the Khedive. This conflict resulted in the invasion of British troops in 1882, which, following the defeat of local forces, reinstated the compromised Khedive Tawfiq and initiated the initial phase of British occupation referred to as the veiled protectorate. British governance in Egypt relied on a relatively limited military presence and an administrative body comprising members of the conventional political elite, predominantly consisting of landowning families, who were co-opted by British authorities and supported by British advisors overseen by the British representative and prominent imperialist, Lord Cromer, for a substantial duration. A new constitution introduced in 1883 would serve as the foundational framework for the subsequent four decades of governance (Arjomand, 2012, p. 205).

Commencing with the reign of Muhammad Ali (1805–1848), a series of fresh legal regulations and contemporary legal establishments were swiftly implemented to oversee trade and expand the influence of the government. The initial consolidated legal system, known as *al-Muntakhabat*, was declared in 1829, while the establishment of the Mixed Courts in 1876 was designed to resolve commercial disputes involving foreign entities, and the National Courts were established in 1883. The surge in commercial operations in the late 19th and early twentieth centuries opened up profitable prospects for a new class of legal professionals. Law also emerged as a prominent career choice among the political elite, with 14 out of the 19 prime ministers between 1919 and 1952 having received formal legal training, and almost all cabinets during this period being dominated by lawyers. The strong link between notable legal practitioners and the nationalist movement further elevated the status of the legal profession. Throughout the interwar era, the legal community emerged as a significant political entity in its own right. The establishment of the Lawyers' Syndicate (*Niqabat al Muhamin*) in

1912 became a focal point for national discussions, as did its professional publication, *al-Muhamah*. The formation of the Judges Association (*Nadi al-Quda*, literally "Judges Club") in 1939 also played pivotal roles in advocating for the rule of law, judicial autonomy and political transformation (Rutherford, 2013, p. 35).

Taking inspiration from the French legal system, the majority of the Egyptian judiciary comprises two distinct hierarchies: one specialising in civil and criminal law and the other focusing on administrative law. Additional judicial entities encompass the SCC and extraordinary courts. At the apex of the regular court system, the Court of Cassation (*Mahkamat al-Naqd*) serves as the ultimate appellate court for all matters related to civil and commercial law, personal status law and criminal law. Judges within the regular judiciary are appointed through a decree issued by the President of the Republic, subject to the endorsement of the Supreme Judiciary Council. The Supreme Judiciary Council comprises the President of the Court of Cassation, the President of the Cairo Court of Appeal, the Attorney General and the two most senior presidents of the Courts of Appeal. While the ordinary judiciary is generally perceived as independent of direct influence from the executive branch of the government, there are several instances indicating that this relative autonomy has diminished over time. At the peak of the administrative court system, the Supreme Administrative Court (*al-Mahkama al-Idariyya al-'Uliya*) operates as the ultimate appellate court for all issues pertaining to administrative law. Serving as a significant platform, the administrative courts enable individuals to contest executive actions or any department within the state bureaucracy. Citizens have the right to challenge state agencies on the basis of violations of administrative laws or in cases where administrative laws themselves contradict the Constitution. The administrative courts maintain a considerable degree of independence concerning appointments, advancements, and other internal functions. While the administrative courts frequently rule against the executive authority, the frequency of these decisions is closely linked to the evolving political landscapes.

After taking control in 1952, Gamal Abdel Nasser swiftly veered away from the existing legal and political framework. The 1923 Constitution, which allowed for a multiparty system and fundamental rights, was invalidated through an executive decree on December 10, 1952. Another decree dissolved all political parties, paving the way for a single-party ruling structure. Nasser significantly undermined Egyptian legal institutions as well. Numerous senior judges were removed from their positions and courts were deprived of their authority to invalidate administrative actions. The government established a series of extraordinary courts, including the Court of the Revolution (*Mahkamat al-Thawra*) in 1953 and The People's Courts (*Mahakim al-Sha'b*) in 1954. These courts possessed extensive mandates, limited procedural guidelines, no appeal process and were staffed by loyalists of the regime, often from the military. Additionally, court cases were frequently transferred from civil courts to both military and state security courts, which offered minimal procedural safeguards (Meital, 2017). The most significant blow to Egyptian judicial institutions during the Nasser era occurred during the 1969 'massacre of the judiciary.' Following a military defeat in the 1967 war and growing calls for judicial reform from the Judges Association and the Lawyers' Syndicate, Nasser dismissed over 200 judicial officials, including the board of the Judges Association and several judges from the Court of Cassation. To prevent the reemergence of resistance to executive power, Nasser established the Supreme Council of Judicial Organisations, granting the regime greater control over judicial appointments, promotions, and disciplinary actions (Brown, 1997).

An effort was made by Anwar Sadat (1970–1981) to create distance from the excessive methods employed during the Nasser era by reintroducing a significant level of institutional autonomy to the judiciary and introducing a new constitution in 1971(Moustafa, 2007). While not entirely progressive, the 1971 Constitution included several provisions that contributed to the reinforcement of the rule of law. Subsequently, in 1972, Sadat also restored the authority and independence of the administrative courts, and further consolidated their position in 1984 by reinstating substantial control over appointments, promotions, and internal disciplinary measures, which had been revoked by the presidential decree in 1959. Likewise, Mubarak (1981–2011) positioned himself as an advocate for political reform. Despite witnessing some advancements in specific aspects of political liberalization during the 1980s, the government reversed these tentative strides during the 1990s (Kienle, 2000). The government enhanced its capacity to employ preventive detention and to subject civilians to trials in military courts under the implementation of Law 97/1992. Professional associations faced increasing regulation and the potential of being taken over by the state as per the provisions of Law 100/1993. Law 26/1994 mandated the selection, rather than the election, of the village umda (mayor) and *shaykh al-balad* (deputy mayor). Democratic institutions within universities were compromised by the enforcement of Law 142/1994. Further limitations were imposed on the press through the enactment of Law 93/1995. Moreover, the emergency law was periodically prolonged throughout the decade. During this entire period, the judiciary demonstrated its efficacy as the most suitable formal avenue for challenging government restrictions.

In the 1980s, there was a notable increase in the number of non-governmental organisations (NGOs) dedicated to rights advocacy in Egypt. This trend began with the formation of the Egyptian Organisation for Human Rights (EOHR) in 1985. Alongside the EOHR, the Legal Research and Resource Center and the Cairo Institute for Human Rights Studies focused on raising awareness about human rights violations in Egypt, both domestically and internationally, through activities such as research and documentation, as well as hosting conferences and publishing materials. The 1990s marked the emergence of a fresh wave of rights organisations that moved beyond the mere documentation of rights abuses to challenging the government in the legal sphere. Among these groups, the Center for Human Rights Legal Aid (CHRLA), established by the proactive human rights activist Hisham Mubarak in 1994, stood out as the most assertive in engaging in public interest litigation (Shash, 2017). Experiencing rapid growth, the Center for Human Rights Legal Aid (CHRLA) swiftly emerged as the most dynamic human rights organisation, initiating 500 cases during its first operational year, 1323 cases in 1996, and 1616 by 1997. CHRLA's primary objective was to offer free legal representation to individuals who had encountered human rights violations perpetrated by the government. Additionally, CHRLA documented instances of human rights abuses and utilised the cases it supported to bring attention to the human rights situation. Similar to other human rights groups in Egypt, CHRLA relied heavily on foreign funding, which remained abundant throughout the mid-1990s. Expanding its reach, CHRLA established two regional offices in Alexandria and Aswan.

In 1996, the Land Center for Human Rights became part of the network of legal aid organisations, focusing its efforts on delivering free legal assistance to peasants. As the land reform law 96/1992 reached full implementation in October 1997, hundreds of thousands of peasants faced the possibility of eviction in the late 1990s, leading to an influx of thousands of lawsuits between landlords and tenants in the courts.

From 1996 to 2000, the Land Center for Human Rights represented peasants in over 4000 cases and offered legal guidance to numerous others. Similarly, the Human Rights Center for the Assistance of Prisoners (HRCAP) furnished legal aid to prisoners and the families of detained individuals, investigating claims of torture, monitoring prison conditions, and combating the issue of repeated detention and torture through legal proceedings. During its initial five years of functioning, HRCAP initiated over 200 court cases annually and offered complimentary assistance, both legal and otherwise, to approximately 7000–8000 victims each year. Concurrently, opposition parties also began to provide pro bono legal aid, with the Wafd Party's Committee for Legal Aid delivering free legal representation in excess of 400 cases each year from 1997 onward. Likewise, the Lawyers' Syndicate actively engaged in supplying legal aid, significantly enlarging its legal aid division until its operations were halted by the regime in 1996 (Moustafa, 2021, p. 268).

By the end of the 1990s, the Egyptian government had become increasingly uneasy regarding the active role of the judiciary in general and the Supreme Constitutional Court (SCC) in particular. Various opposition factions, human rights organisations and political advocates had identified a governmental body capable of restraining executive authority, even if in small increments and with caution. As the regime's impatience grew due to opposition progress and the SCC's expanding support base, the authorities took steps to thwart their activities. Across a span of five years, the government utilised a mix of legal and extrajudicial tactics to undermine the judicial support system and ultimately erode the SCC's previously enjoyed autonomy of two decades. Modifications were made to the appointment procedure, and the SCC was filled with new judges from external sources. Despite internal and external challenges to the political reversal, activists were unsuccessful in halting the regime's retractions, largely due to the substantial power imbalances favoring the state over social movements.

The robust reaction of the Egyptian government towards both the Supreme Constitutional Court (SCC) and the human rights movement implies that constitutional litigation progressively emerged as a genuine threat to the mechanisms employed by the regime to uphold its authority. The SCC served as a viable new pathway for dissenters to contest the state through one of its established institutions. Victories in challenging the government's restrictive NGO legislation and securing complete judicial oversight of elections highlighted how human rights organisations and opposing political groups had grown more proficient in utilising legal avenues to confront the government and safeguard their concerns. Additionally, the SCC's determination to confront the government with groundbreaking verdicts on NGOs and comprehensive judicial monitoring of elections underscored the commitment of SCC judges to a political reform agenda. Meanwhile, opposition efforts extended beyond formal legal routes, evidenced by successful labor movements between 2004 and 2010 (Moustafa, 2021, p. 271).

From January 25, 2011, onwards, masses of Egyptians took to the streets en masse to demand their rights. The momentum of popular mobilisation persisted for several months even after Mubarak's removal, exerting sustained pressure on all fronts of political authority: former NDP members and regime affiliates encountered legal prosecution, labor unions and professional associations fought against the influence of the state, while students and faculty et al.-Azhar University advocated for institutional autonomy and elections for the sheikh al-Azhar position. Concurrently, internal uprisings against Mubarak-appointed figures within the state media and press also transpired. A distinctive feature of these struggles and others was the central role of law as the primary subject of contention. Among the wave of protest movements that swept the region from 2011, the Egyptian movement notably revolved around a contest over the Constitution, oppressive legislation, and the overall state of the rule of law (Moustafa, 2021, p. 272). This heightened focus on legal matters and institutions stemmed from the crucial role that law had historically played in upholding authoritarian control in Mubarak's Egypt. Consequently, opposition activists recognized that meaningful political transformation could only materialse through legal reform. Moreover, as vestiges of the NDP maneuvered their way back into power, law once more emerged as a critical tool through which the Sisi regime sought to solidify its political dominance.

1.3 The Quest for Religious Freedom in Egypt's Sociopolitical History

Before the establishment of the Egyptian nation-state, the concept of religious freedom held little significance in Egypt, unlike other forms of freedom, such as freedom of the press. The notion of religious rights had been part of Protestant missionary activities in the region since the nineteenth century. However, it might not have resonated with local communities, who typically regarded the kind of sectarian conflicts and violence that led to the legal protection of religious freedom as foreign. As early as 1861, representatives of the American United Presbyterian Church, working as missionaries, advocated for religious liberty after one of their members, Faris al-Hakim, a Syrian convert and lawyer, was assaulted in an Islamic court in Assiut and subsequently imprisoned. Al-Hakim's case involved his defence of a Coptic woman whom he had converted to Protestantism. He attempted to arrange her marriage to a Christian man five years after she had converted to Islam, married a Muslim, and given birth to a daughter (Culang, 2018, p. 447).

The *qadi* accused him of misleading her and drawing her away from her faith. In response, al-Hakim denounced Islam as an 'infidelity,' prompting further accusations of 'assailing the Mohammeden religion' and 'instigating doubt among the general public.' Al-Hakim faced physical aggression in the courtroom before being imprisoned, and it was only through the intervention of the U.S. government and Abraham Lincoln himself that he was released. Lincoln echoed the missionaries' plea for religious liberty. However, throughout this incident, the local community never articulated their grievances using the language of religious rights. Furthermore, they did not do so in subsequent controversies involving Muslims who converted to Christianity before the 1920s, including two notable incidents in 1908 and 1911. Beyond these particular cases, the notion of religious freedom was similarly absent from the political and intellectual spheres. When a group of Egyptian Coptic elites arranged a Coptic Congress in 1911 to present demands to the colonial state on behalf of the Coptic community, including several requests related to religious practices, they framed their claims in terms of equality with Muslims rather than religious freedom.

Likewise, in his pre-World War I works on liberty, the prominent figure of liberalism in Egypt, Ahmad Lutfi al-Sayyid, made little mention of this idea. In a 1912 article exploring freedom, he focused on political and personal freedom but omitted any discussion of religious freedom. This topic was also absent from his other writings during that period. The notion of religious freedom entered the realm of Egyptian public life following the global expansion of the nation-state system after World War I, when it became an integral component of state laws. As part of the broader concept of safeguarding religious minorities, religious freedom became a tool used by the newly formed League of Nations, predominantly influenced by the 'Great Powers,' to regulate certain states and national societies through legal means. Many emerging nations perceived religious freedom as a hindrance to complete sovereignty, making it an appealing domain for attempting to extend their influence through the control of religion. The system of rights for minorities equally attracted the attention of missionaries. Fearing that the prospect of political independence might jeopardize their activities, missionaries eagerly rallied behind the cause of religious liberties. The ideals of the League of Nations and missionary organizations aligned in the pursuit of religious freedom. With this context in mind, during the formulation of Egypt's inaugural Constitution in the early 1920s, the pivotal question was not whether to address religious freedom but rather how to approach it. The responses were significantly influenced by Egypt's interactions with Protestant missionaries. It was precisely during the Constitution drafting process, initiated in 1923, that religious freedom became a subject of intense debate (Culang, 2018, p. 449).

The contemporary phase of Egyptian political history can be traced back to 1952, when Col. Gamal Abdel Nasser toppled the British-appointed King in Egypt. The subsequent year saw Egypt being officially declared a republic, accompanied by the implementation of the existing Constitution. Nasser's policies were characterised by their severity and rigidity, allowing no space for political or social dissent to arise. Anwar Sadat's presidency following Nasser's demise brought about significant changes in the social and economic landscape. The government relaxed its control over the economy, promoting both private and foreign investments. There was a relaxation of the political process, reinstating fair legal procedures and prohibiting the use of torture. In the wake of Sadat's assassination in 1981, the incumbent President Mubarak assumed power and enforced a State of Emergency. The Emergency Law places restrictions on many of the reforms initially proposed by Sadat, governing the nation to preempt any uprisings or disturbances. Severe limitations on political opposition persist, including that of the Muslim Brotherhood, which is not officially acknowledged as a political party due to Egyptian laws prohibiting the formation of political groups based on religion. Members of the Muslim Brotherhood participate in elections as independents. Elections are widely suspected to be manipulated, and leaders of opposition groups are frequently detained without substantial cause (Hamzawy & Brown, 2010).

According to Article 2 of the Egyptian Constitution, Islam is designated as the official religion of Egypt, with *sharīʿah*, the Islamic legal system, recognised as the primary basis for legislation. The Constitution contains provisions that broadly ensure freedom of belief and the observance of religious practices, although certain elements of these practices are constrained in practice (Sayed, 2020). For example, Article 40 establishes that all citizens are equal under the law, with equal public rights and responsibilities without any form of discrimination. Discrimination based on race, ethnicity, language, religion, or creed is strictly prohibited. Moreover, Article 46 affirms the state's commitment to safeguarding the freedom of belief and the practice of religious customs. However, the government has chosen to interpret these provisions narrowly, limiting their application to members of the Islamic, Christian and Jewish communities exclusively. The Emergency Law, enacted in 1981, imposes restrictions on various human rights, including religious freedom, freedom of expression, assembly and association.

Critics contend that the law is frequently utilised to stifle political competition and infringe upon human rights without repercussions. The law is primarily invoked in the apprehension of members of the Muslim Brotherhood. According to Article 98(f) of the Penal Code, citizens are prohibited from ridiculing or provoking sectarian conflicts related to divine religions. Breaches of this regulation can result in fines or even imprisonment. The implementation of family law, encompassing aspects such as marriage, divorce, alimony, child custody and burial, is dependent on an individual's religious association. However, the courts overseeing these matters only acknowledge Islam, Christianity and Judaism. *Sharīʿah* law governs Muslim citizens, applying conventional Islamic principles to the rights of both men and women (Office of International Religious Freedom, 2022).

Under this structure, women are significantly restricted in their decision-making abilities and their right to seek divorce. Egypt solely acknowledges marriages conducted within the country, making interfaith marriages nearly impractical. Any interfaith union that does occur might prompt the state to assume custody of any children resulting from the marriage and result in the woman's arrest on charges of apostasy. Law 15 of 1927 was established to recognise religious groups within Egypt. The group is required to submit an application to the Religious Affairs Department of the Ministry of Interior (MOI), which assesses whether the group poses a threat to national unity or disrupts social harmony. The registration application is then forwarded to prominent religious figures for consultation, and if approved, the President makes the final decision. Currently, no groups are awaiting state approval.

The focus on religious freedom in Egypt has traditionally been centered on the challenges faced by minorities, particularly Christians. However, the reality reveals that Muslims have been the primary victims of the absence of religious freedom. While the persecution of religious minorities is more overt and severe, the restrictions placed on Muslims' ability to think independently about religion and to freely believe, practice and worship in accordance with their conscience have resulted not only in oppression but also in a controlled religious environment that has fostered the growth of Islamists. The fundamental Egyptian concept of religious freedom is narrow, often defined merely as the freedom to worship, albeit under significant constraints. There is hardly any understanding of religious freedom as the right of all faiths to bring values derived from their beliefs to the public sphere. This is partly due to priorities, as a religious individual who is not allowed to build a place of worship is unlikely to be concerned with issues such as adoption, which is accepted in Christianity but rejected in Islam, and consequently illegal (Tadros, 2010).

The issue is compounded by the entwining of religion with social customs. Since the state typically upholds these social norms and enforces conformity, the religious establishment has been content with this arrangement. It is only with the increasing radicalisation of the Muslim religious establishment since the 1970s that a conflict with the state has emerged. A similar dynamic has persisted, albeit in a different form, with the Coptic Orthodox Church, which has established a pattern of dependence on Egypt's Muslim rulers. The issue of religious freedom in Egypt, or the lack thereof, revolves around the interplay of four key forces: the regime, the religious establishment, Islamists and society at large. Each of these entities has its own perspective, but it is the interaction among these forces that presents the challenge for religious freedom in Egypt.

1.4 The Scope of Freedom of Expression in Egypt's Constitutional Law

The Egyptian Constitution emphasises freedom of speech and expression as a fundamental aspect of its liberties. Similar to the approach to free speech in the United States of America, the Egyptian Constitution acknowledges the legal entitlement to freedom of expression. The Egyptian *Sharīʿah* Courts were established in the late nineteenth century as a prerequisite for addressing personal-status matters within Islamic society. One could argue that the incorporation of personal status represented the initial move toward broadening the scope of the Constitution to encompass additional Islamic concerns. In the early twentieth century, numerous Arab nations sought to integrate Islamic legal norms into their constitutions in response to the conclusion of the colonial era and to assert their Islamic identity (Brown & Sherif, 2004, p. 56).

As per some analysts, the call for State law to align with Islamic law was particularly evident in Egypt due to the increasing influence of Islamist groups. This demand for the establishment of Egyptian constitutionalism in line with modernity prompted the 1923 Constitution to affirm that the protection of certain human rights must encompass the freedom of opinion. Article 14 of the Constitution stated that 'freedom of opinion is guaranteed and everyone has the right to express verbally, in writing, photography, or any other way within the limitation of law'. According to one commentator, this Constitution represented 'an important step in the constitutional and political development of Egypt and also transferred Egypt from dependency to a legally independent state'. Nonetheless, the constitutional rights were significantly curtailed under British dominance of power and, more notably, the extensive powers of the King (Ahmed, 2008).

The most substantial shift occurred in 1952 when the free officer's revolution "put an end to the era of British influence and the monarchical system and initiated the era of the Egyptian republic" (The Constitution of the Arab Republic of Egypt, 1971). Consequently, the 1923 Constitution was replaced by a new one. Despite the extensive changes during Gamal Abd alNasir's regime, which lasted for nearly seventeen years, no significant transformations were made, particularly concerning human rights and the implementation of Islamic law. The most notable constitutional reform affecting the Islamic judiciary took place with the 1971 Constitution. Article 2 stipulated that 'Islam is the religion of the state, Arabic is its official language, and the principles of Islamic Sharia are a primary source of legislation' identity (Brown & Sherif, 2004, p. 57). The inclusion of *sharīʿah* in the Constitution was regarded as 'a historic first-time consecration of Islam's religious law in an Egyptian constitution'. This Article played a vital role in bridging the gap between Islamic *sharīʿah* and legislation. Additionally, some jurists view this Article as a 'revival of Islamic norms that have always been inherent in the religious tradition and society'identity (Brown & Sherif, 2004, p. 58).

Concerning freedoms, the Constitution affirmed that human rights must encompass freedom of expression. Article 47 explicitly stated, '[f]reedom of opinion is guaranteed. Every individual has the right to express his opinion and to publicize it verbally or in writing or by photography or by other means within the limit of the law…' (The Constitution of the Arab Republic of Egypt, 1971). Therefore, the crucial matter does not revolve around its presence but rather the exercise of this right. The exceptions delineated in Article 47 determine the scope and context of the exercise of freedom of expression. In response to recent developments and to ensure the effective protection and application of human rights, including freedom of expression guaranteed by the Constitution, the Egyptian Government established the Supreme Constitutional Court in 1979, bestowing it with extensive powers. The Supreme Constitutional Court (SCC) has played a significant role in establishing *sharīʿah* principles in two ways. First, the Court nullified all legislations that contradicted *sharīʿah*. Second, the Court has adopted an approach whereby the Egyptian Courts differentiate between laws that are in line with *sharīʿah* and those that are not (Lombardi & Brown, 2005, p. 380).

In Egypt, the concept of the fundamental right to freedom of speech and expression is somewhat unclear. This principle has been consistently upheld in all Egyptian Constitutions, dating back to the 1923 Constitution, and is reiterated in Article 65 of the 2014 Constitution, which affirms that '[a]ll individuals have the right to express their opinion through speech, writing, imagery, or any other means of expression and publication' (The constitution of Egypt, 2014). Despite the explicit assurance of freedom of speech and expression, the Constitution provides detailed clarification regarding the various forms of this right. The article is comprehensive enough to encompass a wide range of communication methods. In case 44, the Supreme Constitutional Court (SCC) provides an explanation that freedom of expression encompasses multiple rights; everyone has the freedom to articulate, write, or portray what they desire, as long as they do not violate the law or the rights of others (Alsubaie, 2018).

Speech and expression can manifest in various conventional and unconventional manners. Conventional communication involves forms such as writing, spoken language, or artistic representation. In contrast, unconventional expression permits individuals to convey their ideas through any medium. This encompasses familiar forms like demonstrations, where individuals can articulate their viewpoints by means such as holding up signs or burning flags, among other methods. Case 160 highlighted the significance of the SCC's emphasis on the right to conduct demonstrations as a form of freedom of expression. Notably, remaining silent or showing no emotion is also recognized as a form of speech protected under Egypt's Constitution. This relates closely to the notion of strikes. A strike constitutes a type of non-verbal communication and should be treated similarly to verbal speech. Article 15 of the Constitution explicitly safeguards this right, affirming that '[s]triking peacefully is a right which is organized by law'. A group of workers can convey their message by ceasing work and maintaining silence in front of a government department to demonstrate their discontent with work policies or other matters (Kameel, 2016).

The press's freedom falls under the umbrella of freedom of speech and expression. It does not matter what title is used to describe it—'freedom of speech,' 'freedom of expression,' or 'freedom of the press'—they all refer to the same thing—namely, the ability to express one's opinions. It is argued that only when artistic nonverbal expression does not threaten public morality, national security, or other people's rights can it be recognised as a form of speech worthy of constitutional protection. There could be a variety of deeds and nonverbal cues that may effectively influence public perception (Alsubaie, 2018). Freedom of expression is greatly aided by the press and publishers, who frequently publish or show films, artwork and music. Therefore, the statements made by the SCC concerning freedom of speech are also applicable to freedom of the press and the reverse holds true as well. This implies that the forms of freedom of expression under the Egyptian Constitution have varied. The analysis of these different forms of expression generally did not give rise to debates regarding their classification as speech or their inclusion under the purview of free speech laws. The aforementioned discussion further revealed that while certain free speech laws, particularly in the Arab world like the Egyptian Constitution, explicitly encompassed different types of speech without imposing specific classifications, the Egyptian Courts tend to approach the issue of communicative conduct cases at a broader, more general level, rather than addressing the specifics of each individual case.

1.5 Malaysia's Legal Trajectory: Islam, Culture and Historical Context

Malaysia is composed of thirteen states and three federal territories, accommodating a total population of 33.57 million individuals. The states that constitute the federation were previously independent Malay states. The Bumiputera group, encompassing ethnic Malays and the indigenous populations of Sabah and Sarawak (East Malaysia), constitutes 66.1 percent of the overall populace. The ethnic Chinese make up 25.3 percent of the population, while the ethnic Indian community represents 7.4 percent. Although the department of statistics does not publicly disclose religious statistics, it acknowledged in a press statement related to the 2000 census that "religion is highly correlated with ethnicity." The majority, 60.4 percent, are adherents of Islam, mainly from the ethnic Malay community. Buddhists make up 19.2 percent, Christians 9.1 percent, Hindus 6.3 percent and followers of Confucianism, Taoism, and other "traditional Chinese religion" account for 2.6 percent. This reveals that Malaysia does not exhibit religious uniformity, with Muslims forming the majority and non-Muslims representing a significant minority. Historically, the region was influenced by various Buddhist and Hindu kingdoms, which left a mark on the Malay states before the rise of Islam in the fifteenth century (Rabasa, 2004, p. 368).

Two notable historical polities were the Buddhist empires of Sri Vijaya during the seventh century and the Javanese-Hindu kingdom of Majapahit in the fourteenth century. It is widely acknowledged that Islam made its way to the Malay states and Southeast Asia through the influence of traders and missionaries originating from Arabia, Persia and India. Its initial establishment took place in Melaka, an important trading hub, during the fifteenth century. Subsequently, Islam not only persisted but also expanded beyond the coastal cities, enduring through the Portuguese takeover of Melaka in 1511 and the subsequent British involvement in the Malay states. The earliest documented British encounter with the Malay states occurred in 1771, when Sultan Muhammad Jiwa of Kedah sought assistance from the East India Company in a dispute over succession. Through treaties with local chieftains or sovereign rulers, the Malay states fell under British sway and settlements. Negeri Sembilan, Pahang, Perak and Selangor were among the Malay states under British protection, collectively referred to as the Federated Malay States. The Unfederated Malay states comprised Johore, Kedah, Kelantan, Perlis and Terengganu, while the colonies or settlements included Penang and Melaka (Mujani & Sulaiman, 2016).

These eleven states came together on August 31, 1957, to establish an independent nation known as Malaya. Subsequently, on September 16, 1963, the union expanded as three additional states, Sabah, Sarawak and Singapore, joined Malaya to form the Federation of Malaysia. However, Singapore withdrew from the Federation in 1965, achieving autonomy as a distinct republic. Since 1965, no changes have been made to the territory, aside from internal reconfigurations that led to the establishment of the federal capital territories of Kuala Lumpur and Putrajaya from Selangor and Labuan from Sabah. While British colonial rule did not directly affect Islam, it notably influenced the administration of Islamic law. The treaties negotiated by the Malay Rulers with the British followed a discernible pattern of incorporating British advice. The initial treaty, known as the Treaty of Pangkor, was established in 1874 between the Sultan of Perak and the English authorities, stipulating that English counsel "must be sought and followed for all matters, except those concerning Malay religion and traditions." Moreover, the formation of the Federated Malay States through a treaty in 1895 safeguarded the authority of the rulers concerning matters related to Islam. There is a widespread consensus that the legal system upheld in the Malay states was a blend of Islamic law and Malay customs. Scholars of law, however, hold divergent views on the nature of the legal framework in the Malay states, debating whether it comprised a fusion of traditional customs, as well as Buddhist, Hindu, and Islamic cultural-legal values, or was primarily based on Islamic law itself.

Some scholars have proposed the idea that the legal texts compiled in the Malay states between the fifteenth and nineteenth centuries, including the Ninety-Nine Laws of Perak, the Pahang Digest (1596), the Kedah Digest (1605), the Johore Digest and the Laws of Melaka (1523), represented a fusion of Malay customary law and aspects of the Shafiʿī school of Islamic law. For instance, an examination of the Laws of Melaka revealed an absence of clear distinctions between constitutional, criminal and civil law. The compilation encompassed a wide array of regulations, covering topics ranging from court protocols and criminal statutes to the jurisdiction of the ruler and his ministries, laws concerning escaped slaves, regulations on libel, contractual laws regarding the hiring of slaves and animals, penalties for acts against the monarch and breaches of engagement agreements. Prior to British intervention in the Malay states, Islamic law served as the predominant legal framework, which to some extent integrated Malay customary practices (Ibrahim et al. 1993). The constitutions of the Malay states of Johore and Terengganu notably emphasised the significance of Islam. The Johore Constitution of 1895 explicitly stated that the state religion was Islam and should continuously be acknowledged as such, while allowing for the peaceful practice of other religions. Similarly, the 1911 Constitution of Terengganu emphasised the ruler's adherence to the "Mohammedan religion," affirming Islam as the state religion. The close association of Islam with the Malay identity is evident in the colloquial expression 'masuk Melayu,' which refers to the act of converting to Islam as a means of becoming Malay (Kumpoh, 2020, p. 89).

These events underscore the deep connection between Islam and the identity of the Malay states and the ethnic Malay populace. In the lead-up to independence and the formulation of the Federal Constitution in 1957, Islam was seen as an essential component of the distinctive status granted to the ethnic Malays and the Federation. Nonetheless, Hooker observes that despite the Malay sultans maintaining their ceremonial roles, their actual authority was largely symbolic, as real power resided with the British Residents who, operating through legislative councils, controlled Islam to a degree where it was treated as a personal religion and private legal system. Consequently, the state underwent a process of secularization, disassociating religion from state affairs. A similar pattern was evident in the Netherlands East Indies. According to Hooker, the Islamic heritage preceding the sixteenth century did not revolve around *fiqh*, the Islamic jurisprudence (Hooker, 1983, p. 11). The earliest known expression of Islamic principles, as evidenced in the late fourteenth-century Terengganu inscription, was restricted to invoking the name of God as a guarantor of the laws. Any components of private law rooted in *fiqh* within the Malay legal compilations were not localised or adapted; they retained their original form as articulated in Middle Eastern texts. The everyday lives of the common people were primarily influenced by local traditions, which were connected to Muslim rulers rather than Islamic law.

The Federation of Malaya gained independence from British colonial rule on August 31, 1957. In addition to the influence exerted by nationalist and anticolonial movements of various persuasions, it is important to note that independence would not have been realised without the agreement reached between the British and the domestic ruling class.

This agreement, commonly referred to as the 'Merdeka compromise,' effectively enabled the ruling class to maintain dominance and govern Malaya. Malaysia's political system bears the fundamental characteristics of a parliamentary system of government, which draws inspiration from the Westminster parliamentary model. It encompasses periodic multi-party elections and a constitutionally defined separation of powers among the executive, legislative and judicial branches (Ahmad, 2005, pp. 3–4).

The implementation of the Federal Constitution was intended to create a harmonious balance among the various communities existing in Malaysia. It introduced several fundamental components, such as a two-chamber government structure, a system of separation of powers inspired by the Westminster model, where the executive was integrated within the legislature and the establishment of an independent judiciary. Moreover, it outlined a process for the selection of a monarch by a group of constitutionally protected sultans, while also acknowledging Islam as the official religion. Special privileges were accorded to Malays and the indigenous populations of Sabah and Sarawak and the Constitution included provisions for the invocation of extensive emergency powers in critical situations. Notably, the Federal Constitution has undergone several amendments since its inception, deviating from the norm. Additionally, the latter portion of the Constitution emphasised the protection of fundamental liberties, encompassing the rights to personal freedom, equality under the law, freedom of movement, freedom of speech and expression, freedom of assembly and association and freedom of religion. None of the freedoms cited are assured, as they are not only confined by explicit constraints within the Constitution but are also susceptible to ordinary laws in practice. After over fifty years of autonomy, numerous uncertainties arose in the practical implementation of the concept of democracy, which progressively intensified over time. The heterogeneous makeup of the populace and the inclination for every political matter to evolve into communalism undeniably represent prominent characteristics in the socio-political landscape of Malaysia. In an ideal democracy, three fundamental elements include widespread political rivalry, a significant degree of political engagement and the assurance of civil and political liberties (Khoo, 2014, p. 46).

The enforcement of strict regulations contradicting democratic ideals implies that Malaysia could be seen as a 'hybrid democracy,' as it only partially embraces the tenets of Westminster democracy. Conversations about Malaysia's political system often revolve around the delicate balance between democratic principles and authoritative tendencies. Since 1955, the dominant political force in Malaysia has been the Alliance regime, also known as Perikatan, maintaining its hold without interruption since the nation's independence. This coalition primarily consists of communal parties representing the major ethnic groups, including Malays, Chinese and Indians. While the government under the BN (Barisan Nasional) integrates certain democratic elements, it also imposes notable constraints on individual civil and political rights. Despite a degree of freedom to establish political parties, the actions of opposition parties are frequently limited by the broader legal framework. In Malaysia, human rights NGOs are often viewed as challenging the national interests of the state or posing a threat to its stability. Simultaneously, these organisations operate as social movements, civil society groups and voluntary associations independent of state influence. Human rights NGOs play a critical role in fostering and preserving a society based on human rights principles. They are regarded as essential for improving governance quality, empowering communities, facilitating development, and strengthening the democratic fabric (Khoo, 2014, p. 48).

In 1957, the Federation of Malaya declared independence amid a state of emergency triggered by the communist insurgency. Despite the existence of a Federal Constitution guaranteeing various political and civil liberties, these rights were curtailed by the Emergency Regulations, which suspended these civil liberties. The Emergency Regulations remained in effect until 1960 when the emergency was lifted, leading to the restoration of most civil liberties. The enactment of the Internal Security Act (ISA) in 1960 replaced the Emergency Regulations. During this period, the Prime Minister, Tunku Abdul Rahman, reassured Parliament and the nation that the ISA would never be utilized to suppress legitimate opposition or stifle lawful dissent. On June 21, 1960, Tun Abdul Razak, the then Deputy Prime Minister and Home Affairs Minister, affirmed in Parliament that the introduction of the ISA aimed to combat the subversive activities of the Communist Party of Malaya (CPM).

During the 1960s, the application of the ISA led to the arrest and detainment of individuals involved in communist activities, specifically targeting members of the former Labour Party, which was a part of the Socialist Front. Notably, on November 26, 1966, the ISA apprehended 70 people associated with various opposition parties, citing their alleged ties to the Communist Party of Malaya. Reflecting on this period, Zakaria Haji Ahmad highlights the years between 1957 and 1969 as a phase of 'testing democracy,' underlining that the adoption of the Westminster model persisted with little modification, despite the communal composition of Malaysia's pluralistic society. In the 1970s, a series of fresh organisations emerged within the nation. Notable among these were the Angkatan Belia Islam Consumer's Society, the Women's Aid Organisation (WAO), and the Environment Protection Society. These entities fervently advocated for various causes, including the fight against corruption, the safeguarding of underprivileged communities, environmental conservation and the promotion of democratic expansion. In 1974, a group of individuals concerned with human rights established the Human Rights Organisation of Malaysia, led by the national poet, Usman Awang. Other temporary committee members included Ahmad Boestamam, V. David, Kassim Ahmad, Azmi Khalid, the lawyer Gamany, and Professor Rohanna Ariffin. However, the organisation's attempts at establishment faced hindrances, ultimately leading to the rejection of its registration application (Khoo, 2014, p. 50).

During the mid-1980s, a range of controversial human rights matters surfaced during Tun Dr. Mahathir Mohamad's leadership. Several laws were introduced in the early 1980s, including the Printing Presses and Publications Act (1984) and the Dangerous Drugs (Special Preventive Measures) Act. In certain aspects, the Printing Presses and Publications Act of 1984 exhibited more rigorous and regressive attributes compared to the Printing Presses Ordinance put forth by the British in 1948, primarily serving their imperial interests. During Mahathir's tenure, a significant step was the establishment of the National Commission of Human Rights (SUHAKAM) through Act 157, which was passed by the Parliament in 1999. However, the government's move to establish the Commission came amid calls from 34 NGOs for public engagement in the drafting process and assurances regarding the transparency, autonomy, and effective execution of its responsibilities (Khoo, 2014, p. 51). The Constitution extensively outlines the rights of Malaysians to participate in civil society and the protection of essential civil liberties, elaborated in the section on Fundamental Liberties. Yet, these rights are essentially conditional, subject to the government's discretion in the interest of national security or public order. Over the years, the consistent expansion of executive powers has effectively curtailed the assurance of individual liberties.

1.6 Understanding Religious Liberty in the Context of Malaysia's Constitution

Being a nation characterised by its diversity, encompassing citizens with varying religious beliefs, the freedom of religion is an integral part of the fundamental rights protected by the.

Federal Constitution (FC). Article 111 explicitly states that 'every person has the right to profess and practice their religion' (Rahman et al., 2021, p. 45). However, there exist two limitations imposed on the freedom of religion. The first limitation pertains to the dissemination of any religious doctrine or belief among individuals who adhere to the religion of Islam, which can be controlled or restricted by the individual states in Malaysia. The second limitation stipulates that the freedom to profess and practice one's religion must not result in actions that contravene any general law concerning public order, public health, or morality. Nonetheless, the freedom of religion, as stated in Article 11, is reinforced by other constitutional provisions. Primarily, Article 149 allows the enactment of laws aimed at combatting subversion, even if these laws would otherwise contradict certain fundamental rights such as freedom of speech or personal liberty. However, it does not allow for any violations of religious freedom. Additionally, even if a state of emergency is declared, any subsequent emergency laws put into effect cannot curtail the freedom of religion. Moreover, Article 8 prohibits discrimination on the basis of religion against public sector employees, in the acquisition or possession of property, and in any trade, business, or profession. It is important to note that Islam is recognized as the religion of the Federation under Article 3 of the FC. However, this does not impede the right of non-Muslims to practice and profess their own religion. This is emphasized by the wording of Article 3(4), which explicitly states that nothing in Article 3 detracts from any other provision of the FC (Abdul Rahman et al., 2021, p. 47).

Moreover, in addition to Article 11(1), other provisions in the Constitution further ensure religious freedom. The Constitution prevents any obligation for individuals to support a religion other than their own, and it prohibits the compelling of any person to pay taxes that are specifically allocated to a religion other than their own (Federal Const. of Malaysia, 2016). Similarly, it prohibits individuals from being required to receive instruction or participate in any religious ceremony or act of worship of a religion other than their own. Furthermore, the Constitution forbids discrimination on religious grounds against public sector employees, in property transactions, and in any trade, business, or profession.In the case of The Minister of Home Affairs v. Jamaluddin bin Othman, the Supreme Court of Malaysia reaffirmed its commitment to upholding the constitutional provision on religious freedom (Thio, 2006, p. i). It dismissed a plea by the Minister of Home Affairs that conversion to Christianity by a Muslim was a punishable offense. The Court found that the grounds for detention in this case, when examined in context, were insufficient. It emphasized that the guarantee provided by Article 11 of the Constitution, which grants the right to freedom of religion, must be upheld unless the actions of an individual clearly exceed the bounds of what can typically be considered as professing and practicing their faith.

As Malaysia is a multiethnic and multireligious society, it becomes crucial to consider how Malaysia approaches the practices of both non-Muslims and Muslims within its borders (Faruqi, 2006). While international law universally acknowledges that the freedom of religion incorporates the right to convert to another faith, the stance of Malaysia on this matter is not entirely explicit. The right to change one's religion is not explicitly mentioned in the Malaysian Constitution (Faruqi, 2006). Nevertheless, it is generally assumed that the freedom of religion for non-Muslims in Malaysia inherently includes the right to renounce their religion. In essence, the constitutional provisions mentioned earlier suggest that non-Muslims in Malaysia are at liberty to profess and practice their religion, which includes the freedom to convert to different faiths.

A non-Muslim individual is also at liberty to propagate their religion to anyone except those who identify as Muslims. It is widely recognised that in countries with diverse religious populations, the constitutional guarantee pertaining to freedom of religion holds considerable importance. Minority religious communities in such nations often express concerns about their right to profess and practice their respective religions. In Malaysia, complete religious freedom has been constitutionally granted to the 39% of the population that does not identify as Muslim, and this guarantee remains inviolable even during times of emergency (Masum & Ahmad, 2013, p. 441). However, for Muslims, the matter of conversion or apostasy brings forth significant religious and political implications. The recognition of Islam as the religion of the Federation and the obligatory submission of Muslims to syari'ah in various aspects contribute to the strong aversion and displeasure among Malay/Muslim citizens when a Muslim renounces their faith. It should be noted that in Malaysia, Islam is established as the religion of the Federation, and the constitutional definition mandates that Malays adhere to the Islamic faith.

All Muslims can be subject to legal action if their behavior is deemed to be in violation of Islamic principles. It is essential to emphasise that no Muslim can lay claim to exemption from syari'ah laws, even in light of the constitutional guarantee of religious freedom. This concept of freedom of belief encompassing the freedom not to believe is unlikely to be widely accepted in Malay society. Despite the intricate religious and political factors surrounding the conversion of a Muslim to a different faith, some individuals interpret Article 11(1) of the Constitution in a broad manner, allowing for the possibility of a change in religious affiliation. It is noteworthy that Article 11(4) does restrict the propagation of any religion to Muslims, but the law does not explicitly prohibit the voluntary conversion of a Muslim to another faith (Masum & Ahmad, 2013, p. 442). The debate concerning the matter of apostasy, particularly in relation to the application of constitutional provisions for religious freedom to Muslims, remains unsettled. Legal and constitutional experts hold varying opinions regarding whether the Constitution permits action to be taken against individuals who renounce their faith (Masum & Ahmad, 2013, p. 443). Some argue that the freedom of religion guaranteed by Article 11(1) is conditional upon Article 3(1) of the Constitution, which designates Islam as the country's official religion and grants it special status.

Thus, initiating legal proceedings against Muslims who choose to renounce Islam or convert to other religions is seen as compliant with the provisions of the Constitution. Advocates of this perspective also reference Article 11(4) to bolster their argument (Malaysia, Federal Constitution, 1957). However, opponents argue that the court should adhere to the spirit of the Constitution. They contend that Article 11(1) is inclusive enough to allow for a change in religious affiliation and that although Article 11(4) restricts the propagation of any religion to Muslims, the law does not explicitly forbid the voluntary conversion of a Muslim to another faith. Numerous state laws implicitly acknowledge conversions out of Islam by mandating the maintenance of a registry of individuals who become *murtad* (infidels), alongside a similar register for those who embrace the Islamic faith (Masum & Ahmad, 2013, p. 445). A number of significant rulings have been issued in both civil and Syari'ah courts regarding apostasy cases (Ahmad, Masum & Ayus, 2016, p.736). For instance, Kamariah Ali, a former religious teacher and follower of the Sky

Kingdom deviant sect, was sentenced to two years in prison for apostasy (Bell, 2008).

Even though Muslim legal scholars hold differing opinions on the matter of apostasy and the right to administer punishment for it, apostasy is generally regarded as a transgression and thus condemned. Citing the Holy Qur'ān, Allah states, 'There shall be no compulsion in religion,' indicating that individuals cannot be forced to adhere to a particular faith. This sentiment is echoed by another verse revealed to the Holy Prophet, which questions the act of compelling individuals to adopt a specific faith. Despite the clarity of the Qur'ānic statements, the issue of religious freedom, particularly in the context of apostasy, remains a contentious topic. Despite the following facts: (1) the absence of consensus on such matters, (2) the noted Maliki jurist al-Baji's observation that apostasy is a sin with no prescribed penalty, (3) the potential punishment of such a sin under the discretionary punishment of *ta'zir* (which is lesser than *hudud*), and (4) the assertion of the renowned Hanbali jurist, Ibn Taymiyyah, many Islamic countries have unequivocally agreed that the punishment for apostasy falls under *ta'zir* (Kamali, 1997).

1.7 The Complex Terrain of Free Speech in Malaysia: Legal Framework and Practical Realities

In the Malaysian setting, the idea of free speech is conceptualised as 'freedom of speech and expression' within the framework of the Federal Constitution. This is clearly explicated in Article 10, where Clause 1(a) guarantees that all citizens possess the entitlement to express their opinions and thoughts openly (Venugopal & Hassan, 2012, p. 1452). Nevertheless, the boundaries of this freedom for Malaysians are not absolute, as they are subject to specific restrictions outlined in paragraphs (2), (3), and (4) of the same Article. As per Article 4(1) of the Federal Constitution, it is firmly established that the Constitution holds the highest authority in the nation, and any subsequent legislation enacted after the country's Independence Day that conflicts with the Constitution will be rendered invalid to the extent of the inconsistency. The subsequent portion of the Federal Constitution pertains to the fundamental freedoms, whereby Section 2 of the Malaysian Human Rights Commission Act 1999 explicitly defines 'human rights' as the fundamental liberties specified in Part II of the Federal Constitution (Venugopal & Hassan, 2012, p. 1453).

Consequently, both laws recognise the importance of privileges explicitly detailed in this section of the Federal Constitution, which encompasses the 'right to freely express one's opinions'. Clause 10(1)(a) of the Constitution grants each person the right to speech and expression. The inclusion of the term 'expression' expands the scope of these entitlements, covering verbal communication, symbols, actions, artistic creations, creative pursuits, media content and digital displays (Faruqi, 2018). Even seemingly harmless remarks about an individual's clothing can fall within the realm of freedom of expression. Acknowledging the non-absolute nature of rights, the Constitution allows for various acceptable limitations. The notion of freedom of speech does not imply immunity from consequences. One evident fact is that while freedom of speech is unquestionably a constitutional right according to Article 10 of the Federal Constitution, it is not without boundaries. Article 10 of the Federal Constitution includes Freedom of Speech, Assembly, and Association. Besides the exceptions stated in Article 10, it can be argued that this freedom is bound by legal, ethical, and societal constraints. Moreover, the protection of fundamental freedoms for Malaysians within the Federal Constitution cannot be easily disregarded, as confirmed in Article 10. This provision empowers individuals to openly articulate their viewpoints without fearing repercussions. Clearly, the fundamental freedoms guaranteed by the Federal Constitution are delicately calibrated to govern and protect the diverse societal framework.

According to legal analysts, government authorities have effectively constrained freedom of expression, freedom of association, and assembly in comparison to other essential liberties outlined in Part-II of the Constitution. A significant portion of these liberties, such as unrestricted speech and protection against double jeopardy, do not substantially deviate from the provisions stipulated in Article 10, paragraphs 2, 3 and 4. Instead, they fail to ensure rights, and the effectiveness of Article 10 relies on the negation of the aforementioned provisions. Despite the privileges enjoyed by Malaysians under Article 10, their capacity for free speech, assembly and association is subject to specific regulations, standards and constraints. Individuals retain the right to voice their opinions and the option of peaceful assembly and association. However, Article 10, paragraph 2 (a) (b) (c) explicitly allows Parliament to impose limitations on these rights. Nevertheless, these freedoms are only limited in terms of public safety, societal needs, morality, or cultural values, as outlined in Article 10(2). Certain matters, such as the status of the national language, the special rights of Malays, the status of Islam as the official religion, and other issues are stipulated in the Federal Constitution and must not be violated.

This suggests that individuals maintain the privilege to articulate their opinions without violating public regulations, disrupting public order, or inciting any public unrest. In general, the extent of unrestricted expression in Malaysia is not comprehensive. The Malaysian Human Rights Commission (SUHAKAM) has emphasised that the use of Article 233 of the Communications and Multimedia Act (CMA) and related statutes, including the Sedition Act of 1948, the Peaceful Assembly Act of 2012, and sections 504 and 505 of the Penal Code, is aimed at monitoring, intimidating, and limiting expression and freedom of speech (Malay Mail, 2020). Suhakam is concerned about the persistent enforcement of restrictive legislations that do not adhere to the fundamental principles of freedom of thought outlined in Article 19 of the Universal Declaration of Human Rights (UDHR) and Article 10 of the Federal Constitution of Malaysia. Suhakam aims to prompt the government to remember that under Article 10 of the Federal Constitution of Malaysia, it is the government's obligation and responsibility to ensure that individuals can freely express themselves. This provision ensures that Malaysian inhabitants have the entitlement to unrestricted speech, opportunities for assembly and the right to associate in order to voice their perspectives on the path the nation should pursue (Mia et al., 2021, p. 49).

1.8 Volume Structure

This volume consists of 6 chapters. Chapter 1 (introduction) gives an outline of the main themes of the book, discussing the importance of examining human rights in countries with Muslim majorities, with a specific focus on Egypt and Malaysia. It emphasises the complexities and difficulties involved in advocating for and safeguarding human rights in these particular contexts. This chapter lays the groundwork for the subsequent chapters that delve into specific aspects of human rights law and practice. Chapter 2 conducts a thorough evaluation of the legal status and challenges of human rights in Muslim majority countries. It examines various contextual elements, such as political frameworks, economic advancements and the impact of religious institutions, which contribute to shaping the landscape of human rights in these nations. The chapter underscores the significance of tailoring human rights initiatives to the distinct socio-political landscapes of Muslim-majority countries to effectively promote and protect these rights. Chapter 3 delves into an exploration of the intricacies and accomplishments associated with the implementation of religious freedom within diverse cultural and societal contexts, particularly focusing on Egypt and Malaysia. The aim of the chapter is to offer valuable insights into the global discourse on human rights by examining the challenges and noteworthy experiences drawn from these countries, thereby contributing to a more comprehensive understanding of the state's role in safeguarding individual liberties. Chapter 4 provides a thorough examination of the constitutional clauses and practical application of freedom of speech and expression in Egypt. It delves into the historical trajectories and legal frameworks that underlie these rights, shedding light on the difficulties and specific contextual intricacies that influence the exercise of these fundamental freedoms within each respective country. Chapter 5 explores freedom of speech in Malaysia's democracy, emphasizing its vital role in socio-economic progress. It raises concerns about imposed restrictions despite constitutional protection and aims to comprehensively examine the nuanced dynamics of this right in Malaysia. Focusing on the constitutional framework, the chapter delves into the legal landscape, scrutinizing laws limiting free expression, to contribute to a nuanced understanding of the practical exercise of this fundamental right in Malaysia. Chapter 5 (conclusion) provides a summary of the key findings and insights from the preceding chapters, highlighting the necessity for tailored and context-specific approaches to advocating for and protecting human rights in diverse sociopolitical contexts. It also presents recommendations for policymakers, civil society actors and international organisations to strengthen human rights protections and ensure the realisation of these rights in Muslimmajority countries and beyond.

References

Abdel-Latif, A. (2014, August). *Egypt and Tunisia underscore the importance of IP*. Retrieved April 8, 2024, from https://www.wipo.int/wipo_magazine/en/2014/04/article_0008.html

Abdul Rahman, S. A. K. B., Sharifuddin, S. B. A., & Hafidz, M. B. M. (2021). Citizenship rights in Malaysia: A constitutional reform. *CLI, 3*, 41–49.

Ahmad, N., Masum, A., & Ayus, A. M. (2016). Freedom of religion and apostasy: The Malaysian experience. *Human Rights Quarterly, 38*(3), 736–753.

Ahmad, S. (2005). Islam in Malaysia: Constitutional and human rights perspectives. *Muslim World Journal of Human Rights, 2*(1), 2–4.

Ahmed, A. (2008). *The student movement and national politics in Egypt, 1923–1973.* American University in Cairo Press.

Alsubaie, S. (2018). The limitations of freedom of expression in theory and practice (Between the First Amendment of the U.S. Constitution and Egyptian law) (PhD Thesis). University of Stirling, School of Arts and Humanities, Law Department. Retrieved April 8, 2024, from https://dspace.stir.ac.uk/bitstream/1893/30387/1/Final%20Copy3.pdf

Arjomand, S. A. (2012). Middle Eastern constitutional and ideological revolutions and the rise of juristocracy. *Constellations, 19*(2), 204–215.

Bell, T. (2008, March 4). *Woman jailed for 'worshipping tea pot'.* Retrieved April 19, 2024, from https://www.telegraph.co.uk/news/worldnews/1580705/Woman-jailed-for-worshipping-tea-pot.html

Brown, N. (1997). *The rule of law in the Arab world: Courts in Egypt and the gulf*. Cambridge University Press.

Brown, N. J., & Sherif, A. O. (2004). Inscribing the Islamic Shari'a in Arab constitutional law. In Y. Y. Haddad & B. F. Stowasser (Eds.), *Islamic law and the challenges of modernity* (pp. 55–60). Altamira Press.

Culang, J. (2018). The Shari'a must go: Seduction, moral injury, and religious freedom in Egypt's liberal age. *Comparative Studies in Society and History, 60*(2), 446–475.

Egypt's constitution of 2014. Retrieved April 10, 2024, from Constitute Project: https://www.constituteproject.org/constitution/Egypt_2014.pdf

Faruqi, S. (2006, June 1). Spotlight on religious freedom. *The Sun*, E7.

Faruqi, S. S. (2018, September 27). Reform needed to protect free speech. *The Star*. Retrieved April, 9, 2024, from https://www.thestar.com.my/opinion/columnists/reflecting-on-the-law/2018/09/27/reformneeded-to-protect-free-speech-we-need-an-independent-law-reform-commission-to-scrutinisethe#cJckxaGsAPQgkuM2

Federal constitution of Malaysia art. 11(2). Retrieved April 9, 2024, from Universiti Putra Malaysia: https://ppuu.upm.edu.my/upload/dokumen/20180726155749RUJ_1_FEDERAL_CONSTITUTION_ULANG_CETAK_2016.pdf

Gutterman, A. (2023, January 9). *What are human rights?* Retrieved April 10, 2024, from SSRN: https://ssrn.com/abstract=4320947

Hamzawy, A., & Brown, N. J. (2010). *The Egyptian Muslim brotherhood: Islamist participation in a closing political environment.* Carnegie Endowment for International Peace.

Hooker, M. B. (1983). Introduction: The translation of Islam into Southeast Asia. In M. B. Hooker (Ed.), *Islam in South East Asia* (pp. 1–22). Brill.

Ibrahim, A., et al. (1993). *The Malaysian legal system*. Dewan Bahasa dan Pustaka.

Institute on religion and public policy. (2010). Report on religious freedom in Egypt. Retrieved April 9, 2024, from United Nations Human Rights Office of the High Commissioner: https://www.ohchr.org/sites/default/files/lib-docs/HRBodies/UPR/Documents/Session7/EG/IRPP_UPR_EGY_S07_2010_InstituteonReligionandP ublicPolicy.pdf

Kamali, M. H. (1997). *Freedom of expression in Islam*. Islamic Texts Society.

Kameel, M. (2016). *Madaa kafalat haqi al'iinsan fi altaebir bayn alfaqih al'iislamii walqanun alwadeii* (pp. 328–329). Munsha'at almaearif.

Khoo, Y. H. (2014). Historical accounts of the human rights development in malaysia from independence to the era of Tun Dr. Mahathir Mohamad. Retrieved April 10, 2024, from: https://eprints.um.edu.my/12877/1/Historical_Accounts_of_the_Human_Rights_Development_in_Ma laysia_from_Independence_to_the_Era_of_Tun_Dr._Mahathir_Mohamad.pdf

Kienle, E. (2000). *A grand delusion: Democracy and economic reform in Egypt*. I.B. Tauris.

Kumpoh, A. A. A. (2020). Masuk Melayu in the context of conversion to Islam. *BITARA International Journal of Civilizational Studies and Human Sciences, 3*(3), 83–94.

Laws of Malaysia. (2009). Federal constitution. Retrieved April 10, 2024, from https://www.jac.gov.my/spk/images/stories/10_akta/perlembagaan_persekutuan/federal_constitution.pdf

Lombardi, C. B., & Brown, N. J. (2005). Do constitutions requiring adherence to shari'a threaten human rights-how Egypt's constitutional court reconciles Islamic law with the liberal rule of law. *American University International Law Review, 21*, 379–435.

Malay Mail. (2020, June 23). Protection of freedom of speech and expression–Suhakam. https://www.malaymail.com/news/what-you-think/2020/06/23/protection-of-freedom-of-speech-andexpression-suhakam/1878253

Malaysia: Federal Constitution, 31 August 1957. Retrieved April 10, 2024, from https://www.refworld.org/docid/3ae6b5e40.html

Masum, A., & Ahmad, N. (2013). Freedom of religion and apostasy under international law: With special reference to article 11 of the Malaysian federal constitution. *Journal of East Asia and International Law, 6*(2), 435–457.

Meital, Y. (2017). *Revolutionary justice: Special courts and the formation of republican Egypt*. Oxford University Press.

Mia, M. T., Islam, M. Z., & Norullah, M. (2021). Freedom of speech and expression in Malaysia: Protection under the federal constitution. *SARJANA, 36*(2), 48–62.

Moustafa, T. (2007). *The struggle for constitutional power: Law, politics, and economic development in Egypt*. Cambridge University Press.

Moustafa, T. (2021). Introduction: Law, courts, and human rights. In R. Springborg, A. Adly, A. Gorman, T. Moustafa, A. Saad, N. Sakr, & S. Smierciak (Eds.), *Routledge handbook on contemporary Egypt* (pp. 263–271). Routledge.

Mujani, W. K., & Sulaiman, W. H. W. (2016). Historical development of the federalism system in Malaysia: Prior to independence. *Advances in Social Science, Education and Humanities Research, 75*, 517–519.

Office of International Religious Freedom. (2021). Report on International Religious Freedom: Egypt. Retrieved November 29, 2024, from https://www.state.gov/reports/2021-report-on-international-religious-freedom/egypt/.

Rabasa, A. M., et al. (2004). Southeast Asia: Moderate tradition and radical challenge. In A. M. Rabasa (Ed.), *The Muslim world after 9/11* (pp. 367–412). Rand Corporation.

Rutherford, B. K. (2013). *Egypt after Mubarak: Liberalism, Islam, and democracy in the Arab world* (pp. 32–76). Princeton University Press.

Sayed, E. S. (2020). Constitutions and religion in Egypt: A comparative study. *Review of Economics and Political Science*. Retrieved April 10, 2024, from https://www.emerald.com/insight/content/doi/10.1108/REPS-06-2019-0081/full/pdf?title=constitutions-and-religion-in-egypt-a-comparative-study

Shash, Y. (2017, August 4). *The formal birth of the human rights movement in Egypt*. Retrieved April 10, 2024, from https://www.arab-reform.net/publication/the-formal-birth-of-the-human-rightsmovement-in-egypt/

Tadros, S. (2010, November 9). *Religious freedom in Egypt*. Retrieved April 10, 2024, from https://www.heritage.org/civil-society/report/religious-freedom-egypt

The constitution of the Arab republic of Egypt, 1971. Retrieved April 10, 2024, from http://Idpbarcelona.Net/Docs/Recerca/Mediterranea/Fichas/Egipto/Constitucion.Pdf

Thio, L. A. (2006). Apostasy and religious freedom: Constitutional issues arising from the Lina Joy litigation. *Malayan Law Journal, 2*, i–xxii.

Venugopal, A. V., & Hassan, K. H. (2012). The law of contempt of court in Malaysia: Considering reforms. *Advances in Natural and Applied Sciences, 6*(8), 1451–1465.

CHAPTER 2

Human Rights Law in Muslim Majority Countries: An Assessment

2.1 Introduction

In Muslim majority countries, constitutional reform is either ongoing or just concluded in the twenty-first century. The extent to which Islamic law should be included into constitutions is one important topic of discussion in these debates, along with the implementation of global human rights norms. People want that their governments follow the Universal Declaration of Human Rights and operate under *sharīʿah* law (Pew Research Center, 2013). There is no contradiction in this. The general public associates social justice and the rule of law with *sharīʿah*, not the other way around. The goals of groups like the Muslim Brotherhood and those of secular democratic reformers, at least in theory, have a great deal in common. This is reflected in Islamic constitutions: the more Islam is referenced in a constitution, the more protections for personal freedoms and rights are often included (Ahmed & Ginsburg, 2014, p. 621).

In addition to Islam, other variables such as political and economic ties with the West, the emergence of pan-Arabism, the struggle for Palestinian self-determination and others have an impact on human rights in countries with a majority of Muslims. The criterion used in any assess ment of human rights—whether it be global, comparative, or unique to the nation or region under consideration—will also have an impact on the results. Many Muslim countries have ratified the Universal Declaration of

A. Mohiuddin, *Human Rights Law in Egypt and Malaysia: Freedom of Religion and Expression, Volume 1*, Political Economy of Islam,
https://doi.org/10.1007/978-3-031-63859-6_2

Human Rights and associated treaties (Arzt, 1990, p. 210), which provide a benchmark. With robust legal frameworks and constitutional protections for civil, political, economic, social and cultural rights, human rights are well-protected and upheld in several nations in the Muslim world. For instance, Malaysia's record on human rights is uneven. Although the country's constitution provides a number of human rights, including as freedom of speech and religion, these rights are frequently curtailed in reality (Roth, 2023). The administration has come under fire for how it handles the media and the political opposition as well as for its limitations on the freedoms of assembly and association. Women are also subject to social and legal discrimination, which limits their access to employment and higher education. The current Egyptian constitution, which was ratified in 2014, on the other hand, consists of a number of clauses that are intended to uphold human rights, such as the freedom of speech, the right to practice one's religion, and the right to a fair trial. Additionally, it forbids discrimination based on gender, ethnicity, or religion, as well as torture and forced labour. In reality, though, the government's and the security forces' activities frequently undercut these safeguards. The constitution also include clauses that have drawn criticism for having the potential to significantly limit human rights.

For instance, the constitution enables the employment of military tribunals for terrorism-related offences and under certain conditions allows the military to undertake trials for civilians. The president is also given extensive authority under the constitution, including the right to dissolve parliament under certain circumstances and to make decrees that have the force of law. Concerns have been raised concerning the executive branch's concentration of power and the possibility of human rights violations as a result. Other nations with a majority of Muslims may have human rights protections in their constitutions, but these rights are not consistently upheld. As an illustration, laws and regulations in certain nations may place restrictions on women's rights and the rights of religious minorities as well as freedom of expression, association, and religion. In these situations, widespread and systemic human rights breaches may exist, and individuals who speak out against them risk harassment, detention, or even physical harm.

The way in which human rights are handled in these countries can also be influenced by religious and cultural issues. Inconsistent with some human rights standards, such as those pertaining to gender equality, freedom of expression, or sexual orientation, are some interpretations of

Islamic law. Religious leaders may occasionally use their power to promote or oppose particular human rights safeguards. Even in nations where there are robust legal systems in place to safeguard human rights, enforcement procedures may be inadequate or ineffectual. For instance, despite the fact that Egypt's constitution protects a number of human rights, such as the freedom of speech and the right to a fair trial, in reality these rights are frequently transgressed. This is partly because human rights violations are not held accountable and the legal system is weak (Schaer, 2022).

The extent to which *sharīʿah* or its amendments or rejections still serve as the foundation for legislation in Muslim countries varies. Islam has been formally recognised as the official religion in seventeen states. The *sharīʿah* is cited as the primary source of law in Syria (Lombardi, 2013, p. 734). Saudi Arabia has adhered to *sharīʿah* without making many changes. Iraq, Jordan, Libya and Syria are examples of former Ottoman Empire nations that generally adhere to the *Majallan* codification of *sharīʿah*. Countries like Algeria, Egypt, Morocco and Tunisia adopted Frenchbased codes, adhering to *sharīʿah* only when it came to laws pertaining to an individual's civil standing. The Egyptian Constitution states that the fundamental basis of law is *sharīʿah* (Sherif, 2012, p.122). The Supreme Constitutional Court is in charge of evaluating whether legislation are compatible with the principles of *sharʿīah*, although it is up to them to interpret and apply *sharīʿah* as they see fit (Lombardi, 1998, p.90). The *sharīʿah* is acknowledged as the basis of law in Malaysia and Islam is designated as the nation's official religion under the constitution (Karcic, 2001, p.208). Due to the dual legal system in place in the nation, *sharīʿah* courts may hear cases involving family law and inheritance.

In Iran, *sharīʿah* law must be upheld by the Supreme Court and Islamic Revolutionary Courts. Islam is recognised as the state religion and the cornerstone of Iranian law under the country's constitution (Arjomand, 2012, p. 142). The authority of Islamic jurists to interpret and apply *sharīʿah* is also recognised by the Constitution. The Supreme Court and Islamic Revolutionary Courts in Iran are responsible for enforcing *sharīʿah* law. The Pakistani constitution stipulates that *sharīʿah* is the only law that has any legal standing in the country (Wolfrum, 2012, p. 78). However, the Constitution also safeguards basic liberties, subject to restrictions put in place for Islam's supreme virtue. While acknowledging the plurality and heterogeneity of the nation, The Indonesian Constitution also stipulates that the concept of the one and only God shall serve as the cornerstone of the nation (Asshiddiqie, 2009). In some regions of the country, especially Aceh, where Islamic law is applied to control interpersonal relations and family problems, *sharīʿah* law is implemented. Islam and other cultures have been blended in various countries. With the notable exception of Saudi Arabia, these countries were affected by a reform movement that originated in Turkey in the 1850s and sought to bring the Islamic world closer to the West in terms of politics and law (David & Brierley, 1978, p. 457). Therefore, the examination of human rights in Islamic governments should take into account both traditional law, which derives from *sharīʿah* and modern law, which takes into account developments after 1850.

Despite the stated goals of Muslim-majority states, the rights envisioned by the human rights accords have not been fully realised for their peoples, who still face the ominous threat of persecution and discrimination. Poor human rights records are a reflection of the historically gloomy constitutionalism in more than fifty nations with a majority of Muslims. Any system may be referred to as constitutional if it upholds the rule of law, offers limited and responsible governance, and protects fundamental rights (Rosenfeld, 1993, p. 497). With *sharīʿah* playing a robust role in the legal system, virtually all nations with a majority of Muslims have accepted the notion that a constitution is an essential component of contemporary government (Lazumirskyy, 2021).

This chapter will explore the potential and difficulties for promoting and defending human rights in nations with majorities of Muslims while also examining the legal status of these rights. A variety of elements, including as political structures, economic progress and the sway of religious figures and organisations, affect the legal status of human rights in Muslim majority countries. These variables may affect how well human rights are upheld in these nations as well as how effectively civil society groups and foreign actors may promote human rights. The chapter makes the case that efforts to advance and defend human rights can be more successfully targeted to the unique settings and difficulties encountered by these countries.

2.2 *Sharīʿah*, Sovereignty and International Order

In the modern world, the historical picture of Islamic law is no longer prevalent. The institutional frameworks that allowed practical application of Islamic law in the Muslim world started to be altered or abolished by the eighteenth century, if not earlier. For instance, non-Muslim Europeans were free from the authority of Ottoman courts in accordance with the Capitulation agreements with the Ottoman Sultan. Application of Islamic law in Egypt was further undermined by the Mixed Court's usage in cases involving non-Muslim parties and interests. *Sharīʿah* courts and the legislation they administered started to lose institutional efficacy in resolving legal issues when Egypt adopted the Napoleonic Code in the late nineteenth century and established national courts to adjudicate it. The colonial history and the relatively recent development of the contemporary Muslim state in an international system of sovereign nations have caused a mismatch between the image of Islamic law today and its historical roots. As a result, while addressing Islamic law today, two characteristics stand out particularly. The first is a focus on source texts and *fiqh* treatises as being infallible descriptions of what Islamic law is and what it entails. The second is the diversity of legal authorities that govern the state, with Islamic law being just one of many legal systems that do so. A state's legitimacy frequently depends on striking a delicate and frequently politically contentious, balance between various and authoritative systems (Christelow, 1985, p. 6).

Islamic law presented a challenge for colonial administrators throughout the time when Europe colonised the Muslim world. On the one hand, it provided an indigenous local culture of law and order that could not be reinstituted forcibly without sparking a fierce backlash against colonial rule. On the other hand, the risk that Islamic law may be used as a tool of an opposition movement against a colonial authority increased the longer it remained a part of the socio-legal and political fabric. Given that Islam 'played a significant role in mobilising against European colonial rule in nearly all Muslim countries' throughout the colonial era, administrators reasoned that supporting the dominant Islamic legal systems would jeopardise the colonial project (Christelow, 1985, p. 7). As a result, the colonial era saw a decline in the scope of Islamic law's application and therefore, its power.

For example, Western nations established "Capitulation" agreements with the Ottoman sultan to safeguard Europeans who lived in the Ottoman Empire and to conduct and regulate economic activities. A portion of these agreements shielded European foreigners from Ottoman legal authority (Brinton, 1968). Consuls who represented the various European nations made decisions in their cases. Commercial disputes between foreigners and indigenous claimants were handled in special tribunals presided over by judges from both the Ottoman Empire and other countries, or they were heard in regular Ottoman courts with a consular representative typically present (Brinton, 1968). Local authorities were encouraged to provide foreigners more exemptions from *sharīʿah* law, therefore extending consular jurisdiction in handling foreigners' legal matters, as they turned to Europe for financial investment and closer commercial links. However, giving consular authorities the authority to hear these matters increased the unpredictability of the results of the judicial process. The Mixed Court, for instance, was established in Egypt to handle cases involving foreign interests, i.e. when one of the parties was a foreigner or where a foreign interest was implicated even though both parties were Egyptian citizens, as a result of the confusion of venues that resulted from consular jurisdiction. The Mixed Court gradually expanded its authority (Brinton, 1968).

The *sharīʿah* legal system that predominated in countries like Algeria in the nineteenth century was reorganised by French colonial officials in order to foster an active land market with positive consequences for colonial businesspeople. A large portion of the land was held in family *waqfs* or trusts that were retained in perpetuity under the prevailing Islamic legal system. The Islamic *waqf* system insured that property would not be divided up into smaller pieces in accordance with Islamic inheritance regulations, allowing it to stay in a family's hands. However, this Islamic system of law hindered French interests in acquiring and cultivating land for industrial uses, ultimately leading to the development of a market for freely alienable property. Two strategies were used to undermine the continuation of these family *waqfs*: marginalising Islamic law by imposing new legal norms and reinterpreting and reinforcing Islamic law for Muslims who were judged incapable to recognise the reality of their own heritage (Powers, 1989, p. 536).

Numerous doctrinal schools, opposing interpretative analytical theories and a diversity of perspectives were characteristics of premodern Islamic law. Through a process of codification throughout the Ottoman reform era, this significant substantive and theoretical diversity was diminished. Muslims had to choose which laws would predominate when they started to codify Islamic law, such as when the Ottomans created the Islamic legal code *'Majalla'*. Would they establish a Hanafi, Maliki, Hanbali, or Shafi'ī code for those predominantly Sunni nations? How would they handle the Shi'a population there? These reformers would frequently pick and choose from several theological schools to arrive at what they saw to be the greatest result. Reformers were able to present a version of Islamic law that was similar to the European model of law in form and structure thanks to this process of selecting (*takhayyur*) and harmonising (*talfiq*) divergent aspects of mediaeval opinions. However, in doing so, they reduced Islamic law to a collection of positivist legal claims that were cut off from the historical, institutional, and jurisprudential context that helped make *fiqh* doctrines understandable in the first place (Hallaq, 1997).

Another illustration is the Egyptian government, which established national courts to carry out the Napoleonic Code's administration in 1883. As a result, three different types of Egyptian courts were established: *Sharī'ah* courts, secular National Courts and Mixed Courts (Brown, 1997). Egypt enacted a civil code in 1949 that was mostly based on the French Civil Code and also had very little Islamic law. The country's *Sharī'ah* courts were subsequently abolished in 1955. It is important to note that these modifications to *Sharī'ah's* authority and capacity to determine the nature of judicial inquiry and the political structure should not be interpreted as proving that *shari'ah* does not apply in today's Muslim majority state. As an illustration, when 'Abd al-Razzaq alSanhuri developed the Egyptian Civil Code in 1949, he substantially drew inspiration from the French Civil Code while keeping in mind the possible influence of Islamic law on the Egyptian legal system. He maintained that defining *Shari'ah* in accordance with the traditional legal principles (also known as *fiqh*) could fill up any gaps in the Code or customary law, provided that no *fiqh* judgement went against a fundamental premise of the Code (Al-Sanhuri, 2007, p. 45).

While Islamic law is unquestionably extant, it is incorporated into a contemporary system of numerous statutes with different origins. It is sometimes described as a set of premodern laws and substantially limited in how it is used in modern legal systems. Islamic family law is one area of Islamic law that is most frequently encountered in contemporary Muslim state legal frameworks. While modernising other legal fields like commercial law, colonial administrators and Muslim nationalist assemblies kept Islamic family law in its codified form. This narrowing of the scope and implementation of the legislation may have appeased Islamists who believed that upholding traditional Islamic family law was essential to preserving Islam in the face of increasing modernity (McClintock, 1993, p. 62). The prevalence of this phenomena throughout the Muslim world has a significant impact on Muslim and European presumptions about what *sharīʿah* is and what it can be. Colonial powers and Muslim elites have contributed to the idea that *sharīʿah* is rigid, static and codified while positioning it as one of many legal traditions that operate within a modern state by redefining it, narrowing its scope, and incorporating it piecemeal into specific statutes without historical context (Kugle, 2001, p. 257).

A centralised sovereign state government that makes laws or decrees establishing the law for a territory that is defined by geopolitical borders is frequently seen as having the right to make laws and to use them as justification for coercion in the contemporary world. The state is a part of an intergovernmental system of states, where every state is regarded as an equal sovereign with a right to territorial integrity. Whether it is through economic agreements, diplomatic connections, or international organisations like the United Nations, these governments interact with one another as players on a global stage. Islamic law is frequently incorporated into the legal systems of countries whose borders formerly belonged to Islamic empires. However, these nations only partially adopt Islamic law. In modern personal status codes, such governments frequently merely adopt premodern Islamic family law while adopting or altering legislative frameworks from European and North American states on issues of responsibilities, process, commercial law, finance and other related topics (Abu-Odeh, 2004, p. 791).

The way Islamic law was formerly taught at premodern madrasas (Islamic law colleges) centuries ago is no longer the norm for modern lawyers in Muslim states that uphold Islamic law; instead, they take a few courses on the subject while concentrating on a 'secularised' legal curriculum for the most part. In fact, Lama Abu-Odeh has vehemently contended that one need not even think about the premodern era in order to comprehend Islamic law in the modern day. Islamic law is currently a part of a complicated, bureaucratic governmental structure where it serves as a minor, if any, source of legal frameworks that are mostly based on European models of civil law and government (Abu-Odeh, 2004, p. 794). That does not, however, imply that society is not governed by *sharīʿah*.

We are unable to readily separate *sharīʿah* from the contemporary setting if it denotes an active participation in regulating society. Studies which work at the nexus of law, politics and the demands of lived experience, continue to be crucial opportunities for critical engagement and reflection on the complexity that attends to any such research.

2.3 Constitutional Protection of Human Rights in the Muslim World

In the constitutions of countries with a majority of Muslims, references to human rights or international human rights might take different forms. Although Saudi Arabia does not legally have a constitution, its Basic Law of Governance (Al-Fahad, 2005, p. 377), mentions human rights with Islam. In line with *sharīʿah*, the state is required to respect human rights. Some constitutions specifically mention the United Nations Charter or the Universal Declaration of Human Rights. In this context, Yemen's constitution serves as an illustration (Constitutional Drafting Committee, 2015). Human rights can also be mentioned in broader terms, without specifically referencing any one particular instrument. The constitutions under consideration often relate to particular human rights in two ways, in addition to generic allusions to the overarching framework of international human rights. Some of them just assert specific legal rights. Other others make general reference of the entire list of liberties and rights contained in the UN Covenants of 1966 (Mahmoudi, 2016, p. 536).

Regardless of how international human rights are viewed in the constitutions of some Muslim countries, there are usually obstacles in the way of their realisation. These issues are not exclusive to these nations; they are present in many other Muslim nations' internal legal structures and constitutions as a whole. One is the broad perspective of a person as the holder of rights and liberties. It is common to discover clauses in various constitutions that emphasise God's rights over human rights, emphasising that people are by nature duty-bearers rather than right-bearers (Mahmoudi, 2016, p. 538). The result of this mindset might be that rights take on a residual aspect and are formed subject to restrictions imposed by the state, religion, or other institutions.

Constitutions may contain provisions limiting certain freedoms and rights. Such restrictions may also be the result of leaving future legislative regulation to address the rights' ongoing development and implementation. The Tunisian Constitution's Article 49, which states that 'the limitations that may be imposed on the exercise of the rights and freedoms guaranteed in this Constitution will be established by law [...],' is an illustration of the latter (Ebel, 2022). The restriction is more frequently written directly into the constitution. 'Freedom of speech is guaranteed within the limits of public interest and the principles of the Revolution,' the 1969 Libyan Constitution's Article 13 said. The restriction on press freedom in Art.24 of the Constitution of Iran is another illustration (Shahidi, 2008, p. 740).

The 2014 Egyptian constitution included legislative safeguards to improve the respect for and defence of human rights. According to Article 53, 'All citizens are equal before the law' (Youssef, 2012). Without distinction on the grounds of race, gender, origin, socioeconomic status, political affiliation, or any other factor, they are all equal in their rights, freedoms and general obligations. A variety of social, economic, civil and political rights are guaranteed under the Constitution. Additionally, it ensures a person's access to courts as well as their right to petition. The current constitution, which was enacted in 2014, ensures that all people have a number of fundamental rights, including the freedom of expression, assembly and religion, as well as the right to a fair trial and the rights to life, liberty and personal security. The constitution also forbids discrimination on the grounds of race, gender, or religion. The National Council for Human Rights (NCHR), the Administrative Prosecution Authority, and the Supreme Constitutional Court are only a few of the autonomous organisations that the Constitution provides to defend human rights in Egypt. The NCHR is in charge of looking into cases of human rights breaches, keeping an eye on jails and detention facilities, and raising awareness of these problems. Government employees may be subject to investigations by the Administrative Prosecution Authority for human rights abuses and legislation that are unconstitutional, including those that violate human rights, may be overturned by the Supreme Constitutional Court (Meyer-Resende, 2014).

Human rights are protected under the Malaysian Constitution. All people are guaranteed certain fundamental rights by the constitution, which was established in 1957 (Azhari & Jiet, 2016, p. 20). These rights include the right to life, liberty and security of person, the freedom of expression and assembly, and the right to a fair trial. The constitution also forbids discrimination on the grounds of gender, ethnicity, or religion. The Human Rights Commission of Malaysia (SUHAKAM) and the Enforcement Agency Integrity Commission are just two of the independent organisations established by the Constitution to defend human rights in Malaysia (EAIC) (Samsudin et al., 2022, p. 16). The EAIC looks into complaints against law enforcement authorities for misbehaviour and abuse of authority, whereas SUHAKAM is in charge of looking into human rights breaches and raising awareness of those concerns.

Despite the fact that the majority of its citizens are Muslims, the Constitution of the Republic of Indonesia (1945) makes no mention of Islam. However, Article 29 mandates that the foundation of the state be the recognition of the One and Only God. Additionally, it protects religious freedom (Ellis, 2005). The constitution stipulates that all international agreements must first get the Dewan Perwakilan Rakyat's (Article 11 Paragraph 2) approval before the president (Article 11 Paragraph 2) may sign them, but it allows all other aspects pertaining to international agreements to be governed by legislation. The list of human rights in Indonesia is found in Chapter XA, which notably emphasises economic, social and cultural rights (Ibrahim, 2020).

Although Art. 2 of the Afghanistan Constitution (2004) provides religious freedom, it also defines Islam as the official religion of the state. There are numerous important allusions to international law in the Afghan Constitution. Its preamble makes reference to both the Universal Declaration of Human Rights and the United Nations Charter. According to Art. 7, the state must uphold the Universal Declaration of Human Rights, international treaties, and the United Nations Charter. The National Assembly is responsible for ratifying international accords (Art. 90 para. 5).

In regards to gender equality, Article 22 states that "The citizens of Afghanistan, man and woman, have equal rights and duties before the law" (Saddique, 2004). The global ideals of human dignity, equality and freedom are recognised by the Pakistani Constitution, which also provides a variety of fundamental human rights to its residents. These rights are protected by a number of Constitutional clauses, such as the fundamental rights, the guiding principles of public policy and the directive principles of state policy.

The right to life, liberty and security of person, as well as freedom of speech, expression, assembly and association, as well as equality before the law and defence against discrimination based on race, religion, caste, sex, or place of birth, are among the fundamental rights guaranteed by the Pakistani Constitution. The Constitution also includes clauses that defend the rights of women, children, minorities and underrepresented groups. For instance, Article 25 of the Constitution forbids discrimination on the basis of sexual orientation, while Article 36 safeguards the freedom of religion for minorities (Mehfooz, 2021, p. 10; Shah, 2006, p.110). Nevertheless, in spite of these fundamental protections, Pakistan has struggled to defend and uphold human rights. The Pakistani government has taken action in recent years to address some of these problems, including creating human rights commissions and implementing legislation to safeguard the rights of women and children.

Numerous human rights, such as fundamental freedoms, religious liberty and minority rights, are protected under the Turkish Constitution, which was established on November 7, 1982 (Yazici, 2006). The Turkish Constitution recognises a variety of fundamental rights, including the rights to privacy, property, a fair trial, and freedom of thought, conscience and expression. It also recognises the rights to life, liberty, and security of the person. The right to life and personal safety is protected under Article 17 of the Constitution. This includes protection against arbitrary imprisonment, arrest and torture (Country Reports on Human Rights Practices, 2021). All people are treated equally before the law under Article 10 of the Constitution, regardless of their race, ethnicity, language, religion, political affiliation, or gender. Freedom of religion and conscience are protected under the Constitution. The state cannot compel someone to practice a specific religion or believe, which means that everyone has the right to practice their own religion or beliefs.

Discrimination based on religion or belief is likewise prohibited under the Constitution. Freedom of religion and conscience are guaranteed by Article 24 of the Constitution (Çınar, 2021). Along with the freedom to alter one's religion or views, this also involves the right to practice and manifest one's religion or beliefs. Minority rights are acknowledged by the Constitution, which also provides protection for them. It forbids discrimination based on racial, ethnic, linguistic, or religious characteristics. Minority groups are also allowed to preserve and advance their own cultures, languages, and traditions. The rights and liberties of minorities are protected under Article 10 of the Constitution (İçduygu & Soner, 2006, p. 449). The ability to preserve and further one's own culture, language, and identity falls under this category. The right to freely express oneself, including via the use of the media and other platforms, is protected by Article 26 of the Constitution. Despite these constitutional guarantees, there have been issues with the defence and advancement of human rights in Turkey, notably with regard to the rights of minorities and the freedom of the press and speech. These constitutional requirements continue to be difficult to execute and enforce across the nation.

One of the main issues with these constitutions is that many of these rights only apply to citizens of the country in question. It is not controversial and has equivalents in the constitutions of many Western countries as long as the restriction relates to fundamental political rights like the freedom of association or the right to vote. The issue is the restriction of rights, such as the right to equality before the law, which should be available to all people, even those who are not citizens (Mahmoudi, 2016, p. 537). The absence of a clear monitoring and enforcement system that may offer redress when a constitutional right is purportedly infringed is a significant general flaw. There are, however, a few sporadic instances of these monitoring systems in the constitutions of several nations. The Sudanese Interim Constitution of 2005 calls for the creation of a Human Rights Commission, which investigates complaints alleging violations of the rights and freedoms guaranteed by the constitution and keeps track of how they are being applied. Art. 19 of the Moroccan Constitution provides another illustration. This creates a body tasked with eradicating all forms of prejudice. The Tunisian Constitution's Article 128 on the creation of a Human Rights Commission and its authority should also be mentioned.

How far the above-mentioned flaws and the inadequate drafting of the constitutions' texts contributed significantly to the actual situation with regard to human rights in the nations under consideration is a pertinent subject. It goes without saying that explicitly stating each of the fundamental rights would make it easier for people to exercise them. Both the Tunisian Constitution and the Sudanese Interim Constitution employ this technique. The confusion that a hortatory reference to the Universal Declaration of Human Rights may imply is completely eliminated by such an extended and thorough reference to rights and freedoms. Each right and freedom can then be used as evidence in court on its own. The question of why the relevant constitutions have not been able to inculcate real respect for these rights arises in light of the recurrent frightening revelations of systematic breaches of human rights in various Arab nations by independent and highly regarded international bodies. How far these constitutions actually represent political life is a related subject, as they all solemnly state that the people are the source of all power (Mahmoudi, 2016, p. 538).

The difficulties involved in establishing a constitution are significant and may hinder the effective and genuine realisation of human rights. A well-equipped and smart administrative infrastructure, on the other hand, guarantees that all laws are implemented correctly and that their intended recipients understand and value each legal provision for what it is. In order to advance human rights, a constitution must include these rights as the cornerstone and framework for all other rights and duties. This must be done while also promoting individual rights awareness and strengthening the state's administrative framework. All of the constitutions mentioned thus far create a connection between international law and domestic law. Nearly all of them adopt a modified dualism philosophy in this regard. After being ratified, international accords are incorporated into national law; in this regard, the role of parliament differs. All of the constitutions described so far reference human rights; some do and some do not comply with international norms. This suggests, at the very least, that the analysed states do not deny the application of human rights on a principled basis. Last but not least, it should be emphasised that the majority of Islamic governments recognise the idea of human dignity and fundamental rights.

2.4 Islamic Law and Human Rights

Regardless of religion or other distinctions, Islamic law regards a number of rights as being universal to all people. The fact that some passages of the Qur'ān expressly address Muslims ('O believers') and others address all of humanity ('O humankind') suggests that all people share a fundamental dignity as God's offspring (Sachedina, 2009). The laws of *jihād*, which defend even atheists as foes in battle (for instance, by forbidding the use of poisoned weapons or the mutilation of bodies), or as prisoners, are another illustration of the universality of dignity and rights in action. The concept of divinely conferred human rights is specifically acknowledged in the constitutions of Somalia, Saudi Arabia and Iran (McDonough, 2021). It is important to highlight that pre-modern jurists did not establish a specific human rights *fiqh* sub-field. However, a set of rights is discernible in *shari'ah*, for instance inferred in the mirror-image obligations due to each person or expressed plain in the proofs by instructions telling people to use their own judgement or adhere to their own preferences in particular situations. Muslim jurists have recognised an overarching system of rights (*haqq*) within Islam since the Middle Ages. These rights include rights of God, such as observance of the five pillars of Islam, but they also include rights of people, which 'can be general, like the right to health, to have children, to safety or, they could be specific, like protecting the right of a property-owner or the right of a purchaser and seller in commercial transactions' (Moosa, 2001). In addition to rights that are unalienable, people also have obligations (Kamali, 2002a). The proofs specify particular rights and obligations in addition to demonstrating guiding principles that will help to further guide a system of individual rights that has striking resemblance to contemporary international human rights regimes.

Islamic human rights are based on the universal human dignity, individual freedom and equality. Respect for the inherent dignity of every individual, whether or not they are Muslims, is shown by the Qur'ān and the Prophet's teachings. *Ibahah*, the fundamental tenet that states that everything is not prohibited is permissible, denotes the freedom for people to think and behave whatever they like, with the exception of clear legal requirements based on *shari'ah* or the needs of the society. Finally, Islam introduced a revolutionary 'vision of creating an egalitarian society' to seventh-century Arabia, even though its conception of equality may not quite align with a current western or international perspective (Kamali, 2002b). Among the most crucial elements for legislators and judges to take into account as they continue to create the Islamic law of human rights are dignity, freedom and equality. The fundamental tenant of *sharī'ah* is the respect for human dignity (Kamali, 2002b). The dignity of 'all human beings without limitations or qualifications of any kind' is affirmed in the Qur'ān. Kamali equates the obligation of the ruler to defend human dignity with acknowledgment of and adherence to the *maqasid al-shari'ah* (Kamali, 2002b).

According to Weeramantry, Islam highlights the same inherent dignity that serves as 'the fundamental precept of contemporary doctrines of human rights' (Weeramantry, 1988, p. 152). Despite not going nearly as far, Sachedina contends that acknowledging such dignity might 'serve as a minimalist foundation for human rights in Islam' together with the Qur'ān's universalist vision of a unified society under God and the fact that God gave mankind an innate moral sense (Sachedina, 2009). An Islamic state must undoubtedly work to uphold human dignity, but this is not enough on its own. Human dignity must also be respected in order for human rights to be respected (Donnelly, 1982, p.305). The protection of dignity does not always preclude actions like state intrusion into private affairs, excluding people from political involvement, or granting different rights depending on social standing.

In Islam, personal liberty is a second source of human rights. It derives from fundamental principles like *ibahah* and from countless directives urging believers to seek knowledge and insight and engage in civil discourse. God made it possible for people to make their own decisions since only those who voluntarily want to do so can properly follow *sharīʿah* (Weeramantry, 1988). Even though the proofs and classical jurists hardly ever use the word freedom (*hurriyyah*), according to Kamali, they nonetheless establish a presumption of freedom through the language of permission, which is made even more expansive by al-Shatibi's observation that the proofs point to a state of forgiveness that lies between what the *sharīʿah* has deemed forbidden and permissible (Kamali, 2002b). The Maldives constitutionalises this principle, guaranteeing citizens' freedom to engage in any conduct or activity within the confines of *sharīʿah* and express provisions of law (Weeramantry, 1988). Although individual freedom is the presumption, it is constrained by the needs of society and by the fact that the individual is a social being.

The third essential tenet of Islam is equality, the interpretation of which has caused controversy among supporters of Islamic law and international human rights. The arguments for equality are compelling (McDonough, 2021). This fundamental idea, which is demonstrated by the Prophet and the early Muslim emperors, is in fundamental conflict with the early, powerful jurists who supported hierarchical elements of local social systems and treated them as though they were required by Islamic law (McDonough, 2021). For instance, Baderin argues that the notion of men being superior to women derived from Qur'ānic verses such as 2:228 (which states, in part, 'And women shall have rights similar to the rights against them, according to what is equitable; but men have a degree above them') and 4:34 (which states, in part, 'Men are the protectors and maintainers of women') is too general because those verses specifically addressed the institution of the family (Baderin, 2003). Instead, the verses mirrored the protective and leadership roles that men filled in society, where being in charge of a group effort did not entail superiority over other members of the group and being responsible for protecting and upholding the family did not involve having control over women (Baderin, 2003).

2.5 Islam and International Human Rights Law

International human rights, in the eyes of their supporters, are unquestionably universal, much like *sharīʿah*. With a few exceptions and reservations, the vast majority of governments abide by at least the first generation of UN human rights accords, which is essentially true in positive law. But it is unclear what the actual legal foundation of human rights is. The 'orthodox international view' holds that people have rights by nature, that it is wrong to deny anybody their basic liberty and that rights belong to specific people (Cox, 2013, p. 313). The international human rights instruments' preambles only state their own universal reality. The Enlightenment-era thinkers who applied these old religious and moral principles to governance in Europe and North America in the seventeenth and eighteenth centuries laid the foundation for the modern human rights framework (Bates, 2014, p. 16). The human suffering caused by the two wars sparked global consciousness, leading to the Universal Declaration of Human Rights (UDHR) and efforts to carry out its values in the years that followed (Bates, 2014, p. 28). This legacy is referenced in the constitutions of Algeria and Palestine, which promise to defend, respectively, fundamental liberties, citizen rights and human rights (McDonough, 2021). The origins of international human rights legislation are the same as those of international law more broadly, including treaties, customs from other countries, universally accepted rules of law and judicial or scholarly opinion as 'subsidiary means' (McDonough, 2021, p. 55). International courts, in theory, do not create law, but the parties to the case are bound by their rulings. Resolutions passed by the UN Security Council have legal force. Through the General Assembly resolutions that include the UDHR and organisations like the Human Rights Council and the High Commissioner for Human Rights, the UN has a significant impact on the soft law of human rights.

States engage in (or refrain from) activities because they feel compelled to do so by the law, which is an example of state practice, and thus is an example of opinio juris. A custom is when most states, or most states in a region, regularly operate in the same way while acting within the bounds of the law. Resolutions of the General Assembly, the Human Rights Council and other inter-state organisations, which show how nations perceive their responsibilities, as well as their participation in international affairs, might serve as indicators of custom. When custom and treaty clash, the treaty takes precedence; nevertheless, a treaty may not contradict a peremptory norm of general international law (*jus cogens*), which is a norm that the international community of States as a whole has accepted as a standard from which no deviation is authorized (McDonough, 2021). In the field of human rights law, custom came first. The powerful General Assembly resolution that the ambitious UDHR adopted in 1948—with Saudi Arabia, South Africa and the Soviet Union abstaining—declared an emerging set of principles.

Many of the rights outlined in the UDHR are implemented by the International Covenant on Civil and Political Rights (ICCPR) and the International Covenant on Economic, Social and Cultural Rights (ICESCR), both of which were created within the scope of the UN Human Rights Commission (Bantekas & Oette, 2013). They were declared by the General Assembly in 1966 and state ratifications put them into effect in 1976. International human rights legislation is built around these three documents, which are sometimes referred to as the international bill of rights. There are now seven more UN human rights treaties in effect, each with a monitoring committee: the Convention on the Elimination of All Forms of Discrimination Against Women (CEDAW), the Convention against Torture and Other Cruel, Inhuman or Degrading Treatment or Punishment (CAT), the Convention on the Rights of the Child (CRC), the International Convention on the Protection of the Rights of All Migrant Workers and Members of Their Families (ICMW), the International Convention on the Elimination of All Forms of Racial Discrimination (CERD) and the International (CRPD).

Traditional treaties and human rights treaties have different concepts. They demonstrate nations' consent to give up some of their sovereignty for the benefit of all people, rather than benefiting states as a whole (as, for instance, trade or security accords do). The UN treaty system consists of several monitoring, reporting and other entities, some of which have general mandates and others which are connected to specific treaties. The Human Rights Council, a subsidiary body of the General Assembly and the Human Rights Committee, formed under the ICCPR primarily to assess reports from states parties documenting actions taken to implement the rights the treaty safeguards, are the two most notable (Chinkin, 2018, p. 86). The worldwide system is supplemented by regional agreements in Africa, the Americas, and Europe, as well as the Arab Charter on Human Rights for select League of Arab States members. The creation of a worldwide civil society devoted to advancing human rights, whose participants include non-governmental organizations, academia, and multinational enterprises, was aided by the treaties and monitoring bodies. The profusion of monitoring and reporting that has resulted has substantially augmented the academic and legal sources that have historically served as the primary secondary way of understanding international law (Chinkin, 2018, p. 89).

Although only governments have standing to appear before the International Court of Justice, it has comprehensive authority over international law. Most judgements concerning a person's human rights are made by regional and national courts. Only the European Court of Human Rights handles individual complaints, but all three courts have the authority to render binding judgements. The African Court on Human and Peoples' Rights, the Inter-American Court of Human Rights, and the European Court of Human Rights. The Human Rights Council has the authority to examine specific complaints and express judgements. States who have ratified the ICCPR's Optional Protocol consent to the Committee's right to consider any individual complaints brought against them.

Only Algeria, Djibouti, Libya, the Maldives, Somalia and Tunisia are Islamic countries that have ratified or acceded to the agreement, out of the 120 nations that have done so. Western culture strongly influences international human rights legislation (Wa Mutua, 1996, p. 589). Many of the modern Islamic governments were not independent at the time the bill of rights was being written, which was in the late 1940s. Muslim countries were first underrepresented in terms of the number of delegates and participants, but as more became independent, they began to participate more frequently. Seventeen of the present-day Islamic countries participated in the unanimous adoption of the ICCPR and ICESCR by the General Assembly (Waltz, 2004, p. 807). In a few places, the wording of these accords was altered by representatives of Muslim states. Waltz categorises their main contributions under the following five headings: 'religious freedom, particularly the right to change religion; marriage equality; social justice and the interdependence of political and socioeconomic rights; right to self-determination and the right to petition' (Waltz, 2004, p. 803).

The majority of Islamic countries have embraced international human rights legislation, although Islamic law continues to be relatively understated on a global scale. Nevertheless, the two paradigms have a certain gravitational pull towards one another, particularly now that a modern Islamic interpretation of international human rights legislation is emerging. Islamic law is applied internationally as Islamic states' involvement in institutions and agreements is guided by their ideals. According to Mutua, this presents a chance to reconsider some norms in accordance with Islamic principles because the social welfare state of the twentieth century, which replaced the minimalist republican model of the nineteenth century, is more reminiscent of an ideal Islamic state (McDonough, 2021). By pushing Islamic governments to pursue *sharīʿah* interpretations that adhere to international standards, international law has an impact on Islamic law.

2.6 The Islamic Factor: How Muslim States Address Human Rights in Their Constitutions

Both through highlighting the governmental system's Islamic roots and by designating Islam as the state's official religion, Muslim countries have found ways to display their distinct Islamic identities. For instance, 'Algeria, land of Islam' is mentioned in the preamble of the Algerian Constitution. The Kingdom of Bahrain is a recognised Islamic Arab State, according to Article 1(a) of Bahrain's Constitution. The Yemeni Constitution's Article 1 has the same clause. The Tunisian Constitution, which is perhaps the most advanced and comprehensive constitution in the Arab world in terms of including universal human rights in the country's fundamental legislation, declares in its Art. 1 that Islam is its religion and that this item can be construed as a declaration of the state religion. In virtually every Arab country's constitution, Islam is referred to as the state's official religion, the people's religion, and the religion of the state (Brown, 2017). The Basic Law of Saudi Arabia is unquestionably distinctive in that it references the Islamic nature of the kingdom and does so in nearly every article of the constitution.

As was already indicated, the majority of pertinent constitutions cite Islamic law (*sharīʿah*) as the primary basis of legislation. In the constitutions of Kuwait (Article 2), Iraq (Article 1), Syria (Article 3) and Bahrain, for instance, this is the situation. (Art. 2). Islamic law is regarded as the primary source of law in certain constitutions. Examples include Libya, Qatar and Egypt (Article 2) (Art. 1). Some states have taken things a step further and made Islamic law the only source of law. Sudan (Art. 5) and Yemen are two examples. (Art. 3). The question of whether a state is in accordance with its international human rights commitments may arise given the Islamic character of the political system and, in particular, references to Islamic law as a source or as a source of legislation. The underlying assumption of equality of rights in international human rights discourse, which many non-Muslim states more or less take for granted, is at odds with a number of justifications for discrimination in Islam, leading to the question. The two of them are religion and gender. Furthermore, it has been questioned whether certain criteria of Islamic law, such as those pertaining to the form and content of criminal law, are compatible with international human rights (Alidadi & Foblets, 2012, p. 388).

The majority of constitutions in Muslim countries have generic clauses on equality of rights. Some adhere to the structure found in international legal documents that guarantee equality of rights by outlawing discrimination on a variety of reasons. According to Article 53 of the Egyptian Constitution, 'Citizens are equal before the law, possess equal rights and public duties, and may not be discriminated against on the basis of religion, belief, sex, origin, race, color, language, disability, social class, political affiliation, or for any other reason' (Virgili, 2010). Similarly, Article 31 of the Sudanese Constitution states that 'All persons are equal before the law and are entitled to equal protection without discrimination on the basis of race, color, sex, language, religious creed, political opinion, or ethnic origin' (Mujuzi, 2020, p. 156).

The Malaysian constitution, also known as the Federal Constitution, affirms the principle of equality of rights among all citizens of Malaysia. Article 8 of the constitution expressly prohibits discrimination on the grounds of race, religion, descent, gender, or place of birth. Specifically, Article 8(1) states that 'All persons are equal before the law and entitled to the equal protection of the law' (Wong, 2021). This provision guarantees that every person in Malaysia, regardless of their background or status, is entitled to equal treatment under the law. Article 8(2) further elaborates on the principle of equality by prohibiting discrimination on the grounds of religion, race, descent, place of birth, or gender in any law, or in the appointment to any office or employment under a public authority. This provision ensures that no one is excluded from public office or employment based on their race, religion, gender, or other discriminatory factors. However, it is important to note that the Malaysian constitution also includes affirmative action policies known as the New Economic Policy (NEP) and the National Development Policy (NDP) that aim to redress economic imbalances among different ethnic groups in the country. These policies have been controversial and have been criticised for perpetuating inequalities in certain instances. In summary, while the Malaysian constitution enshrines the principle of equality of rights for all citizens, the implementation of this principle has been complicated by affirmative action policies and ongoing debates about their effectiveness and fairness (Dass, 2019).

The principles of equality of rights are all guaranteed by the constitutions of Indonesia, Pakistan and Turkey, albeit the details and interpretations may vary. The 1945 Constitution of Indonesia has Article 28I, which declares that "every person shall have the right to be treated equally before the law and government and shall be entitled to protection of the law," which upholds the equality concept in Indonesia (Eddyono, 2015, p. 122; Ibrahim, 2022, p.122). According to how this clause has been construed, all citizens are entitled to the same rights regardless of their race, ethnicity, religion, gender, or other traits. In a similar vein, Article 25 of the Pakistani Constitution upholds the ideal of equality before the law and equal protection under the law. According to the clause, there shall be no discrimination on the basis of race, color, creed, or sexual orientation and every citizen shall have the equal protection of the law (Yousaf, 2014). In Article 10 of the Turkish Constitution, which stipulates that "all persons are equal before the law without any discrimination based on language, race, color, sex, political opinion, philosophical belief, religion and sect, or any other reason," the concept of equality is also guaranteed. Equal protection under the law is another promise made by the Constitution (Oguz, 2011).

Although the concept of equality is guaranteed by all these constitutions, there may be variations in how this ideal is applied in actuality. For instance, concerns with discrimination based on religion, ethnicity, or gender may be more prevalent in some nations than others and the methods used to resolve these issues may vary. Nevertheless, the constitutional frameworks of Turkey, Pakistan and Indonesia all fundamentally uphold the idea of equality. The constitutions of these nations have provisions that address particular concerns relating to equality and discrimination in addition to generic equality ideals. For instance, the Indonesian Constitution has clauses that safeguard minorities' rights and the rights of women and children. In a similar vein, the Pakistani Constitution forbids discrimination based on gender, caste, or religion as well as slavery and forced labour. Along with prohibiting discrimination in work and education, the Turkish Constitution also contains measures defending the rights of minorities, women, and children (Süral, 2007, p. 815; Roznai & Yolcu, 2012, p. 178). Notably, prejudice and inequality persist in these countries as well as other regions of the world despite these constitutional protections. It is up to governments, public society and people to make sure that these ideals are followed in reality even if the constitutions offer a legal foundation for fostering equality. This calls for continual campaigns to increase public awareness of discrimination and inequality as well as the creation of laws and other measures that support equality and discourage prejudice.

In some cases, a constitution does not explicitly and completely recognise the equality of rights. Sometimes, some grounds for discrimination are not included, usually due to national political considerations or a potential conflict between that right and Islamic law. The Kuwaiti Constitution's Article 29 forbids discrimination on the grounds of race, national origin, language, or religion. It does not include things like sex being a basis for discrimination. The basis of discrimination are listed as sex, race, language, and religion in Article 35 of the Constitution of Qatar. No mention of ethnicity as a potential factor is made (Mahmoudi, 2016, p. 539). In terms of equal rights, Morocco has employed a different strategy. The civil, political, economic, social, cultural, and environmental rights and freedoms guaranteed by the Moroccan constitution or the international accords that Morocco has joined are equally enjoyed by men and women, according to Article 19 of that nation's constitution. This should obviously imply that Morocco should not be allowed to discriminate on any of the reasons listed in the 1966 Covenants (Mahmoudi, 2016, p. 540). The topic of whether potential discrimination pertaining to rights owing to the conflict between Islamic law and international human rights is being, or can be, addressed continues, notwithstanding states' diverse constitutional approaches to equality of rights. The current situation can be better understood by taking a closer look at minorities' and women's rights as two specific forms of discrimination (Mahmoudi, 2016, p. 541).

Islamic law's treatment of women's rights is frequently cited as a classic case of discrimination. This assertion is supported by a comparison of Islamic law's protection of women's rights with the most significant piece of legislation in this field, the Convention on the Elimination of All Forms of Discrimination Against Women (CEDAW) (Brandt & Kaplan, 1995–1996, p. 110). The Convention affirms that men and women are entitled to the same freedoms and rights in all areas, including the political, economic, social, cultural, and civic ones. According to certain analysts, the Convention's provisions are incompatible with *sharīʿah*. They use passages from the Qur'ān that deal with inheritance, divorce and polygamy to bolster their claim (AlQur'ān; 2:228, 4.3, 4:11 & 4:12). Naturally, some commenters attempt to defend the prejudice by outlining the social, political, and economic elements that contributed to the inequality (Baderin, 2003). Supporters of gender equality frequently criticise Qur'ānic verse 4:34 because they believe it to be permissive of males to abuse women (Al-Qur'ān; 4:34). Modern interpretations, however, contend that the text should not be read literally. These interpretations contend that the consequences outlined in the passage are only symbolic and are not required to take the shape of actual physical retribution. Islamic jurists can be loosely divided into two groups with regard to gender equality. The conservative school of interpretation contends that the equality principle conflicts with Islamic law because it attempts to treat equally people who, according to *sharī'ah*, should be treated differently. The other side, which takes a more contemporary stance in its interpretation, insists that the Qur'ānic texts that appear to be discriminatory may really be reconciled with the idea of equality (Baderin, 2003).

The majority of Arab League members ratified the Convention without making any reservations. One claim is that because women's and children's rights are so vigorously upheld in Islam, there is no need for reservations (Cole, 2013, p. 234). This group includes Bahrain, Iraq, Jordan, Lebanon, Morocco, Oman, Qatar, Saudi Arabia, Syria and Tunisia. Reservations have been included by a few more countries to their ratification or accession documents. It is unclear how some of these nations can uphold their Convention responsibilities given that their constitutions explicitly state that Islamic law serves as their primary source of legislation. The constitution of Qatar, which states in Art. 51: 'The right of inheritance is inviolable and is governed by Islamic law,' is an excellent example. In Egypt, women's rights have been a major concern, and the constitution of the country includes provisions for gender equality and women's rights. The Convention on the Elimination of All Forms of Discrimination Against Women (CEDAW), which strives to safeguard and advance women's rights and gender equality, has also been ratified by Egypt.

In addition to recognising the value of women in society, the constitution prohibits discrimination based on gender. In addition, the constitution mandates that the state take action to safeguard women from abuse and grant them equal access to political participation, work prospects, and educational possibilities. Egypt adopted CEDAW in 1981 and has moved forward with putting its provisions into practice. The nation has implemented legislation to defend women from abuse and discrimination, including the Law on the Elimination of Violence Against Women, which makes a number of gender-based types of violence illegal. To properly implement CEDAW and safeguard women's rights in Egypt, however, advocates for women's rights contend that more work has to be done. There are still numerous instances of discrimination and injustice against women, and there have been questions about how Islamic law is interpreted and applied when it comes to inheritance and family problems. The constitution of Malaysia has clauses that prohibit gender discrimination and support gender equality. Malaysia adopted CEDAW in 1995 and has made great strides in putting its principles into practice, including raising the political engagement of women and expanding access to healthcare and education. However, there are still issues that women must deal with in areas like marriage, inheritance and work where cultural and religious customs may be in conflict with women's rights (Sheikh, 2010, p. 56).

The constitution of Pakistan ensures gender equality and forbids gender-based prejudice. Pakistan adopted CEDAW in 1996 and has made progress in putting its principles into practice, including adopting legislation to safeguard women from domestic abuse and raising the role of women in politics (Gondal, 2017). Gender equality and the ban on discrimination based on gender are both guaranteed under Turkish law. Turkey adopted CEDAW in 1985 and has made strides towards putting its principles into practice, including adopting legislation to safeguard women from abuse and raising the role of women in politics (Müftüler-Baç, 2012).

Although the constitutions of these countries include clauses promoting gender equality and women's rights, considerable work has to be done before these clauses are completely implemented and women's rights are fully safeguarded. In these nations, ratifying CEDAW was a significant step towards advancing women's rights and gender equality and ongoing work to put its provisions into practice is crucial to attaining gender equality. Other Arab nations have added reservations to the Convention. Regarding a number of clauses, such as Art. 16 related to the right to marriage, Kuwait has reservations (Mahmoudi, 2016, p. 541). Libya has stated that its acceptance of the Convention is 'subject to the general reservation that such acceptance cannot conflict with the laws on personal status derived from the Islamic Shari'ah' (Mayer, 1998, p. 26). Regarding Islamic law, the United Arab Emirates have likewise expressed a reluctance.

Another area of dispute is the issue of religious equality. Despite significant distinctions between Muslims and non-Muslims in terms of status under Islamic law and practice, some Islamic scholars hold that the Qur'ān and the Sunnah make clear that Muslims and non-Muslims are equal in a number of instances. Verse 49:13 is mentioned in this context. Islamic governments now have different policies towards religious minorities. The discrimination is more overt and complex in nations where Islamic law is the rule of law. As People of the Book, Christians and Jews often possess certain guaranteed rights, but other faiths seldom have any particular rights that are codified in legislation. By placing various types of restrictions on the activities of religious minorities, discrimination is tacitly practiced in several Islamic countries (Mayer, 2013). Access to public office is another instance of prejudice with significant practical repercussions. In the majority of Islamic nations, entry is frequently restricted to religious minorities. Even though it is not often stated in laws, this type of discrimination still occurs. In different nations, there are varying degrees of restrictions on the ability to hold public office. In some, the restriction only applies to high-ranking posts like those of cabinet ministers, high-ranking military officers and high-ranking judicial authorities. A non-Muslim's ability to hold public office is a very unusual exception that requires special permission in other countries, especially those that have Islamic law as their state legislation. Scholars who promote modern interpretations of Islamic law think that there may be some room for agreement with Western state policies on matters pertaining to the rights of women and religious minorities. They emphasise that internal politics and constitutional shortcomings in these governments, rather than the requirements of Islamic law, are to blame for the dismal human rights record of many Islamic states (Mayer, 2013).

The domain of criminal law is another potential area where Islamic law and international human rights law may clash. What is commonly referred to as Islamic criminal law is made up of a variety of laws governing how certain types of crimes should be punished as well as features of how these crimes should be prosecuted. Islam classifies crimes according to their gravity, much as all other legal systems. The most severe sins are those that are deemed to be crimes against God, or '*hudud*' (an Arabic term meaning limitations) (Kamali, 1998, p. 205). Which offences are covered by *hudūd* are a matter of debate among all schools of Islamic law. Apostasy, rebellion against the authorities, intoxication, robbery on the highway, adultery and defamation are a few instances of crimes that fall under this heading. *Sharīʿah* imposes obligatory punishments for *hudūd*. They include death, occasionally by stoning, hand amputation and whipping. The second category of offences is referred to as *qisās*, which is Arabic for 'retaliation' and encompasses offences like murder and causing bodily harm. Retaliation or financial recompense for the victim or his or her family are the penalties for *qisas*. The term '*ta'zir*' refers to the third group of offences. Islamic law does not specify a punishment for certain offences; instead, the court or a parliamentary act may determine the appropriate sentence (Usmani, 2006, p. 288).

The term of torture as stated in the Convention against Torture includes *hudūd* and *qisās* penalties, such as amputating hands and feet or stoning. However, only Qatar has said that it will not ratify the Convention if any of its articles are interpreted in a manner inconsistent with the principles of Islamic law and the Islamic religion among the Islamic nations that have so far done so. This reservation has drawn criticism from some Western nations. In addition to ratifying the Convention, Pakistan included a declaration stating that the provisions 'shall be applied to the extent that they are not repugnant to the provisions of [...] the Shariah law' (Mahmoudi, 2016, p. 542).

It is a known fact that most of the Organisation of Islamic Cooperation's member states do not implement Islamic criminal law. Therefore, no reservations are required for the Convention. However, there are several nations that have accepted the Convention that apply Islamic criminal laws. Yemen and Saudi Arabia are two instances. For these nations as well as other Islamic governments that adhere to Islamic law to the letter but are not Convention parties, like Sudan, Islamic penalties are not equivalent to torture because they are predetermined in *sharīʿah* as God's will. These countries contend that the Convention's definitions of torture and harsh treatment are artificial constructs. The Iranian Constitution's Article 38 expressly forbids using any kind of torture to coerce confessions or gather information. This implies that Iran does not view the Islamic criminal penalties that are applied there as torture or other forms of cruel, inhumane, or humiliating punishment.

2.7 Human Rights Conventions and Muslim Response

Constitutionalism had been seen as a way of safeguarding civil and political rights, negative rights that imposed restrictions on the authority of government, long before the emergence of international human rights legislation. Later, the constitutions of Europe and the United States served as models. Limits on political authority and protections for individual liberty, which is to be shielded from state interference, are central to these constitutions. The regulations creating these limits are responses to tyranny and bad governance, and they are intended to remedy these problems. The drafters of constitutions attempted to identify and limit the arguments that governments may rely on to restrict rights because they understood that occasionally individual rights would need to be restricted in the public interest or in exceptional situations. International law on civil and political rights, which extensively borrows from formulations initially produced in the West, is motivated by similar goals.

The scope of potential international sources of human rights legislation is too broad for us to examine here, even with an emphasis on civil and political rights. The International Bill of Human Rights will serve as the main reference for the comparisons made here. The 1948 Universal Declaration of Human Rights, the 1966 ICESCR, the 1966 International Covenant on Civil and Political Rights, and the Optional Protocol to the ICCPR make up the International Bill of Human Rights. In 1976, the accords from 1966 came into effect. The UDHR has grown in significance through time and is now regarded as obligatory on all governments, regardless of whether they have ratified any agreements. Numerous countries have declined to ratify one or both of the two primary covenants. Saudi Arabia and the United Arab Emirates (UAE) are two examples of Muslim-majority nations in the Middle East that have not ratified the ICCPR and the ICESCR. The same covenants, however, have been ratified by a variety of nations, including Afghanistan, Algeria, Egypt, Iran, Iraq, Jordan, Kuwait, Libya, Morocco, Pakistan, Sudan, Syria and Tunisia. Only a small portion of the body of literature produced by Muslims that purports to explain where Islam stands on human rights may be presented here (Henkin, 1981, p. 260). Abu'l A'la Mawdūdī, a well-known Sunni religious figure from the Indian subcontinent, wrote a booklet titled Human Rights in Islam. The pamphlet's main feature is an English translation of a speech delivered by Mawdūdī in 1975 in

Lahore, Pakistan. It was initially published in 1976. Jama'at-I-Islami, a political organisation established by Mawdūdī in 1941, has been active in Pakistani politics for the last few decades. Its members are dedicated to the restoration of Islamic law and the creation of an Islamic state in Pakistan. Mawdūdī wrote a lot about how to apply Islam to modern issues before he passed away in 1979, and his works were widely translated. He received the King Faisal Prize from Saudi Arabia in honour of what were reportedly his exceptional services to Islam. Mawdūdī sought to speak to a broad public audience, without the usual religious education obtained by highly qualified religious scholars. His remarks found an audience among Muslims who shared his profound disdain of Western dominance. In his confrontational approach towards the West, he criticised Western society and culture for its corruption and materialism while asserting that Islamic civilisation was much better to that of the West. His booklet on human rights exemplifies the polemical viewpoints that influenced his work in general (Mawdudi, 1977).

Also covered is the Universal Islamic Declaration of Human Rights (UIDHR), which was published in 1981. Representatives from Egypt, Pakistan, Saudi Arabia and other nations worked on this paper under the direction of the Islamic Council, a private organisation with a base in London that is connected to the Muslim World League, which has its headquarters in Saudi Arabia. The proclamation was sent to the United Nations Educational, Scientific, and Cultural Organisation (UNESCO) in Paris amid much public hoopla. On first glance, the English translation of the UIDHR appears to be identical to the UDHR, however many of the parallels are deceptive. The Arabic version, which expresses concepts that greatly depart from the UDHR, differs dramatically from the English version.

We look at the discrepancies between the UIDHR's English and Arabic versions. Although the UIDHR usually reflects the views of traditional Muslim scholars, it is doubtful if we may be able to agree on all of the clauses due to the complexity and ambiguities in the document. Al-Azhar University, the most prominent school of higher learning in Sunni Islam and a centre of traditional Islamic thinking, is linked with the Islamic Research Academy of Cairo, which developed the rights provisions in the "Draft of the Islamic Constitution" (Mohiuddin, 2022, p. 167). One view of Sunni Islam's perspective on human rights is reflected in this draft constitution, which was published in 1979 in Volume 51 of the al-Azhar periodical *Majallat alAzhar*. The al-Azhar draft may be viewed as an attempt to show that Sunni Islam has the ability to create a constitution for a contemporary government because it was published at a time when the Shiʿī leadership of Iran's Islamic revolution was gaining support in the Sunni world.

Also evaluated are the rights clauses in the Iranian constitution from 1979, which, according to its preamble, 'is based upon Islamic principles' (Mayer, 2013). One effort to define what rights should be included in a document that establishes a theocratic government rooted on Twelver Shiʿism is the Iranian constitution. The Saudi foreign minister delivered the Cairo Declaration on Human Rights in Islam during the 1993 World Conference on Human Rights in Vienna. He said that it represented the global Muslim community's position on human rights (Mayer, 1994, p. 375). The endorsement of the declaration by the OIC's foreign ministers in August 1990 has led to it being regarded as the primary Islamic statement on human rights, reflecting trends that had already been established in earlier Islamic human rights frameworks.

It seemed, at least on the surface, to represent a more broad understanding of how Islam should influence rights—even if it was just at the governmental level. The real positions on rights taken by OIC member states and the rights formulations in their constitutions, which continued to differ as significantly after the release of the Cairo Declaration as they had before, belied the impression of unanimity in practice. The OIC declared that a charter on human rights will replace the Cairo Declaration, although this proposed charter has not yet been published. The OIC has been taking an active part in the UN's human rights system in the meanwhile, advocating for the Cairo Declaration and trying to convince the UN to pay consideration to what are portrayed as Islamic issues in the human rights arena.

Muslim countries were inspired to clarify their positions on human rights by the 1993 Vienna World Conference on Human Rights. The conference's main topics of contention were whether or not human rights were inexorably related to Western civilisation and whether or not they could or should be universal (Mayer, 1994, p. 377). Saudi Arabia and Iran were ardent supporters of the 1990 Cairo Declaration in the time leading up to the meeting. The Saudi Basic Law, which was published on March 1, 1992, is also examined (Aba-Namay, 1993, p. 296). Saudi Arabia, unlike Iran, Pakistan, or the Sudan, had chosen to keep premodern Islamic law as the rule of law in the majority of its jurisdictions, choosing not to pursue Islamisation. Instead, Saudi Arabia was tardily starting a programme of cautious reforms of the sort that the majority of countries had previously implemented by the early twentieth century. Although very basic, the 1992 Basic Law was the closest thing Saudi Arabia had ever had to a constitution. The Basic Law's provisions claimed to be derived from Islam and to set up a government that was also derived from Islam (Mayer, 2013). The inconsistency in Saudi human rights policy is shown by the differences between the rights that the Basic Law guarantees and those in the Cairo Declaration, which Saudi Arabia has previously formally approved.

Since the previous governments had been deposed by US military invasions in Iraq and Afghanistan, US advisors had a substantial influence on the constitution-drafting procedures. However, just as it was in many other Muslim countries, the issue of how to strike a balance between the conflicting claims of Islam and human rights emerged as a major point of dispute in both nations. For comparison, aspects of Islamisation initiatives in Pakistan and Sudan as well as some other works on Islam and human rights are also explored. It should be emphasised that just because something is called 'Islamic,' it does not necessarily mean that all or even most of the more than 1 billion Muslims in the world would agree with it. The same goes for the fact that the word 'Islamic' is used to describe the human rights programmes that are presented here. The relationship between Islamic tradition and the preservation of human rights is still a hotly debated topic in the Muslim world.

Asserting that Islam does support human rights—as long as such human rights are subjected to Islamic principles, the Islamic human rights publications examined here represent compromise stances in many ways. The end result is an amalgamation—often a very difficult one—of international law with ideas that are either appropriated from or portrayed as having Islamic roots. The literature supporting the compromise viewpoints is an intriguing picture of what occurs when elements of two very different legal systems meet, creating a combination without any prior precedent. Interestingly, the compromise position that holds that Islam recognises some kind of human rights but sets limitations and conditions on them also has significant political implications.

2.8 Conclusion

Human rights are a key component of a just and equitable society. These rights, which are frequently enshrined in both domestic and international law, guarantee that everyone is treated equally under the law and with respect and dignity. However, there has been considerable discussion and examination around the legal status of human rights in nations with a majority of Muslims. Depending on the nation and its political structure, different Muslim-majority nations have different constitutional protections for human rights. Many nations with a majority of Muslims have accepted international human rights treaties, which have been used to enshrine human rights in their constitutions and legislation. However, there can be vast variations in how effectively these rights are safeguarded and upheld (Kayaoglu, 2020).

Despite having references to Islam in their constitutions, several of these nations, like Syria, clearly have secular administrations. Others, such Saudi Arabia and Sudan, are said to have Islamic regimes and are devoted to the rigorous enforcement of Islamic law. The alleged incompatibility of these rights with the norms of Islamic law cannot be the only explanation for why Arab nations may fall short in implementing international human rights. Thus, in a constitutional reform, consideration must be given to both the typical shortcomings of a Third World nation's legal system and the potential barriers that these nations' strong Islamic identities may pose to the realisation of international human rights (McCrudden, 2008, p. 661).

Why these nations should use international human rights as a basis for their constitutions is one conceivable question. It is possible that these nations' adoption of international documents like the 2005 Covenant on the Rights of the Child in Islam, the 2004 Arab Charter of Human Rights, and the 1990 Cairo Declaration on Human Rights in Islam show that they do not view international human rights as fully adequate or sufficient for their needs. These Islamic writings all have the trait of being mute on the most contentious topics pertaining to women's and children's rights. Therefore, it might be argued that they cannot be as thorough and in-depth as those international legal instruments that have explained the whole list of international human rights as accepted by the majority of countries. Islamic human rights documents should not take the place of international human rights standards, even if they may be a significant tool for furthering their protection while taking into account cultural variation. Furthermore, the majority of Arab and Muslim nations actively contributed to the creation of international agreements and joined such agreements, eliminating the need for outdated debates between Western and Islamic standards (Robinson, 2021).

Those who support finding answers inside Islam have been led by Abdullahi Ahmed An-Na 'im. Based on the writings of Sudanese Muslim scholar Mahmoud Mohamed Taha, he adopts an approach that holds that *sharīʿah* is not the entirety of Islam but rather the understanding of the early Muslims of Islam's sources in response to the practical challenges of establishing an Islamic state in seventh-century Arabia. He recommends permitting contemporary Muslim jurists to express and interpret the law for their peers, even if those statements and interpretations deviate from the conventional knowledge in certain ways. It has been suggested that previous, more liberal passages of the Qur'ān, such as the ban of force in matters of faith, were repealed in order to make room for the ideology of *jihad* and other severe directives. Similarly, the argument that the very life of the young Muslim community is at risk cannot be used to justify the practice of putting people to death for apostasy (Arzt, 1990, p. 215). The current status quo, however, is intolerant of political or religious disagreement, which prevents the research and debate required to create novel solutions. Taha's movement was outlawed, his writings were destroyed, and he was put to death in Khartoum in 1985. Internal reformers require the credibility of postings in internationally renowned academic institutions as well as the support of outside allies (Arzt, 1990, p. 219).

It is encouraging to see Morocco's commitment to universal human rights and reiteration of its membership in the Islamic ummah in the preamble to its new constitution (Blitt, 2017, 780). It also emphasises how it upholds and advances the principles of humanitarian law and human rights and how doing so advances its universality and indivisible nature. Additionally, it forbids and opposes discrimination of any kind based on a person's sex, race, religion, culture, nationality, place of origin, nationality, language, disability, or other characteristic. It prioritises and harmonises national law with the international agreements ratified by the nation before its national laws. These sentences demonstrate a shift in perspective on the value of international human rights as a reliable foundation for drafting a new constitution (Blitt, 2017, 789).

The inclusion of all fundamental international human rights in the constitution and the establishment of the necessary oversight bodies are two actions that can be taken to bring the constitutions of the Arab countries and their actual performance with international human rights law into compliance. Practically speaking, one solution to the issue of inconsistencies between Islamic law and human rights legislation, such as polygamy and underage marriage, is to enact laws that are so stringent that these actions are almost impossible. In certain national laws and customs, practical solutions to problems like inheritance and custody or guardianship of the kid can be found. If allowed to function freely, voluntary organisations in Arab governments may help bring about systemic transformation. For instance, the Cairo-based Union of Arab Jurists has taken a prominent role in defending the legal rights of political offenders. With its conferences examining the issue of human rights and democratic freedoms in the Arab world, a recently established Arab Organisation for Human Rights may potentially assist reform. The charter of the organisation does, however, permit Arab nations to declare emergencies that would allow them to reject the Charter's obligations (Rishmawi, 2015). Women's rights are being pushed by feminist authors in Morocco, Pakistan, Saudi Arabia, and other countries with restrictions that take into account Islamic customs (Rishmawi, 2015).

It could be advisable to urge lawyers and other professionals in other Arab countries to adopt these patterns. Even more directly, proposals for the creation of an Arab Court of Justice would entrust Islamic jurists and legal institutions with the duty of developing a contemporary understanding of the function of international law in Islamic courts if they were to be repeated after the first proposal in the 1950s. Such chances to harmonise conventional values with global human rights conventions shouldn't be passed up.

References

Aba-Namay, R. (1993). The recent constitutional reforms in Saudi Arabia. *International and Comparative Law Quarterly, 42*, 295–331.

Abu-Odeh, L. (2004). The politics of (mis)recognition: Islamic law pedagogy in American academia. *American Journal of Comparative Law, 52*, 789–824.

Afghanistan Constitution. (2004). Retrieved November 28, 2024, from https://www.constituteproject.org/constitution/Afghanistan_2004#:text=Article%202,performance%20of%20their%religious%rituals

Ahmed, D. I., & Ginsburg, T. (2014). Constitutional Islamization and human rights: The surprising origin and spread of Islamic supremacy in constitutions. *Virginia Journal of International Law, 54*(3), 615–695.

Al-Fahad, A. H. (2005). Ornamental constitutionalism: The Saudi basic law of governance. *The Yale Journal of International Law, 30*, 376–395.

Alidadi, K., & Foblets, M.-C. (2012). Framing multicultural challenges in freedom of religion terms: Limitations of minimal human rights for managing religious diversity in Europe. *Netherlands Quarterly of Human Rights, 30*(4), 388–416.

Al-Sanhuri, A. R. (2007). *Al-wasit fi sharh al-qanun al-madani al-jadid* (A. al-Maraghi, Ed., Vol. 1, pp. 44–50). Dar al-Nahda al-'Arabiyya.

Arjomand, S. A. (2012). The kingdom of jurists: Constitutionalism and the legal order in Iran. In R. Grote & T. Röder (Eds.), *Constitutionalism in Islamic countries: Between upheaval and continuity* (pp. 141–170). Oxford University Press.

Arzt, D. E. (1990). The application of international human rights law in Islamic states. *Human Rights Quarterly, 12*(2), 202–230.

Asshiddiqie, J. (2009). *The constitutional law of Indonesia*. Maxwell Asia.

Azhari, A. N. A., & Jiet, L. W. (2016). Separating the Attorney-General and public prosecutor: Enhancing rule of law in Malaysia. *Policy Ideas, 34*, 2–28. Retrieved April 5, 2024, from https://www.ideas.org.my/wp-content/uploads/2021/04/PI34-Separating-the-Attorney-Generaland-Public-Prosecutor.pdf

Baderin, M. A. (2003). *International human rights and Islamic law*. Oxford University Press.

Bantekas, I., & Oette, L. (2013). *International human rights law and practice*. Cambridge University Press.

Bates, E. (2014). History. In D. Moeckli, S. Shah, & S. Sivakumaran (Eds.), *International human rights law* (2nd ed., pp. 16). Oxford University Press.

Blitt, R. C. (2017). Equality and nondiscrimination through the eyes of an international religious organization: The organization of Islamic cooperation's (OIC) response to women's rights. *Wisconsin International Law Journal, 34*(4), 755–821.

Brandt, M., & Kaplan, J. A. (1995–1996). The tension between women's rights and religious rights: Reservations to CEDAW by Egypt, Bangladesh and Tunisia. *Journal of Law and Religion, 12*(1), 105–142.

Brinton, J. Y. (1968). *The mixed courts of Egypt*. Yale University Press.

Brown, N. (1997). *The rule of law in the Arab world: Courts in Egypt and the gulf*. Cambridge University Press.

Brown, N. J. (2017). *Official Islam in the Arab world: The contest for religious authority*. Carnegie Endowment for International Peace.

Bureau of democracy, human Rights and labor. (2021). 2021 Country reports on human rights practices: Turkey. Retrieved April 7, 2024, from https://www.state.gov/reports/2021-countryreports-on-human-rights practices/turkey/

Chinkin, C. (2018). Sources. In D. Moeckli, S. Shah, & S. Sivakumaran D. Harris (Eds.), *International human rights law* (4th ed., p. 86). Oxford University Press.

Christelow, A. (1985). *Muslim law courts and the French colonial state in Algeria*. Princeton University Press.

Çınar, Ö. H. (2021, June 15). Freedom of religion and belief in Turkey: Recent challenges and recommendations in the context of European integration. Retrieved 7 April, 2024, from https://talkabout.iclrs.org/2021/06/15/freedom-of-religion-and-belief-in-turkey-recent/

Cole, W. M. (2013). Government respect for gendered rights: The effect of the convention on the elimination of discrimination against women on women's rights outcomes, 1981–2004. *International Studies Quarterly, 57*(2), 233–249.

Constitutional drafting committee. (2015). The 2015 Draft Yemeni constitution. Retrieved April 5, 2024, from https://constitutionnet.org/sites/default/files/2017-07/2015%20%20Draft%20constitution%20(English).pdf

Cox, N. (2013). The clash of unprovable universalisms—International human rights and Islamic law. *Oxford Journal of Law and Religion, 2*, 312–313.

Dass, D. (2019, June 9). Is equality a problem for Malaysia? *Malaysiakini*. Retrieved April 27, 2023, from https://www.malaysiakini.com/news/478935

David, R., & Brierley, J. (1978). *Major legal systems of the world today: An introduction to the comparative study of law*. Free Press.

Donnelly, J. (1982). Human rights and human dignity: An analytic critique of non-western conceptions of human rights. *American Political Science Review, 76*, 303–307.

Ebel, F. (2022, July 29). New constitution gives some Tunisians hope, others concern. *AP News*. Retrieved April 2, 2024, from https://apnews.com/article/middle-east-africa-tunisia-constitutions-06c915ec08ed05686a09081d74287cb6

Eddyono, L. W. (2015). The first ten years of constitutional court of Indonesia: The establishment of the principle of equality and the prohibition of discrimination. *Constitutional Review, 2*(1), 120146.

Ellis, A. (2005, March). Constitutional reform in Indonesia: A Retrospective. Retrieved March 19, 2024, from https://constitutionnet.org/sites/default/files/AEpaperCBPIndonesia.pdf

Gondal, A. R. (2017, October 31). Violence against women in Pakistan and Pakistan's obligations under international law. Retrieved March 20, 2023, from https://ssrn.com/abstract=3062673

Hallaq, W. (1997). *A history of Islamic legal theories*. Cambridge University Press.

Henkin, L. (1981). International human rights as rights. In J. R. Pennock & J. W. Chapman (Eds.), *Human rights: NOMOS XXIII* (pp. 258–259). New York University Press.

Ibrahim, M. (2022). The judicialisation of discrimination in the Indonesian constitutional court. *International Journal of Discrimination and the Law, 22*(2), 121–151.

Ibrahim, R. (2020, June 28). Status of international agreements in national law. Retrieved April 2, 2024, from https://udayananetworking.unud.ac.id/professor/scientific/1633/status-ofinternational-agreements-in-national-law-471

İçduygu, A., & Soner, B. A. (2006). Turkish minority rights regime: Between difference and equality. *Middle Eastern Studies, 42*(3), 447–468.

Kamali, M. H. (1998). Punishment in Islamic law: A critique of the hudud bill of Kelantan, Malaysia. *Arab Law Quarterly, 13*(3), 203–234.

Kamali, M. H. (2002a). *Freedom, equality and justice in Islam*. Islamic Texts Society.

Kamali, M. H. (2002b). *The dignity of man: An Islamic perspective*. Islamic Texts Society.

Karčić, F. (2001). Applying the sharī'ah in modern societies: Main developments and issues. *Islamic Studies, 40*(2), 207–226.

Kayaoglu, T. (2020). *The Organization of Islamic Cooperation's declaration on human rights: Promises and pitfalls*. Retrieved November 28, 2024, from https://www.brookings.edu/research/the-organization-of-islamic-cooperations-decleration-on-human-rights-promises-and-pitfalls/.

Kugle, S. A. (2001). Framed, blamed and renamed: The recasting of Islamic jurisprudence in colonial South Asia. *Modern Asian Studies, 35*(2), 257–313.

Lazumirskyy, V. (2021). *Legal and practical challenges to the fulfilment of fundamental rights in Muslim-majority states*. Retrieved November 28, 2024, from https://www.lai.lv/viedokli/legal-and-practical-challenges-to-the fulfilment-of-fundamental-rights-in-Muslim-majority-states-927

Lombardi, C. B. (1998). Islamic law as a source of constitutional law in Egypt: The constitutionalization of the sharia in a modern Arab state. *Columbia Journal of Transnational Law, 81*, 81–121.

Lombardi, C. B. (2013). Constitutional provisions making Sharia 'A' or 'The' chief source of legislation: Where did they come from? What do they mean? Do they matter? *American University International Law Review, 28*(3), 733–774.

Mahmoudi, S. (2016). International human rights law as a framework for emerging constitutions in Arab countries. In R. Grote & T. J. Röder (Eds.), *Constitutionalism, human rights and Islam after the Arab Spring* (pp. 535–544). Oxford University Press.

Mawdudi, A. A. (1977). *Human rights in Islam*. Islamic Publications Ltd.

Mayer, A. E. (1994). Universal versus Islamic human rights: A clash of cultures or a clash with a construct? *Michigan Journal of International Law, 15*, 375.

Mayer, A. E. (1998). Islamic reservations to human rights conventions. *Recht Van De Islam, 15*, 25–45.

Mayer, A. E. (2013). *Islam and human rights: Traditions and politics* (5th ed., pp. 138–139). Westview Press.

McClintock, A. (1993). Family feuds: Gender, nationalism and the family. *Feminist Review, 44*, 61–80.

McCrudden, C. (2008). Human dignity and judicial interpretation of human rights. *European Journal of International Law, 19*(4), 655–724.

McDonough, P. (2021). *Human rights commitments of Islamic states: Sharia, treaties and consensus*. Hart Publishing.

Mehfooz, M. (2021). Religious freedom in Pakistan: A case study of religious minorities. *Religions, 12*(1), 1–16.

Meyer-Resende, M. (2014). *Egypt: In-depth analysis of the main elements of the new constitution*. Directorate-General for External Policies of the Union.

Mohiuddin, A. (2022). Islam, religious authority and the state: The case of Egypt. *Asian Journal of Middle Eastern and Islamic Studies, 16*(2), 165–188.

Moosa, E. (2001). The dilemma of Islamic rights schemes. *Journal of Law and Religion, 15*, 191–192.

Müftüler-Baç, M. (2012). *Gender equality in Turkey*. European Parliament.

Mujuzi, J. D. (2020). The right to freedom from discrimination in Rwanda. *International Journal of Discrimination and the Law, 20*(2–3), 156–180.

Mutua, M. W. (1996). The ideology of human rights. *Virginia Journal of International Law, 36*, 589.

Oguz, O. (2011, July 8). The impact of the amendments of 2010 in Turkish constitution to the working life. Retried April 27 2023 from https://ssrn.com/abstract=1881527

Pew Research Center. (2013, April 30). *The world's Muslims: Religion, politics and society*. Retrieved November 27, 2024, from https://www.pewresearch.org/religion/2013/04/30/the-worlds-muslims-religion-politics-society-overview/

Powers, D. S. (1989). Orientalism, colonialism, and legal history: The attack on Muslim family endowments in Algeria and India. *Comparative Studies in Society and History, 31*(3), 535–571.

Rishmawi, M. (2015). *The league of Arab states human rights standards and mechanisms*. Open Society Foundations and Cairo Institute for Human Rights Studies.

Robinson, K. (2021, December 17). Understanding sharia: the intersection of Islam and the law. *Council on Foreign Relations*. Retrieved April 27, 2023, from https://www.cfr.org/backgrounder/understanding-sharia-intersection-islam-and-law

Rosenfeld, M. (1993). Modern constitutionalism as interplay between identity and diversity: An introduction. *Cardozo Law Review, 14*, 497–531.

Roth, K. (2023, April 10). Events of 2020. *Human rights watch*. https://www.hrw.org/world-report/2021/country-chapters/malaysia

Roznai, Y., & Yolcu, S. (2012). An unconstitutional constitutional amendment—The Turkish perspective: A comment on the Turkish constitutional court's headscarf decision. *International Journal of Constitutional Law, 10*(1), 175–207.

Sachedina, A. (2009). *Islam and the challenge of human rights*. Oxford University Press.

Saddique, A. (2004, August 3). Constitutional guarantee of equal rights for Afghan women so far brings little change to everyday life. *ReliefWeb*. Retrieved April 27, 2023, from https://reliefweb.int/report/afghanistan/constitutional-guarantee-equal-rights-afghan-women-sofar-brings-little-change

Samsudin, I. S., Rajamanickam, R., & Nordin, R. (2022). Roles of human rights bodies on chain remand complaints in Malaysia. *Cogent Social Sciences, 8*(1), 1–18.

Schaer, C. (2022, February 3). UN asked to monitor Egypt human rights. *Deutsche Welle*. Retrieved April 27, 2023, from https://www.dw.com/en/un-asked-to-monitor-egypt-humanrights/a-60649827

Shah, N. (2006). *Women, the Koran and international human rights law: The experience of Pakistan*. Brill.

Shahidi, H. (2008). Iranian journalism and the law in the twentieth century. *Iranian Studies, 41*(5), 739–754.

Sheikh, S. S. (2010). The implementation of CEDAW in Malaysia: A human rights-based analysis. *Sarjana, 25*(3), 55–72.

Sherif, A. O. (2012). The relationship between the constitution and the sharī'ah in Egypt. In R. Grote & T. Röder (Eds.), *Constitutionalism in Islamic countries: Between upheaval and continuity* (pp. 121–134). Oxford University Press.

Süral, A. N. (2007). Legal framework for gender equality at work in Turkey. *Middle Eastern Studies, 43*(5), 811–824.

Usmani, M. T. (2006). The Islamization of laws in Pakistan: The case of Hudud Ordinances. *The Muslim World, 96*(2), 287–304.

Virgili, T. (2010). *Islam, constitutional law and human rights: Sexual minorities and freethinkers in Egypt and Tunisia*. Routledge.

Waltz, S. (2004). Universal human rights: The contribution of Muslim states. *Human Rights Quarterly, 26*, 806–807.

Weeramantry, C. G. (1988). *Islamic jurisprudence: An international perspective*. Palgrave Macmillan.

Wolfrum, R. (2012). Constitutionalism in Islamic countries: A survey from the perspective of international law. In R. Grote & T. Röder (Eds.), *Constitutionalism in Islamic countries: Between upheaval and continuity* (pp. 77–88). Oxford University Press.

Wong, J. (2021, October 7). Malaysia: High court recognises the right to citizenship of children born overseas to Malaysian mothers. *Mondaq*. Retrieved April 7, 2024, from https://www.mondaq.com/human-rights/1118996/high-court-recognises-the-right-to-citizenshipof-children-born-overseas-to-malaysian-mothers

Yazici, S. (2006). *A guide to Turkish public law and legal research*. Retrieved November 28, 2024, from https://www.nyulawglobal.org/globalex/Turkey.html.

Yousaf, F. (2014, December 16). Pakistan's minority-rights challenge. *openDemocracy*. Retrieved April 30, 2023, from https://www.opendemocracy.net/en/opensecurity/pakistans-minorityrightschallenge/

Youssef, N. (2012, November 30). Egypt's draft constitution translated. *Egypt Independent*. Retrieved April 3, 2024, from https://www.egyptindependent.com/egypt-s-draft-constitutiontranslated/

CHAPTER 3

Constitutional Status of Religious Freedom in Egypt and Malaysia: A Cross-National Analysis

3.1 Introduction

Religion has always had a significant impact on how communities and cultures evolve in different parts of the world. Any democratic society must take seriously the constitutional guarantee of freedom of religion because it demonstrates how seriously a country takes the protection of religious diversity and individual liberties. This chapter compares and contrasts the constitutional protections for religious freedom in Egypt and Malaysia. It explores the intricacies of religious rights and how they affect social cohesion, individual liberty and the operation of the state by looking at their constitutional provisions respecting freedom of religion.

The protection of religious freedom is essential in a democratic society for a number of reasons. First of all, it acknowledges and respects people's autonomy to select, practice and modify their religious beliefs in accordance with their conscience. It defends the idea that people should be allowed to practice their religion without interference or force, allowing them to do so openly and without concern for retaliation or persecution. Second, the constitutional guarantee of freedom of religion encourages racial and religious diversity to live in peace and concord with one another. It offers a framework that promotes communication, comprehension and tolerance, creating an atmosphere where people of

A. Mohiuddin, *Human Rights Law in Egypt and Malaysia: Freedom of Religion and Expression, Volume 1*, Political Economy of Islam,
https://doi.org/10.1007/978-3-031-63859-6_3

all religions may get along peacefully, learn from one another, and collaborate to achieve shared objectives. An inclusive and peaceful society is made possible by a constitution's protection of religious freedom, which fosters the notion that people's differing religious views and practices should be valued rather than suppressed. The guarantee of religious freedom provided by the constitution also serves as a restraint on the authority of the state. It guarantees that the government would not intervene excessively in religious affairs or favour one religion over another. A constitution aids in maintaining the harmony between religious freedom and legitimate concerns of public order, security and the defence of other basic rights by defining the limits of official participation in religious issues (Shah, 2021, p. 3).

It is especially important to investigate how freedom of religion is protected by the constitution in Muslim majority countries. Due to their distinct historical, cultural, and religious backgrounds, these nations provide a wide range of case studies. Countries like Egypt offer a unique chance to examine the relationship between religion and the state as well as the difficulties and successes in preserving religious freedom in nations that are predominately Muslim because of their rich Islamic legacy and impact (Report on International Religious Freedom, 2021). However, in countries like Malaysia, multireligious and multiethnic settings make it possible to examine the challenges of governing religious diversity within a legal framework. The example of Malaysia sheds light on the delicate balancing act that must be struck in a country where Islam is the official religion between upholding societal cohesion and safeguarding the rights of religious minorities (Rahman & Khambali @ Hambali, 2013, p. 81). We may better comprehend the difficulties and achievements in implementing freedom of religion in other nations by comparing and contrasting the constitutional provisions, legal interpretations and sociopolitical settings of Egypt and Malaysia. Discussions on human rights, democratic government and the state's role in preserving individual liberties are all influenced by these comparative perspectives, which also help to improve our comprehension of the preservation of religious freedom globally.

Although the scope and actual application of this right may differ depending on the nation, Egypt and Malaysia both have the constitutional status of freedom of religion established in their respective legal systems. The *sharīʿah* is the primary source of law in Egypt, according to the country's constitution, which also recognises Islam as the state religion. For followers of the three Abrahamic religions—Islam, Christianity and Judaism—the Egyptian Constitution also provides freedom of thought and the performance of religious rites. It is specifically stated in Article 64 of the Egyptian Constitution that "Freedom of belief is absolute," guaranteeing everyone's freedom to practice their faith. There have been times in which Egypt's freedom of religion has been threatened, notwithstanding this constitutional protection. Certain limitations on non-Muslim religious practices, particularly those of minority communities, have been enforced by the government. There have also been some reports of social prejudice against religious minorities, as well as sporadic acts of violence.

The freedom of religion is protected under Article 11 of the Malaysian Constitution. Every person has the freedom to declare, practice and spread their faith in accordance with this clause. The freedom of religion is subject to several restrictions under the constitution. While stating that Islam is the official religion of the Federation, Article 3 also protects the right of non-Muslims to practice any faith they want. There are several restrictions on how the freedom of religion is actually interpreted and practiced in Malaysia. In the nation's dual legal system, *sharīʿah* law coexists with civil law. *Sharīʿah* courts have authority over issues pertaining to personal status, such as marriage and conversion to Islam. For those looking to convert from Islam to another religion, this has occasionally resulted in disputes and difficulties (Shah & Mohd, 2011, p. 649). Concerns regarding Malaysia's limits on religious freedom have arisen in recent years. There have been incidents of disagreement and prejudice against religious minorities, as well as challenges certain non-Muslim organisations have had in acquiring permission to construct houses of worship (Musa, 2022, p. 11).

In summary, a nation's dedication to preserving individual rights and religious diversity is reflected in the constitutional position of freedom of religion, which is a critical component of any democratic society. In this chapter, we will investigate the difficulties of enforcing religious freedom in various sociocultural situations by looking at particular examples, such as Egypt and Malaysia. Understanding the difficulties, triumphs, and lessons from these nations helps to advance knowledge of religious freedom throughout the world and enriches conversations on human rights and the function of the state in preserving individual liberties.

3.2 Historical and Legal Context

Egypt, following its independence in 1923, saw the emergence of a constitution that acknowledged the significance of state religion. The drafting committee, comprised of influential figures from various religious backgrounds, including representatives of Islam, Christianity, Judaism and even the Bedouin community, worked under the authority of the King and his Prime Minister (Hillal, 2011). However, it is worth noting that the Wafd, the dominant political party at the time, criticised this constitution (Brown, 2014). The aristocracy of the Egyptian constitution drew inspiration from European models, where the notion of an official state religion prevailed in the majority of constitutions. Notably, the Constitution of Estonia stood out as an exception, stating that there was no official religion (Sayed, 2020, p. 10). While Islam was declared the official religion of Egypt in the 1923 constitution, it did not make any specific mention of influential Islamic institutions such as Al-Azhar. The elite who shaped this constitution had been exposed to French education, which likely influenced their perspectives on religion. Their respect for Egypt's traditionally conservative culture and their awareness of the public's Islamic sentiments could also have played a role in the absence of debates on religious inclusion or the placement of religious provisions within the constitution (Sayed, 2020, p. 11).

On the other side of the world, prior to its independence in 1957, Malaya had a ruling system deeply rooted in religious guidance. Islamic law, known as *sharīʿah*, was integrated into the existing state laws, such as the Undang-undang Kedah, Undang-undang Pahang and Undang-undang Melaka. The Undang-undang Melaka, with its incorporation of *sharīʿah* principles, had been introduced during the reign of Sultan Muhamad Syah (1422–1444). However, one of the conditions for Malaya's independence was the establishment of a legal system based on English common law, with Islam designated as the official religion of the Federation. Following independence, Malaysia made efforts to reconcile civil and religious laws within its government structure (Ahmad Mohamed Ibrahim, 1996). The legal system was built upon a foundation that combined Islamic law, customary laws and English common law (Liaw, 1976). Discussions regarding the implementation of Islamic law, also referred to as *hudūd*, emerged (Shah, 2010, p. 135). Some argue that if colonisation had not introduced and enforced English law in Malaysia, Islamic law would have held a more prominent position (Ibrahim, 1997).

However, the implementation of English law through the judicial process and legislation effectively displaced Islamic law from its previous position of prominence (Ahmad & Rajasingham, 2001).

While both Egypt and Malaysia embarked on journeys shaped by their historical, cultural and political contexts, their approaches to state religion diverged. Egypt acknowledged Islam as the state religion, but with limited specifics, while Malaysia sought a balance between Islamic law and English common law within its legal framework. These paths demonstrate how nations navigate the intricate relationship between religion, governance and the influences of external forces throughout their respective histories. In the realm of historical context, delving into the foundations of Islamic law in Malaysia reveals intriguing parallels and divergences. Unveiling a rich tapestry of heritage, the earliest trace of Islamic law in Malaysia dates back to 1303, discovered etched upon the Batu Bersurat Terengganu, an ancient stone inscription in Terengganu (Nor et al., 2012, p. 1233). Meanwhile, during the fifteenth century, when Malacca thrived as a Malay kingdom, a compendium of laws known as the Malacca Laws (Undang-undang Melaka) was commissioned by the ruling authority, signifying the infusion of Islamic influence into Malay customary laws (Ibrahim, 1997, p. 56). A fascinating amalgamation, the Undang-undang Melaka emerges as a hybrid text, meticulously composed by binding together several distinct manuscripts. Despite its integration into a single body of work over time, the distinct components remain discernible, reflecting its complex evolution (Liaw, 1976). Capturing the essence of tradition, the Sejarah Melayu (Malay Annals) depicts the societal customs of the era and unequivocally affirms the adoption of Islam as the state religion in Malacca, further demonstrated by the appointment of Qādīs (judges) as religious advisors to the rulers, including prominent figures like Kadi Yusof, Kadi Monawar, and Maulana Abu Bakar (Kheng, 1998).

On the contrasting landscape of Egypt, a different narrative unfolds, shaped by a distinctive historical trajectory. The 1930 constitution served as a template for subsequent constitutional iterations, laying the foundation for the nation's political framework (Nor et al., 2016, p. 6). With time, Egypt's political system underwent a significant transition, shifting from monarchy to republicanism with the advent of the 1956 constitution, which materialised in the wake of the 1952 Free Officers' Movement. Notably, this constitutional shift held a more advanced position, occupying Article 3 rather than Article 149. Initially integrated into the 'General Provisions Section,' it evolved over the years, finding its place in the first section, known as 'The Egyptian State' or, in 2012, 'The Elements of the State and Society,' ultimately returning to simply 'State' as per the 1971 Constitution. Across Egypt's various constitutional manifestations, a recurring provision became entrenched: 'Islam is the state religion.' While the planned 1954 constitution, drafted by a committee under the guidance of the nation's first president, Mohamed Naguib, was discarded, Nasser spearheaded the formation of a committee to craft a new constitution, mirroring the process undertaken for the 1964 constitution. Curiously, information regarding the preparation of this constitution remains elusive, leaving no trace of discussions or sessions in the parliamentary library. Subsequently, with the dissolution of the Egypt-Syria union, the 1964 constitution came into effect until an updated version was promulgated in September 1971, marking a momentous turning point. Intriguingly, with the exception of the 1958 United Arab Republic constitution, all of Egypt's constitutional frameworks encompassed the provision acknowledging Islam as the state religion, whereas the aforementioned constitution omitted any reference to a state religion, possibly due to its temporary status or President Nasser's inclination to avoid constitutional disparities that could undermine unity. Thus, this constitutional landscape endured throughout both the royal and republican eras until a transformative shift in 1971 (Zemni & Bogaert, 2009, p. 151).

Malaysia, on the other hand, has witnessed a tumultuous history of foreign domination and shifting colonial powers. Beginning in 1511, the Portuguese arrived in Malacca with ambitions of establishing a monopoly on trade in the Far East. Their rule lasted for over a century, until 1640, as they aimed to control the lucrative commerce routes in the region. Following the Portuguese, the Dutch took charge of Malacca from 1641 to 1824, driven by their desire to outmaneuver their commercial rivals, particularly the Portuguese and the English, in the Malayan waterways. However, amidst these foreign occupations, the indigenous Malays upheld their Islamic law and Malay customs as the supreme legal system. The Portuguese and Dutch rulers did not seek to impose their own laws in Malacca, allowing the Malays to continue practicing their legal traditions. Nevertheless, without resistance, the Dutch ultimately handed over Malacca to the British in 1795, primarily as a preventive measure against potential French capture during the era of the French Revolution. The British returned Malacca to the Dutch in 1818 as part of the Vienna Peace Treaty, but in return, the Dutch ceded Bencoolen on the West Coast of Sumatra to the British in 1824. This marked the beginning of British colonial authority over various states on the Malay Peninsula, with Penang being the first region to fall under their control when Captain Francis Light conquered it on behalf of the East India Company in August 1786. Despite acknowledging the sovereignty of separate states, the British found ways to exert influence and enforce English law through the appointment of a British adviser known as the Resident in each state. The British Resident acted as a counselor to the Sultan in all matters of state, with the exception of Malay religion and tradition. The British introduced several laws from British India into the Federated Malay States through the Resident, thereby impacting the legal landscape (Nor et al., 2016, p. 7). Prior to British arrival, the Sultans held both political and Islamic leadership within their respective states, known as Tanah Melayu. Islamic law governed the states, with the Sultans regarded as representatives of God on earth and responsible for upholding the law established by Islam. However, the British colonization led to a division of Islam into public and private strands through a series of treaties with the Sultans, starting with the Treaty of Pangkor. Islam became more ceremonial and symbolic, while the ruler's authority transformed into a secular institution. The idea of attributing sovereignty to a human ruler clashed with the Islamic belief that only God possesses sovereignty (Nor et al., 2016, p. 8).

This change diminished the religious foundation of legal authority, as the British introduced secular decrees to validate all laws, including the application of Islamic law. as the British introduced secular decrees to grant validity to all laws, including the administration of Islamic law. The treaties between the Anglo-Malay limited the ruler's power, allowing the colonial administration to govern the nation under the guise of advice. Consequently, the position of the ruler gradually weakened and Islam's societal aspect became marginalised, serving as little more than an insignificant appendix to the ruler's autonomy. During the British colonisation, the application of Islamic law gradually diminished and its scope was narrowed down to private matters and inheritance. The development of the imperial administrative structure and secular bodies further restricted the reach of Islamic law. Only laws pertaining to family and inheritance were left within the purview of Islamic law, but even these were not considered geographically applicable to all individuals, regardless of religion and ethnicity, residing in the state. Only Muslims were allowed to use Islamic law as their personal code. Therefore, it becomes evident that under British colonial rule, the implementation of Islamic law was gradually reduced to a limited domain, confined to private matters and inheritance, as the imperial administrative structure and secular institutions took precedence. The erosion of the ruler's authority and the marginalisation of Islamic law within the broader legal framework contributed to this transformation. The influence of the British colonial administration led to the relegation of Islamic law to a secondary position, primarily confined to personal and familial affairs.

The founding of the Federated Malay States in 1895 further solidified the diminishing authority of the rulers. The establishment of the Council of States, along with other administrative measures, continued to erode the ruler's power and further marginalised the societal aspect of Islam. Islam, once considered the guiding force for governance, was reduced to a mere ceremonial aspect, detached from the realm of state affairs. The British colonial administration operated under the pretext of providing 'advice' to the rulers, yet it effectively governed the nation according to its own agenda (Ali & Ahmed, 2021, p. 21). This manipulation of power caused a continuous deterioration of the ruler's position and weakened the overall influence of Islamic law within the legal system. With the gradual decline of the Sultan's authority, the British introduced their own legal principles and structures, based on English law, to govern the Malay Peninsula. The British legal system was enforced through the Resident, who acted as a conduit for the implementation of English law, further displacing the prominence of Islamic law. As a result, during the era of British colonisation, Islamic law underwent a significant transformation. Its scope was reduced and its authority was superseded by the introduction of secular legal frameworks. Islamic law became a marginalised aspect of the legal system, limited to personal and familial matters, while the broader governance and administration were shaped by British laws and institutions (Hooker, 1984).

In Egypt's constitution, the positioning of the religion clause emerges as a reflection of the socio-political context in which it unfolded. A pivotal moment arose with the ascension of President Sadat in 1970, leading to the implementation of the 1971 constitution. While his predecessor, President Nasser, attempted to bolster his credibility, Sadat embarked on a quest for a distinct form of legitimacy, one intertwined with religion. Harnessing the power of Islam, Sadat skillfully attempted to win the trust of the populace. Strategic maneuvers, such as the symbolic destruction of the Torah jail and the purging of Egyptian intelligence files, aimed to dismantle remnants of the previous regime and signify a new era under his leadership. Moreover, he signaled a shift towards democracy by endorsing the possibility of multiple political parties. Thus, the 1971 constitution's focal point became the inclusion of the principles of *sharīʿah* within the religion clause, designating it as a source of law (Hashish, 2013, p. 122).

Considering the growing influence of Islamist organisations and the burgeoning Islamic sentiment in society since Sadat's collaboration with them to suppress communist movements in 1967, he believed that incorporating a clause on *sharīʿah* would grant him credibility and legitimacy within the community. However, Sadat's aspirations extended beyond this initial amendment. He revisited clause 2, positioning *sharīʿah* as the primary source of law, a strategic move to advance his political agenda, including altering the clause governing presidential terms. To divert attention from his self-serving motives for constitutional change, Sadat pursued additional modifications. In exchange for the passage of the amendment to *sharīʿah* principles, serving as the primary source of legislation, the elites acceded to the amendment on presidential term limits and other concessions, such as the establishment of the *Shura* Council. While substantive change remained elusive despite the compromise, this maneuver could be perceived as an evolution in the views held by the ruling elite.

The complex interplay of power dynamics and political maneuvering unfolded within this constitutional landscape. President Sadat's strategic deployment of religion and subsequent revisions to the constitution reflect the negotiations between those in power and their adversaries. The constitution evolved into a dynamic framework where the aspirations, negotiations and fluctuations in political influence intertwine, leaving a lasting imprint on Egypt's constitutional trajectory.Amidst the labyrinthine legal challenges that beset the Supreme Constitutional Court, a profound shift was set in motion by the deluge of constitutional complaints preceding the amendment date. Faced with this formidable task, the court laid the cornerstone of a transformative principle: the non-retroactivity of Article 2. Henceforth, legislators were bound to draw inspiration primarily from *sharīʿah* law after the amendment's enactment, ushering in a new era of legal interpretation and application (Dupret, 2016). However, the situation changed with the ousting of former President Mubarak in 2011, as a resolute public movement sought to redefine the system and challenge the entrenched elite. Seizing the reins of power, the Supreme Council of Armed Forces assumed control, heralding an era that, despite the absence of tangible change, whispered of an evolution in the views held by the ruling class.

In this tumultuous period, the Supreme Constitutional Court found itself confronting an array of constitutional complaints, further testing its resolve and resilience. Undeterred, the court etched the principle of non-retroactivity into the annals of legal doctrine, a guiding light that mandated *shari'ah* law as the primary source for legislative inspiration henceforth (Dupret, 2016). Amidst the ebb and flow of Egypt's political tides, a critical juncture emerged with the introduction of the 2012 constitution. This document not only enshrined the significance of Al-Azhar in Article 3 but also unveiled a new article, numbered 219. As the reins of power passed to the Muslim Brotherhood, the nation grappled with social and political contractions, which would eventually culminate in another uprising. The interim leadership, led by President Adly Mansour, heeded the call for change and summoned the 10th /experts committee—a group steeped in legal and constitutional expertise—to edit the constitution. This transitional phase paved the way for the emergence of the Fifty Committee, led by Amr Moussa.

In the context of constitutional evolution, both Egypt and Malaysia embarked on transformative paths, shaping the course of their respective nations. While Egypt's Fifty Committee encompassed a diverse array of esteemed individuals from various sectors of society, Malaysia's Reid Commission comprised legal luminaries entrusted with defining the country's identity. The compositions of these committees were distinct, with Egypt's encompassing a heterogeneous body and Malaysia's emphasising intercommunal agreements. The Fifty Committee in Egypt undertook the arduous task of drafting a new constitution, navigating the complexities of a changing political landscape. Through the interplay of courts, committees and public sentiment, Egypt's constitutional was crafted, leaving an indelible mark on the nation's trajectory (Brown & Lombardi, 2006). Similarly, in Malaysia, the Reid Commission, led by Lord William Reid, sought to craft a constitution that would define the country's identity. The deliberate omission of an explicit designation of Islam as the religion of the Federation underscored the Commission's belief in maintaining the state's secular character. This decision was influenced by the opposition of the Malay Rulers and the intercommunal agreement among the Malaysian Chinese Association (MCA), Malaysian Indian Congress (MIC) and United Malays National Organisation (UMNO), reflecting a delicate balance between religious considerations and the state's secular nature.

Both Egypt and Malaysia grappled with challenges and made crucial decisions that shaped their constitutional landscapes. These nations strived to strike a balance between tradition and the need for change, leaving an enduring legacy on their constitutional journeys (Hamid, 2011, p. 68).

The findings of the Reid Commission shed light on the reservations expressed by the Malay Rulers, effectively thwarting the establishment of a state religion. Non-Muslim organisations echoed concerns over the preservation of the state's secular character and the safeguarding of freedom of worship. These appeals, coupled with a private letter from Secretary of State for the Colonies Alan Lennox-Boyd, stressing the importance of protecting religious freedom in the Constitution, had a profound impact on the Commission's decision to forgo including an article enshrining a state religion. However, contrasting UMNO's position, several Malay and Muslim groups advocated for Islam to be recognised as the official religion while ensuring the freedom to practice other faiths. The Malay Forum, spearheaded by senior Malay officials from the Malayan Civil Service, explicitly called for this balance in their memorandum to the Commission (Fernando, 2006, p. 253). The absence of a state religion clause in the drafted Constitution provoked disappointment among UMNO leaders when the Reid Commission's report was released in February 1957. Subsequently, during the Working Party's review of the Commission's draft, Tunku Abdul Rahman, the leader of the Alliance and UMNO, pushed for the inclusion of an article designating Islam as the Federation's religion. Assuring that the state would remain secular, the Tunku responded to the concerns of the Malay Rulers by pledging that any federal department overseeing religious matters would solely serve as a liaison body. This suggestion stemmed from lobbying within UMNO and the rival Malay parties, who vehemently opposed the Reid constitutional amendments on this specific point. Their argument rested on the significant psychological impact that an official religion would have on Malays. Nonetheless, the Alliance recognised the need for two key provisions in the proposed amendment: preserving the Rulers' position as Heads of Faith in their respective states and guaranteeing the practice and propagation of other religions throughout the Federation (Fernando, 2006, p. 254).

The Working Party engaged in extensive deliberations, resulting in multiple drafts of the article establishing Islam as the Federation's official religion before arriving at the final version. Discussions between the Rulers' delegates and UMNO representatives were particularly intense.

Minutes from the Sixth Meeting of the Working Party reveal broad support for an article stating that Islam would be the official religion, with safeguards in place to protect the practice of other faiths (Article 11). It is evident from the source records that the Working Party intended for the state to remain secular while recognising Islam as the official religion by inserting Article 3(1). Neither UMNO nor the Alliance leaders harbored intentions of establishing a theocratic or quasitheocratic government. They provided assurances to the Colonial Office that Article 3(1) would not infringe upon the civil and political rights of non-Muslims or impede religious freedom. The leaders' objectives were clear throughout the discussions, as stated in the initial recommendation of the Alliance Party, which read: 'The religion of Malaysia shall be Islam.' The inclusion of this clause did not impose limitations on non-Muslim citizens practicing and professing their own religions, nor did it imply that the state was anything other than secular. This statement explicitly articulated the initial goals of the UMNO and Alliance leaders, and the MCA and MIC did not oppose the inclusion of this provision in their joint memorandum, as it was a compromise reached within the Alliance parties (Fernando, 2006, p. 255). In the Malaysia's constitutional journey, the Reid Commission and the subsequent Working Party played pivotal roles in shaping the nation's identity. The delicate balance struck between recognising Islam as the official religion while safeguarding the secular character of the state reflects the nuanced aspirations of a diverse society. The constitutional architects navigated the concerns of different stakeholders, aiming to establish a Malaysia that respects religious freedom, preserves the rights of all citizens, and upholds the principles of a secular state. It is within this complex interplay of perspectives and compromises that the Malaysian Federal Constitution emerged, a testament to the ongoing dialogue and evolution of Malaysia's constitutional landscape.

In the realm of constitutional deliberations, the Malaysian case presents a distinct perspective compared to the situation in Egypt. The resistance exhibited by the Malay Rulers in Malaysia influenced the omission of the Alliance's plan to designate Islam as the official religion in the constitution. The Rulers' concerns stemmed from their perception that such a clause would encroach upon their authority as the Heads of the Faith in their respective jurisdictions. This resistance created a challenge for the Reid Commission, as they grappled with the contradiction posed by the Alliance's desire for an official religion alongside a secular state. However, the subsequent discussions at the Working Party stage shed light on the intentions of the Alliance and UMNO leaders. It became evident that the inclusion of the new article was requested by the leaders themselves, with Tunku Abdul Rahman emphasising that the entire Constitution was framed on the basis of a secular state. The goal of the clause was not to alter the secular character of the state but to serve as a symbolic and ceremonial affirmation. The term "innocuous" used by Justice Abdul Hamid accurately captured the Alliance's aims, ensuring that the article had no adverse effects in any domain. Nonetheless, interpretations of the clause's meaning have varied over time, often clouded by inadequate analysis of the original materials (Fernando, 2006, p. 255).

Contrasting this with the Egyptian context, religious identity holds a significant place in the country's culture and legal framework. The national identification card in Egypt explicitly mentions an individual's religious affiliation, highlighting the entrenched role of religion in Egyptian society. The religious identity of an individual is generally determined by birth and is closely linked to their familial background, especially if born to a Muslim father. Despite this, Egyptians also share a strong national identity, transcending religious divisions. Both Muslims and the Coptic Orthodox Church are seen as having a historical presence in Egypt, and the notion of being Egyptian is shared by the majority.

Interfaith relations, particularly between Muslims and Christians, are considered essential for social cohesion and national unity in Egypt. Challenges to interfaith harmony are viewed as threats to public peace and safety. Conversions from one faith to another can often lead to conflicts and even violence between religious groups, potentially endangering public welfare and causing societal unrest. Consequently, conversions are seen as matters that implicate broader public interests and can ignite prolonged disputes. While the Malaysian case grappled with the delicate balance between recognising Islam and maintaining a secular state, Egypt faces challenges in navigating interfaith relations and preserving social harmony. These differing dynamics reflect the unique historical, cultural, and religious contexts of the two nations and underscore the complexities involved in constitutional arrangements and societal coexistence.

Within the complex fabric of Egyptian legal norms, a perplexing dichotomy emerges, where the absence of an explicit law against proselytising belies a clandestine reality. In practice, the act is rendered illegal for all but the followers of Islam and even within that realm, certain circumstances raise concerns. Religious clashes, ignited by conversions from one faith to another, become fertile ground for discord and occasional violence. As a result, proselytisers, converts and their loyal adherents find themselves entangled in the grasp of the Penal Code, facing charges of inciting public disturbance or undermining national unity, a recurring phenomenon. Under the auspices of this code, the prohibition to insult, disdain, or exhibit contempt for the "heavenly religions" of Islam, Christianity and Judaism, as well as their various sects, finds its voice. Moreover, it serves as a tool to enforce the punitive measures of blasphemy dictated by Islamic law (Minority Rights Group International [MRG], 2019).

Curiously, while Islam lacks a specific law that punishes apostasy, Muslims who are accused of such face the weight of traditional legal repercussions, save for physical death, which in Egypt takes the form of civil death. The apostate's marital bonds are severed, forever nullifying their union and forever barring the possibility of marrying, even a non-Muslim. Furthermore, inheritance rights evaporate like fleeting mirages in the desert. The organisations and individuals responsible for the majority of these assaults, often justified by religious beliefs cloaked in Islamic or pseudo-Islamic rhetoric, have engendered mounting concerns within the public and government spheres, coinciding with the rise in terrorist attacks. Fueled by these apprehensions, the government deems it essential for social and public safety to exert control over both preachers and the content of Friday sermons (Minority Rights Group International [MRG], 2019).

Consequently, the path to the pulpit becomes intertwined with bureaucracy as mosques must obtain licenses from the Ministry of Islamic Endowments (*Awqaf*). Since September 2013, under the guidance of an esteemed Al-Azhar scholar, the Ministry has mandated Al-Azhar graduation and certification for recruitment, leaving countless imams bereft of their preaching licenses. Compensation is extended to those who deliver sermons in selected mosques, but now the Ministry's voice resonates through every licensed imam, dictating the themes of tolerance and nonviolence that must be woven into their Friday orations. As for matters of family and personal status, religious regulations govern the landscape. Muslims find themselves entangled in the threads of Islamic law, Christians bow to the dictates of Christian canon law and Jews submit to the precepts of Jewish law (International Religious Freedom Report, Egypt, 2016).

In the context of matrimony, Egypt forsakes the notion of civil unions, recognising only the unions of Jewish, Christian and Muslim couples. However, the absence of legal recognition for Baha'i weddings gives rise to a myriad of complications, entangling banking, real estate, inheritance and occasionally even school enrollment. Muslim men enjoy the liberty to marry nonMuslim women, while the reverse remains forbidden, casting a shadow of inequality over these unions. Within the Coptic Orthodox Church, divorce is traditionally forbidden unless one spouse commits adultery or embraces another faith. In stark contrast, for Muslims, the dissolution of marital bonds assumes a straightforward nature. Should a non-Muslim woman convert to Islam while her non-Muslim husband remains steadfast, their union is deemed null and void, often igniting violent conflicts between these two communities. The labyrinthine complexity of inheritance law weaves its intricate patterns, intricately entwined with the religious affiliations of the parties involved. Contemplating the opening clause of Article 53 in the 2014 Constitution, one is impelled to seek justification for the profound disparities in the legal standing and treatment of individuals. Ostensibly, citizens are promised equal treatment under the law, with equal rights and responsibilities, safeguarded against discrimination based on race, gender, ethnicity, national origin, disability, socioeconomic class, political opinion, or geographic association. However, the enigma unfolds when Article 53 is juxtaposed with the intertwined provisions of Articles 2 and 3, which demand the fusion of religious laws with the fabric of governance (Risley, 2017, p. 176).

In this complex interplay of constitutional principles, the task befalls the Supreme Constitutional Court (SCC) to shed light on the harmony between faith and law. Litigants who raise these questions beckon the SCC to elucidate the underlying complexities that shroud the legal landscape. The constitutional promise of equality, though seemingly absolute in isolation, reveals its true contours within the intricate tapestry of interconnected provisions, where religion and governance converge (Risley, 2017, p. 177).

The analysis revealed several intriguing trends and distinctions in how Islamic law is incorporated and treated in the various legal systems. An early mention of a state religion in Egypt's 1923 constitution—in which Islam was declared to be the national religion—is highlighted in the discussion. There may have been an effort to achieve diversity and representation given the membership of the writing committee, which comprised members from many racial and religious communities. The absence of discussion and the exclusion of particular Islamic organisations, however, point to a top-down approach in determining the place of religion in the constitution. It is also stated that European constitutions, which frequently referred to an official religion, had an impact. The comparative context clarifies the elements influencing Egypt's constitutional treatment of religion. But the debate of Malaysia places more emphasis on the historical background of Islamic law in the Malay states, where it predominated as the supreme law before British colonialism. The influence of colonial rule on the legal system is best seen by the introduction of English common law and the consequent restricted application of Islamic law to private affairs. The split of Islam into public and private threads as a consequence of the talks between the British and the Malay monarchs reduced Islam's significance from a complete legal system to a more constrained religious character. It shows how colonial influence significantly impacted how Islamic law was viewed and used. Overall, the analyses of Egypt and Malaysia highlight the complex relationships that exist between religion, colonialism and the evolution of legal systems. Malaysia's debate highlights the alteration and marginalisation of Islamic law under colonial rule, in contrast to Egypt's emphasis on the incorporation of Islam as the official religion inside the constitutional framework. Understanding these historical and contextual elements is crucial for understanding both countries' current legal systems as well as the interaction between religion and the state.

3.3 Constitutional Provisions

In Egypt, the constitutional landscape regarding religious freedom is complex, intertwining beliefs, practices and legal regulations. The constitution strongly asserts that 'freedom of belief is absolute,' celebrating the diverse spiritual fabric of the nation. It allows the practice of religious rituals and the establishment of places of worship, guided by specific laws. However, amid the constitutional commitment to equality, there exists a contrasting reality (Office of International Religious Freedom, 2021). While Islam, Christianity, and Judaism are explicitly recognised and supported, other faiths lack the same level of constitutional protection. Followers of these three Abrahamic religions enjoy the privilege to build sacred spaces and publicly express their faith, while those outside these traditions find themselves in a zone without explicit constitutional safeguards (Report on International Religious Freedom: Egypt, 2021).

The constitution acknowledges the primacy of Islam as the state religion, with the principles of Islamic *sharīʿah* serving as the guiding compass for legislation. This acknowledgment sets a distinctive tone, reflecting the entwined relationship between religion and the affairs of the state. Within the folds of governance, Christian and Jewish canonical laws assume their positions, shaping regulations that delve into the intricacies of personal lives, religious practices and the selection of spiritual leaders. Article 64 of the 2014 Constitution stands as a pivotal cornerstone, illuminating the delicate balance between belief and practice. The unbridled freedom to hold individual beliefs exists as an inviolable right, standing tall and unregulated. Yet, as the boundaries shift from belief to action, the contours of legislation emerge, marking the point where religious convictions find themselves subject to legal frameworks. It is within this realm that the followers of Islam, Christianity and Judaism find solace and legal protection, while those beyond these borders navigate uncharted territories, lacking the clear constitutional moorings intended by the framers (Risley, 2017, p. 171). The constitution's intent to ensure equality and non-discrimination shines brightly, but its reach selectively embraces certain faiths, leaving others in a state of ambiguous constitutional status. In Egypt, there is a concerted effort to strike a balance between religious freedom and constitutional guarantees. This aims to be inclusive and respect diversity within society.

Article 18 of the ICCPR consists of two main sections. The first section emphasises the freedom of individuals to express their thoughts, conscience, and faith without restrictions. This includes the right to hold and manifest one's beliefs openly, whether in private or public settings. The second section underscores the prohibition of coercion in matters of faith, asserting an individual's right to follow their chosen beliefs without compulsion or restraint. A third aspect of Article 18 introduces the concept of limitations. It specifies that restrictions on the freedom to express religious beliefs are acceptable only if they are deemed necessary by law and are consistent with other permissible standards. This acknowledges a balance between the right to religious expression and the legal boundaries established for societal well-being (UN Human Rights Committee [HRC], 1993).

In Egypt and similar nations, where the laws governing religious practice and affairs hold sway, the interpretation of these guidelines becomes a subject of intense contemplation. Supporters of such laws find solace in their perceived necessity, but the absence of language confining exceptions to religion-neutral laws casts a haze of uncertainty. It raises questions about the extent to which these laws could engulf the very essence of freedom, blurring the lines between religious practice and government control. Amidst this conundrum, a beacon of hope emerges in Article 92 of the 2014 Constitution, illuminating the path towards preserving individual rights and freedoms. Its resolute proclamation reverberates through the chambers of power, declaring that the fundamental essence of citizens' rights may not be tampered with or diminished. It stands as a guardian, shielding the vibrant tapestry of liberties from any rule that would compromise its very fabric (Egypt's Constitution, 2014).

The Federal Constitution of Malaysia serves as the foundation for the principles of religious freedom in the country, establishing both conceptual and legal frameworks. It designates Islam as the official religion of the Federation, primarily due to the prevalence of this faith among the native Malay population. However, the Constitution recognizes the peaceful practice of other religions throughout the nation, as stated in Article 3(1). Article 11(1) ensures that every individual has the freedom to profess and practice their own religion. Nonetheless, there are certain regulations regarding the propagation of religion, particularly in relation to Malays, outlined in Article 4 (Husina & Ibrahim, 2016, p. 1220). This article imposes restrictions and limitations on the methods of spreading one's religion specifically to Malays. The Constitution, under Article 160, defines Malays as Muslims who speak Malay, adhere to Malay customs, were born in Malaya or Singapore before or on the day of independence, and currently reside in Malaya or Singapore. This connection between Malays and Islam is explicitly stated, indicating that the Constitution safeguards the faith of the Malay people and protects them against conversion. While there is ongoing debate regarding whether Malaysia is an Islamic or secular state, it is worth noting that the Constitution does not explicitly endorse a fully Shariah-based system. In terms of religious liberty, the Malaysian Constitution highlights three aspects: the freedom to declare, practice, and propagate one's faith (Husina & Ibrahim, 2016, p. 1221).

Regarding the right to profess a religion, Article 11 of the Malaysian Constitution guarantees individuals the freedom to practice and proclaim their faith. However, specific provisions regarding the freedom of religion for Muslims are addressed within the Constitution. Matters pertaining to Muslims fall under the jurisdiction of the *Sharīʿah* Court, as they are governed by Islamic laws. Nonetheless, the Constitution does not explicitly prohibit non-Muslims from professing a different faith or converting to another religion. Even individuals who were previously Muslims are allowed to exercise this freedom (Choon, 1999). Article 160 of the Malaysian Constitution defines Malays as individuals who practice Islam, speak Malay as their primary language, and follow Malay customs.

Within the realm of religious practice, the Federal Constitution grants every follower the right of practicing their faith, establishing religious institutions and prospering in abundance, as articulated in Article 11(3). This provision goes even further, bestowing upon believers additional rights: the privilege to form religious organisations, participate in congregations, construct shrines, establish centers of knowledge, foster welfare organizations, cherish sacred texts, amass wealth, and propagate the tenets of their faith (Tan & Thio, 1997, p. 12). Embracing the spirit of inclusivity, the Constitution entwines the freedom to establish religious organisations, empowering any ethnic group to create registered entities, be they organizations or corporations. The government's resolute stance on the matter has paved the way for numerous religious organizations to flourish, many of which have been acknowledged as esteemed corporate bodies. Notable examples include the Methodist Church of Malaysia Ordinance of 1955 and the Roman Catholic Bishop Incorporation Ordinance of 1957, testaments to the government's commitment to safeguarding the continued existence of these revered institutions (Koh Tong Ngee, 1987). As these organisations navigate the complex landscape of rights, they emerge as pillars of strength, fostering a shared awareness that supports the aspirations of diverse communities (Faruqi, 2001).

The Constitution extends its protective shield to constructing houses of worship by any ethnic group. Although the creation of these houses of worship can give rise to delicate questions and conflicts, the government, in accordance with Islamic Laws, has enacted a constitution that generously affords 'each ethnic community the opportunity to erect their sacred structures.' However, when the right to build is put into practice, challenges arise. The local council and state authorities bear the responsibility of granting approval for these holy places of worship. For instance, in the year 2000, the government made headlines when it temporarily abolished the requirement for a holy edifice to secure the consent of at least 2000 members of the local religious community. However, spurred by protests from concerned parties, the requirement was eventually reinstated, underlining the complex interplay between authority and communal sentiments

(International Religious Freedom Report, 2001). Past instances of unauthorised construction of structures have engendered legal disputes, as local governments grappled with the task of demolishing these contested buildings. One such event unfolded in the 'Kuah village's Muniandy A/L Subramaniam v. Langkawi City Council' court case, where a shrine, steeped in history and cherished by estate workers since the days of British colonisation, stood in the face of demolition (Faruqi, 2001). While the court ultimately ruled against the plaintiff, tensions simmered between the local government and the Hindu community, underscoring the profound emotions and aspirations enshrined within these sacred spaces.

The freedom to propagate one's religion is limited by the Constitution, specifically concerning Malaysians. The Constitution defines Malays as Muslims, making it illegal to promote religions other than Islam among Malays. Article 11(4) grants authority to State's Law and Federal Territories of Kuala Lumpur, Labuan and Putrajaya, allowing them to control and restrict the spread of other faiths to Muslims. Consequently, certain laws were enacted under State Acts to restrict the religious freedom of Muslims in Kelantan, Terengganu, Pahang, and Kedah. Similar acts were implemented in Melaka, Johor, and Perak to limit the growth of other religions among Muslims. However, some states, such as the Federal Territories of Labuan, Kuala Lumpur, and Putrajaya, Pulau Pinang, Sabah, and Sarawak, have not adopted these measures. In 2006, the former prime minister introduced legislation to prevent conversion to another faith among Malaysia's Muslims, as reported by Utusan Malaysia on May 25, 2006. One notable case that exemplifies the inviolability of the Constitution is the story of Azlina Jailani, a Malay Muslim who sought to change her Islamic status on her identity card through the National Registration Department (NRD) (Mohammad & Kusrin, 2017, p. 220).

Azlina Jailani's case garnered significant attention from non-Muslim organisations and foreign observers who disagreed with the court's decision. Critics called for the establishment of the Inter Faith Commission, an NGO advocating for the freedom of religious practice among Malays. A protest titled 'Federal Constitution Protects all parties' was organised by 500 individuals, objecting to Article 11. The Inter Faith Commission also raised concerns about Article 121 (A) of the Constitution, arguing that its enforcement imposed norms and regulations that contradicted their faith, while challenging the position of Islam as the Federal religion (Harding, 2012, p. 357). The government staunchly supported the court's ruling, asserting the irrevocability of the Apostasy Act. Eventually, Azlina Jailani's request was brought before the Syariah Court, where it was rejected. After examining the three categories of freedom and the struggle for their implementation, this article will explore the significance of freedom in various aspects, including its general meaning as interpreted in the Qur'ān, its application in Muslim jurisprudence and its connection to *ijtihād* and legal judgments within the Muslim community.

The analysis conducted sheds light on significant disparities in the approaches adopted by Egypt and Malaysia in the realm of religious freedoms. In Egypt, there is a discernible inclination towards embracing religious diversity, underscored by the explicit allowance for various communities to construct houses of worship. However, despite this apparent openness, the emergence of challenges and conflicts during the approval process indicates the existence of potential intricacies in translating the theoretical endorsement of religious freedoms into seamless practical implementation. Conversely, Malaysia takes a divergent stance, particularly concerning the propagation of religions other than Islam among Malays. The imposition of limitations in this context has not only triggered debates but has also elicited protests, underscoring a contentious space surrounding the delineation of boundaries for religious freedoms. The restrictions on the dissemination of non-Islamic beliefs among Malays suggest a regulatory framework that may pose constraints on the unrestricted exercise of religious expression.

These observed disparities bring to the fore diverse dynamics in the interpretation and application of religious freedoms in the two countries. Egypt's approach, while explicitly affirming the value of diversity, may encounter challenges in translating the policy into effective practice. In contrast, Malaysia's adoption of restrictions points to a more nuanced and regulated understanding of religious freedoms. This reflects ongoing debates within the country about the appropriate scope and limitations concerning the propagation of non-Islamic beliefs, adding layers of complexity to the landscape of religious freedoms. The variations in these approaches not only underscore the multifaceted nature of religious freedoms but also illuminate the intricate interplay between legal frameworks, societal expectations, and the lived experiences of religious freedoms in distinct cultural and political contexts. The evolving dynamics within each nation underscore the ongoing dialogues and negotiations surrounding the delicate balance between protecting religious harmony and preserving individual freedoms in the face of religious diversity.

3.4 Interpretation and Implementation

In the Egyptian constitution, Islam is designated as the official religion and *sharīʿah* law holds its position as the primary source of legislation. The constitution enshrines the principle of absolute freedom of belief, emphasising that the right to practice religious rituals and establish places of worship for followers of Abrahamic religions is protected by law. It further declares the equality of all individuals before the law, explicitly prohibiting discrimination based on religion, as well as incitement of hatred towards religion, belief, sex, origin, race, or any other grounds. Additionally, the constitution expressly prohibits the formation of political parties based on religion, as well as political actions rooted in religious affiliation. Discrimination based on sex, ethnicity, sect, or place of residence is also forbidden (Harding, 2012, p. 357).

Under the government's authority, Christian, Jewish and Sunni Muslim believers are the only ones permitted to openly practice their religions and construct places of worship, with formal recognition granted to these three faiths. Al-Azhar, the institution dedicated to the study of Islamic theology and related matters, is described in the constitution as an independent scientific Islamic establishment with exclusive competence over its own affairs. Its responsibilities extend to the preaching of Islam, dissemination of religious sciences, and promotion of the Arabic language on an international scale. The selection of the Grand Imam of Al-Azhar is entrusted to the Council of Senior Scholars of Al-Azhar, with formal appointment granted by the President for a lifetime tenure. The President does not possess the authority to dismiss the Grand Imam. Recognised as an independent institution within the constitutional framework, Al-Azhar is mandated to receive sufficient funding from the government to fulfill its objectives. According to the legislation, the Grand Mufti, the highest Islamic legal authority in the nation, must be consulted before capital punishments can be carried out. However, it is important to note that the Grand Mufti's judgment in these matters is advisory in nature and does not hold legal influence over the court that imposed the sentence (Report on International Religious Freedom in Egypt, 2021).

In Malaysia, Article 11 of the Federal Constitution ensures the right to practice and express one's religion, while also allowing for certain limitations. The state has the power to regulate the spread of religious beliefs among Muslims, reflecting Malaysia's protective stance towards Islam. However, this prohibition can lead to discriminatory legislation and practices. For instance, the Syariah Criminal Offences (Federal Territories) Act of 1997 criminalises the spreading of other religious beliefs among Muslims. It is important to note that this clause only applies to Muslims spreading other faiths among fellow Muslims. The extent of religious freedom in Malaysia is a topic of ongoing debate and the case of 'Minister of Home Affairs v. Jamaluddin Othman' is a notable example. In this case, the plaintiff was detained under the Internal Security Act of 1960/72 for his involvement in a campaign to promote Christianity among Malays. The plaintiff challenged his detention, arguing against the reasons given by the Minister of Home Affairs. The trial court ruled in favor of the plaintiff, stating that the Minister lacked the authority to deny someone their constitutional right to practice their faith. However, the Minister appealed the judgment.

The Supreme Court expressed agreement with the trial court's decision, emphasising that the freedom to practice religion, as stated in Article 11(5) of the Constitution, is subject to the general laws of the nation. It clarified that religious freedom does not protect criminal or immoral activities that endanger public health, morals, or order. Actions that pose a threat to national security cannot be justified by claims of religious freedom. The Supreme Court concluded that the plaintiff's participation in conferences and workshops did not endanger national security, and the conversion of six Malay individuals alone did not constitute a threat. This ruling is significant as it recognizes and upholds religious freedom in Malaysia, affirming the guarantees of Article 11 in the Federal Constitution. Furthermore, it sheds light on the notion that leaving Islam is seen as such a societal threat that it warrants detention under the Internal Security Act (Report on International Religious Freedom in Egypt, 2021).

When it comes to religious freedom, Egypt and Malaysia have faced their fair share of challenges and controversies. In Egypt, the interpretation and implementation of constitutional clauses related to religious freedom have predominantly been handled by the courts. However, these courts have faced criticism for their perceived bias towards Sunni Muslims, often neglecting the rights of religious minorities, particularly Coptic Christians. One prominent example is the case of Alber Sabre, a Coptic Christian blogger who was arrested on blasphemy charges in 2012. Despite evidence proving his innocence regarding a video he had allegedly posted, Sabre was found guilty and sentenced to three years in prison. This verdict sparked outcry from human rights organisations and activists who argued that it reflected religious prejudice rather than an impartial assessment of the evidence. Additionally, the control and regulation of religious organisations and practices in Egypt have been problematic, with accusations that such laws have been utilised to suppress non-Muslim groups, especially Christians. An illustrative example is the 2016 rule requiring Christians to obtain official permission for church construction or renovation, which has been condemned for its discriminatory nature.

In Malaysia, although the Federal Constitution's Article 11 guarantees freedom of religion, exercising this right can prove challenging, particularly when it involves leaving or renouncing Islam. In the case of 'Daud bin Mamat & Ors v. Majlis Agama Islam & Anor,' the court controversially ruled that the right to convert out of a religion is not encompassed within Article 11's freedom to profess and practice religion. The court asserted that connecting the freedom to leave a religion with the freedom to practice or proclaim one's religion would be an excessive interpretation, contrary to the principles of constitutional construction. This ruling contradicts Article 18 of the United Nations Universal Declaration of Human Rights, which explicitly safeguards the freedom to adopt another religion or belief. If such a stance were upheld, it would undermine and render meaningless the freedom to profess and practice religion as enshrined in the Constitution. In Malaysia, although *aqidah* (personal belief) is considered a private matter for Muslims, it is often publicly regulated by law. Consequently, religion is no longer solely an individual's relationship with their faith, going against the Qur'ān's emphasis on religious freedom and recognition of religious diversity in Malaysia's multicultural society. Instead, laws pertaining to Islamic practices, traditions and Syariah offenses have been used to impose restrictions on religious expression, raising concerns about their constitutionality (Abdullah @Chew Li Hua, 2007, p. 265).

The idea of religious freedom has been discussed by some scholars in relation to statist policy. According to Hirst, statism entails hierarchical authority and constrained personal freedom (Hirst, 2000, p. 281). This entails a move on the part of the government to increase state authority and gain more social control. Hirst states that "the state does come to control more and more affairs of the society" as a result. When religion and religious matters are examined within the framework of statism, we frequently observe attempts on the part of the government to regulate and, in some cases, restrict religious activity, often involving hierarchical oversight of religious organizations and people (Hirst, 1997).

The military takeover in 1952 and Nasser's administration, according to Rutherford, are what led to the emergence of statism in Egypt (Rutherford, 2008). The state attempted to dominate many facets of Egyptian society, particularly its political system and the economy, during Nasser's administration. Nasser also favored governmental regulation of religion and religious organisations in society. This can be seen in the nationalisation of Al-Azhar with Law 103 of 1961, which gave the Ministry of Religious Endowments control over the institution. The appointment of the Grand Sheikh of Al-Azhar by the president rather than top clerics is another sign of the loss of autonomy (Rutherford, 2008).

The discriminatory and abusive treatment of religious minorities by the government in Egypt is well-documented. There were not many religious minorities in the parliament or the cabinet (Cairo Institute for Human Rights Studies. 2013). Baha'i, Shiite, Ahmadiyya and Coptic Christians all experienced prejudice in the workplace. Government agents have been known to intimidate and detain Shiites, considering their religion as rebellious and contrary to 'genuine Islam' (Cairo Institute for Human Rights Studies. 2013). The political and institutional barriers to the development or refurbishment of religious buildings and places of worship in Egypt have been highlighted by the US Commission on International Religious Freedom (United States Commission on International Religious Freedom Annual Report, 2013). More than 100 proposals to construct new churches were made in 2006, but many of these requests have been pending for over ten years. This situation disproportionately affects religious minorities, such as Coptic Christians, who make up a significant portion of the population. Sunni Muslims, on the other hand, do not face the same difficulties when building mosques (United States Commission on International Religious Freedom Annual Report, 2013). While economic pressure and the Arab Awakening may have caused the statist order that prevailed throughout Mubarak's administration to wane, it did not completely disappear (Scott, 2014, p. 63). Political and institutional barriers to religious freedom persist, although they may have been somewhat mitigated by the changing circumstances in recent years.

During their period of governance from 2011 to 2013, the Muslim Brotherhood in Egypt and their acceptance of statism have drawn attention from experts, despite statism's origins lying in Nasser's secular ideology. Scott argues that the Justice and Development Party and the Muslim Brotherhood under Morsi did not significantly deviate from the statist stance of their secular predecessors (Scott, 2014, p. 65). However, it is worth noting that the Muslim Brotherhood underwent an evolution towards a unique form of secularism, where the state assumes the authority to define the boundaries of religion and politics (Scott, 2014, p. 71). Scott's analysis sheds light on how the Muslim Brotherhood strategically utilized governmental institutions, including the 2012 constitution, as tools to exert control over religious affairs.

Comparatively, both the 1971 constitution and the 2012 constitution in Egypt exhibit similarities in their approach to religion. Article 2 of both constitutions emphasises the primacy of *sharīʿah* law as the foundation for legislation. However, these constitutions do not explicitly guarantee religious freedom or tolerance for religious minorities such as Baha'is, Shiites, or Quranists (Hamzawy, 2014, p. 402). Under the 2012 Constitution, the Supreme Constitutional Court, a governmental entity, retained the authority to determine the compliance of laws with Article 2 and *sharīʿah,* despite the Muslim Brotherhood and the Justice and Development Party having the option to involve senior religious experts from Al-Azhar as the ultimate authority on the matter (Hamzawy, 2014, p. 403). Notably, there were no efforts made to restore the financial independence of Al-Azhar or relinquish control over its finances. Additionally, Morsi's administration appointed several Muslim Brotherhood members to positions within the Ministry of Religious Endowments, further consolidating their influence. Had it not been for the military takeover, the Muslim Brotherhood's statist strategy, including the appointment of judges aligned with their ideology, might have persisted (Hanna, 2015, p. 23).

Following the military takeover led by El-Sisi in 2013, which led to the overthrow of Morsi and the Justice and Development Party, Egypt witnessed an increase in statism, even within the realm of religion. According to Wahid Hanna, religion has been instrumentalised to reinforce state authority and legitimacy, aligning with the regime's statist vision (Hanna, 2015, p. 24). Despite the presidential elections in 2014 and the implementation of the 2014 constitution, El-Sisi's administration has maintained control over religion and religious institutions. The 2014 constitution upholds Article 2 and guarantees freedom of religion for specific faiths. However, it falls short in ensuring equal rights for non-Muslim citizens (Hanna, 2015, p. 29). While Articles 64 and 65 of the constitution provide guarantees for freedom of religion and practice, concerns persist regarding the rights of non-Muslims.

Shifting our focus to Malaysia, the question arises as to whether state legislatures can pass laws based on religion. The authority of state legislatures in Malaysia is limited to issues specified in the State List. This includes Islamic law and personal and family law applicable to Muslims (Abdullah@Chew Li Hua, 2007, p. 275). Notably, the State List does not explicitly address religious conversion or renunciation Furthermore, state legislatures possess the power to enact laws related to offenses committed by individuals adhering to the religion of Islam, except for matters included in the Federal List. This prompts us to reflect on the constitutionality of criminalizing the exercise of the freedom to reject Islam and whether such an act contradicts the principles of Islam (Abdullah@Chew Li Hua, 2007, p. 277). In the context of Malaysia, there is a contention that state laws governing religion infringe upon Article 11 of the Federal Constitution by seeking to restrict and eliminate the right to renounce, which is an integral aspect of the freedom to practice one's chosen religion (Neo, 2018, p. 578). However, it is noteworthy that the State legislature lacks the authority to pass legislation on this subject as it is not even included in paragraph 1 of the State List. Nonetheless, until a court deems such provisions unconstitutional, they remain enforceable, and individuals can challenge their legality through legal action seeking a declaration of their illegality. However, so far, such attempts have not been successful.

In the case of "Kamariah Ali and Yang Lain Iwn v. Kerajaan Negeri Kelantan and satu lagi," the applicants were granted leave to appeal on the grounds that the limitations imposed by section 102 of Kelantan's Council of Muslim Religion and Malay Custom Enactment 1994 are in conflict with various articles of the Federal Constitution. However, the Federal Court summarily dismissed the issue as unimportant, rather than engaging in a substantive debate (Abdullah@Chew Li Hua, 2007, p. 279). The Federal Court argued that section 102, which pertains to converts, should not be interpreted in a literal or rigid manner. It is widely accepted that constitutional provisions should be interpreted more liberally and less strictly, particularly when it comes to safeguarding fundamental rights. However, laws aiming to restrict basic freedoms should be subject to strict and literal interpretation. In the Kamariah case, the Federal Court also ruled that the renunciation by the applicants did not impact the severity of the penalty imposed by the Syariah court, as allowing such a scenario would create the potential for individuals to renounce their faith solely to evade charges (Marican & Adil, 2004, p. 170). The court noted that this would have implications for the administration of Malaysian Islamic law.

However, this ruling sidestepped the underlying issue of limitations on the exercise of the fundamental right enshrined in Article 11. It is argued that the decision's flawed logic and avoidance of the core problem have left the matter unresolved.

From the above analysis, it becomes evident that both countries have distinct approaches towards the protection of individual rights, particularly in the realms of free speech, thought and religious practice. Article 64 of the Egyptian Constitution asserts the fundamental nature of free speech, while Article 65 guarantees the right to free thought. In Malaysia, the Federal Constitution also guarantees freedom of speech and expression under Article 10, albeit subject to certain restrictions (Noor, 2020, p. 290). However, when it comes to religious freedom, disparities arise. In Egypt, the right to practice one's faith is limited to the three major religions, while publicly expressing different views is not permitted.

Apostasy legislation is another contentious issue in Egypt. While apostasy is not a criminal offense, it carries civil repercussions, impacting matters related to personal status. The consequences of apostasy include nullifying marriages, prohibiting new marriages (even with nonMuslims), and exclusion from inheritance (Berger, 2002, p. 556). The Court of Cassation and the Supreme Court have upheld the view that apostasy's legal repercussions are grounded in public order and the constitutional provision (Berger, 2002, p. 556). Hamad further emphasises the legal repercussions of apostasy in Egypt, noting that apostates are denied inheritance and marriage rights (Hamad, 1999, p. 219). The case of Nasr Hamid Abu Zayd, an Egyptian professor, exemplifies the consequences of apostasy, as he was declared an apostate and divorced from his Muslim spouse due to his academic writings on Islamic law and history (Moustafa, 2010, p. 611). While Egypt does not specifically criminalize apostasy, blasphemy laws can be utilised to prosecute individuals who belong to non-recognized religions, atheists, or Muslims who convert to other faiths (O'Sullivan, 2003, p. 97). Blasphemy is considered a felony in Egypt, punishable by imprisonment (Article 98(f) of the criminal code). Some intellectuals have faced accusations of insulting Islam under the guise of blasphemy laws, although many cases did not result in conviction and imprisonment.

A notable example is the case of Egyptian blogger Karim Amer, who received a three-year prison sentence in 2007 for posting writings on his personal website deemed offensive to Islam and Al-Azhar Islamic institution (Amnesty International, 2010). In contrast, Malaysia takes a different stance on religious freedom, although some limitations exist. While the Federal Constitution guarantees freedom of religion, including the right to profess and practice one's faith (Federal Constitution of Malaysia), the Constitution also allows for the restriction of these rights on grounds of public order, morality, and the interests of Islam (Federal Constitution of Malaysia). This has resulted in certain limitations on religious conversion and restrictions on proselytization, particularly from Islam to other faiths.

In 2012, Egypt witnessed a surge in blasphemy accusations, leading to convictions and imprisonment for individuals expressing critical views about Christianity and Islam (Amnesty International, 2010). Alber Saber, an Egyptian atheist of Christian heritage, was sentenced to three years in jail for blasphemy after posting critical articles about both religions on his personal website and Facebook page (Amnesty International 2010). Similarly, another Egyptian Muslim Shi'i was found guilty of blasphemy and given a three-year jail term (El Fegiery, 2013, p. 3). Article 44 of Egypt's 2012 Constitution prohibits disrespect towards religious messengers or prophets, making blasphemy a punishable offense and creating a chilling effect on the expression of religious ideas by atheists and converts.

When examining the State Council's approach to religious freedom, three distinct themes emerge: a rigid stance, a liberal stance, and a pragmatic stance. Judges adopting a strict stance dismiss objections from Muslim residents seeking to change their religious affiliation on identity cards, citing Islamic law's traditional prohibition of apostasy and the need to maintain public peace in a predominantly Muslim nation (Brown, 2014). This rigid stance has long been considered the norm, but a pragmatic approach has recently emerged, which maintains the traditional definition of apostasy while accommodating converts from Christian backgrounds in order to uphold law and order and meet the needs of the contemporary nation-state. The liberal perspective justifies religious freedom by considering Egypt's obligations under international human rights treaties and finding a balance between constitutional protections for religious liberty and Islamic law.

In a specific case before the State Council, Nabil Hassan Sabry, an Egyptian Muslim seeking to change his identity card to reflect his conversion to Christianity, was denied the opportunity. The Civil Records Office argued that Islam forbids apostasy, and thus the change could not be made. Sabry argued that changing one's faith is not against the Civil Code and invoked the Law of Civil Status, which allows for the updating of personal information on documents. He also referred to Article 46 of

Egypt's 1971 Constitution, which safeguards religious freedom, asserting that Islamic law was irrelevant in this situation since the Law of Civil Status explicitly allows for changes in religious information. The government contended that the Law of Civil Status is constrained by Islam's prohibition on apostasy, which is considered a norm of public order, and cited Article 2 of the Constitution, which establishes Islamic law as the primary basis of law. The argument put forth was that since apostasy is forbidden by the Qur'ān, the primary source of Islamic law, the Law of Civil Status clause governing the change of religious affiliation on identification papers is nullified (Brown, 2014).

In Egypt, the implications of apostasy under Islamic law are striking. Apostates are denied civil rights, with only non-Muslims permitted to change their religious affiliation. Muslims, on the other hand, are prohibited from doing so, whether by embracing a non-religious stance or converting to another faith. The Egyptian courts have affirmed the necessity of prohibiting apostasy in accordance with Islamic *sharīʿah*. They contend that the failure to allow such changes is justified due to the state's inability to tolerate apostasy, as it would contravene a law essential to maintaining public order (Berger, 2003, p. 730). Delving further, the Egyptian courts have invoked the relationship between constitutional provisions and Islamic law. They argue that Article 47 of the Egyptian Constitution, which guarantees religious freedom, should be interpreted in harmony with Article 2, which designates Islamic law as the primary source of legislation. This indicates that the courts view the protection of religious freedom as compatible with upholding the primacy of Islamic law (Berger, 2003, p. 735).

Another case that exemplifies these perspectives is that of Jerjes Malak Wassef. Born into a Christian family, Wassef's life took a different course when his father converted to Islam, leading to a change in the child's birth certificate to reflect his new religion. The courts made a distinction between an individual's freedom to adopt religious beliefs and their right to express those beliefs publicly. While the former is considered a personal matter, the latter, with its potential impact on society, may be subject to limitations in the interest of public order and public morals. The courts emphasized that although Islam respects the freedom of non-Muslims to practice their respective faiths, it forbids those who embrace Islam from renouncing it, considering this prohibition a crucial component of national public order (El Fegiery, 2013, p. 24). Similarly, in the case of Mohamed Hegazy, who converted from Islam to Christianity, the court denied his petition to change the religion designation on his identity card. The court invoked the Islamic prohibition of apostasy and the need to uphold the rule of law in a Muslim society. Hegazy, invoking the government's international obligation under Article 18 of the International Covenant on Civil and Political Rights (ICCPR), argued that such obligations had been incorporated into national laws under the 1971 constitution. However, the court maintained that the provisions of the ICCPR are constrained by Islamic law, citing the same justifications as in the Wassef Case and referencing a judicial decision on apostasy issued by *dar al-ifta'* in May 2001.

The plaintiff in the case of Mohamed Mahdy Abdullah was a Christian who had been born to Christian parents (El Fegiery, 2013, p. 25). The Ministry of Interior declined to amend the religion shown on his citizenship card when he converted to Islam but afterwards returned to Christianity. In this instance, the court upheld the claim and issued a directive to the interior ministry. 22 cases were successfully resolved by the Court between April 2004 and September 2006, including this one. Abdel Qader, who presided over the Court of Administrative Justice at the time and used liberal reasoning, led the institution (Human Rights Watch and Egyptian Initiative for Personal Rights, 2007). The Ministry's reluctance to change the identity card in these instances was viewed by the Court as an unjustified intrusion on the man's personal autonomy. The act, according to the Court, is only an administrative process that reflects reality, and registration is required to create rights and obligations based on the appropriate religious status. The Egyptian Constitution's Article 40 guarantees that all citizens be treated equally in terms of their rights and obligations without distinction on the grounds of religion, language, origin, or sex, the Court stated in response to the public order argument. It also made reference to Article 46, which safeguards people's freedoms to express their religious beliefs as well as their right to freely practice their chosen religions. In addition to asserting that Islam clearly recognised freedom of religion many centuries ago, the Court cited the Arab Charter of Human Rights as well as the UN Declaration of Human Rights. A number of Qur'ānic passages that emphasise the values of freedom and non-compulsion in religious belief were quoted by the Court to demonstrate the compatibility between Islam and religious freedom (Rieffer-Flanagan, 2016, p. 11).

A brief discussion of apostasy is included in the Malaysian Human Rights Commission's 2005 Annual Report. The Malaysian government's entire reaction is as follows: The problem of apostasy is not a recent one (Martinez, 2008, p. 121). In order to foster understanding and prevent the incidence of apostasy, the government has taken suitable and harmonious action to handle this issue. The government has also discussed this topic and the laws that are accessible to the various parties through various organised events. A person who joins Islam is obligated to uphold its rules and ideals, according to Islamic beliefs. Islam considers apostasy to be a crime for which there must be a penalty (Annual Report of the Human Rights Commission of Malaysia, 2003). Rights and freedom of religion are not addressed in the government's response to concerns highlighted by the Malaysian Human Rights Commission under the category of basic freedoms and rights. Instead, the teachings of Islam are loosely and broadly referred to, along with a moral warning that anybody who embraces Islam is obligated to uphold its values and precepts, and the contentious idea that temporary punishment is required for apostasy.

According to reports, the Mufti of the state of Perak announced to the Malay daily the Utusan Malaysia on March 16, 2006, that more than 250,000 Muslims had abandoned their faith and more than 100,000 had converted to Christianity. According to the chairman of the state-level Islamic development and mission committee for Kelantan, the government of Kelantan is paying its missionaries RM 10,000 to marry indigenous women in exchange for free accommodation, a RM 1000 per month, as well as a car (Ahmad, 2006). This is part of an effort to convert the indigenous population. The problem of converts wanting to reject Islam is a major one given the relentless proselytising. Islamic law derives its legitimacy from Article 74(2) of the Federal Constitution, although the constitutional framework holds that the Constitution is the highest law of the state. Any inconsistency between state legislation and the constitution, such as those governing faith or establishing the crime of apostasy, renders the state law invalid to the degree of the conflict. Every citizen is given the constitutional freedom to profess and practice the religion of their choosing under Article 11 of the Federal Constitution. It is noteworthy to mention that section 46(2) of the Islamic Family Law (Federal Territories) Act 1984 states that a party's conversion to Islam by itself would not cause a non-Muslim marriage to dissolve, as long as the Syariah Court confirms this (Shuaib, 2008, p. 443). In addition to the aforementioned issues, getting compensation from the spouse who adopted Islam might also be problematic because that person is a Muslim and the provisions of section 77 of the Law Reform (Marriage and Divorce) Act 1976 does not apply to Muslims. Despite the fact that her ex-husband had later converted to Islam, the Supreme Court held in Tan Sung Mooi v. Too Miew Kim that the civil court had the authority to adjudicate on the appellant's motion for ancillary relief after their divorce (Hak, 2012, p. 227). Article 121(1A) has frequently rebuffed requests before the High Courts seeking declarations in respect to Article 11, far from settling jurisdictional problems between the civil courts and Syariah courts as envisaged (Hak, 2012, p. 228). The Syariah Courts, who have thus far interpreted the regulations as outlined in the state legislation, have been tasked with addressing the substantive issue of the exercise of religious freedom and the challenge to the legality of measures governing faith. The legality of such clauses cannot be addressed by the Syariah Courts since it is beyond of their purview to do so. The High Court is the appropriate forum for this matter.

There are effectively two sets of rules for Muslims: civil law, which extends to all Malaysians, and *sharīʿah* law, which historically deals with marriage, inheritance and other family-related matters. This is at the heart of the apostasy problem. *Sharīʿah* laws have, however, expanded beyond marriage, divorce, and inheritance as politics and government have become more Islamic throughout time in Malaysia's many states. *Hudūd* laws have been passed in the states of Terengganu and Kelantan, but they have not yet been put into effect because of the Federal Constitution's ninth schedule. Federal courts, not state laws or courts, have the authority to impose sentences such as the death penalty. It is becoming more and more contentious to distinguish between constitutionally guaranteed freedoms and rights and *sharīʿah*-compliant laws. In wellknown decisions before the Courts, the gaps and overlaps between Islamic law, or *sharīʿah*, and the common-law system contained in the Constitution have grown further clearer. One of these is whether Muslims have full rights under Article 11 of the Malaysian Constitution, which protects religious freedom. This is because convictions under the *sharīʿah* that criminalise apostasy have been upheld, and the *sharīʿah* courts continue to prosecute people who identify as Muslims and who declare they have renounced Islam even after they have served their prison sentences and paid fines as punishment handed down by the same courts and who describe themselves as having done so (Martinez, 2008, p. 120).

For instance, four followers of a Muslim who was labelled and tried as a "deviant" were found guilty and given a two-year jail term in 1992. These four people were once more summoned before the *Sharīʿah* High

Court in 2000 for disobeying the request to repent. They disclosed to the court throughout this trial that they had rejected Islam in 1998 in accordance with the Statutory Declaration Act (1960). However, the four were found guilty and given three years in prison by the *Sharīʿah* High Court. They faced apostasy charges a month later. The Kota Baru High court denied the people's request for declaratory relief while also ruling that the four people continued to be Muslims. As with the majority of Malaysian states, this state's *sharīʿah* law does not have a clause allowing Muslims to renounce their faith. The main offences against apostates and deviants include "insulting Islam" and/or defying *sharīʿah* law, which includes fatwas. Although a fatwa is a mufti's interpretation of the law, Malaysia's *sharīʿah* laws make it illegal to disagree with a fatwa or to defy one as well. More recently, the same adherents and "deviant" are again contesting the *sharīʿah* laws for which they are once more being punished. Two of them have filed an application to submit the identical issue to the Federal Court and are requesting a new determination from the High Court in Kuala Lumpur that the *sharīʿah* system has no authority over them since they have forsaken Islam. The ninth schedule of the Constitution, which is being contended as a delimiting element, only specifies penalty for violating the precepts of religion (not its mediators, dispensers, or arbiters), is being used by another plaintiff to contest the authority of state law (Martinez, 2008, p. 122).

In the year 2004, the conversion of two young children without the knowledge of their nonMuslim parent, who had been granted custody after their mother's divorce, sparked widespread concern among Malaysia's non-Muslim minority. The public outrage was a reflection of the rising concern of non-Muslims about how Islam affects them. Instead of deciding on the validity of the conversions, the civil courts finally determined that the mother would keep custody of the kids but would be responsible for bringing them up as Muslims despite not being a Muslim herself. The petition filed on behalf of Azalina Jelani (Lina Joy), who wanted the National Registration Department to remove the word "Islam" from her Identity Card (I.C.), is another case that is indicative of numerous similar cases that are pending in the legal system (Martinez, 2008, p. 123). The verdict in this case is still uncertain. In light of the glaring inconsistencies between state Islamic law and the federal constitution, there appears to have been a growing reluctance on the part of the Federal Court to explain basic issues relating to the freedom to personal beliefs.

3.5 Challenges and Controversies

Religious freedom for citizens is guaranteed under the constitutions of Egypt and Malaysia. However, in reality, both nations have difficulties and disagreements in relation to religious freedom. Blasphemy legislation, prejudice against religious minorities and the interaction of religion and the state are a few of the major concerns. The legal system in Egypt is a crucial lens through which to view the situation of religious minorities there. According to the 2014 Constitution of Egypt, religious freedom is unrestricted. According to Article 64, adherents of the "revealed religions," which are regarded as being Islam, Christianity and Judaism, are granted the freedom to engage in religious ceremonies and create houses of worship. Al-Azhar is recognised as the "main authority for religious sciences and Islamic affairs" under Article 7 (Feuer, 2020). Requests for official approval from religious groups that have not yet been recognised by the Egyptian government must be made to the Department for Administrative and Religious Affairs within the Ministry of Interior, which then determines whether or not the group constitutes a threat to social harmony or national cohesion after consulting with official religious institutions. The legal structure of the nation prohibits anyone who do not adhere to the "revealed religions" from performing their religious ceremonies. Even followers of the "revealed religions" may encounter limitations in this regard.

All Malaysians are equal before the law and get equal protection under the law, according to Article 8(1) of the Federal Constitution. The remainder of the text forbids discrimination as well. The protection offered by Article 153 for Malays is confined to quotas and a few other items; after 1963, it was also extended to Sabah and Sarawak residents. The Federal Constitution's Article 153 poses no issues for non-Malays. For the purposes of Article 153, 'Malay' is defined in Article 160 as include both the original citizens of Malaya and their offspring. The government has been pursuing an intensive social engineering effort to elevate the Malays to the perceived status of the more prosperous non-Malays for years after the riots of 1969. The New Economic Policy was the name of such project. There was nothing wrong with the NEP's formulation. In the execution of it. However, it was discriminatory in many ways. As a result, non-Malaysians and nonbumiputeras were shut out of several government activities and institutions (Dass, 2019).

Article 153 of the Federal Constitution made it legal to give more favorable treatment to Malays (also known as Bumiputera) and the New Economic Policy and other economic policies were put into place with the goal of reducing and ultimately eradicating "the identification of race with economic function". While the effectiveness of such programmes is debatable, others contend that in reality the main gainers have been an expanding middle class of ethnic Malays. As a result, prejudice exists against other ethnic groups, such as the Chinese, Indians and some indigenous tribes, in the areas of political involvement, employment and housing. Malaysia's public schools employ Malay as their primary language of teaching, which has resulted in the majority of schools and institutions being racially divided. The uneven financial assistance given by the government, which prioritises Malay schools and students, disadvantages colloquial national type institutions and students. In order to exercise their right to equality, individuals must be treated equally in all spheres of economic, social, political, cultural, and civic life. This applies to people of all religious and philosophical beliefs as well as non-religious individuals. Islam, Buddhism, Christianity and Hinduism are the four primary faiths practiced in Malaysia, and there is a strong correlation between race and religion. No statistics that break down data on education, employment, health care, and other topics based on religion were discovered while conducting research for this study. Therefore, it is impossible to make exact judgements about how a person's religion affects their capacity to engage in these activities equally. The freedom of a person to freely practice their religion, to change their faith, and to exercise particular human rights has been linked to discriminatory practices that have been established via research. All religious groups, both the dominant Muslim population and the minority communities like Hindus and Christians, are subject to discrimination in Malaysia. However, Article 3(1) of the Malaysian Constitution gives Islam a special status that is mirrored in other parts of the Constitution (Allen & Gledhill, 2016).

Minority faiths that are seen to be 'threatening' to Islam's status have had their members' right to practice their religion restricted in order to preserve the integrity of the state's official religion. Hindu temples have been demolished, Christians have been detained for purportedly attempting to convert Muslims to Christianity, Malay-language Bible translations and other printed materials have been banned, and violent attacks against people of other faiths have all been committed in the name of discrimination against non-Muslim religious groups. Regarding the funding of religious institutions and religious education, non-Muslims suffer from discrimination. Such behaviours exacerbate the problems with race prejudice mentioned above, given the close connection between ethnicity and faith in Malaysia.

In Egypt, Shi'a Muslims and adherents of other Muslim sects, for instance, are subject to limitations since the position given to al-Azhar is often perceived as a support for Sunni Islam. Additionally, the Supreme Administrative Court maintained a ban on the yearly Jewish holiday of Abu Hasira in September 2020, claiming "moral offences and disturbances to public order." The legal system of the nation prohibits the capacity of unrecognised sects, faiths and denominations to ask the state for formal recognition, and the courts have mostly upheld this position, particularly in disputes involving Jehovah's Witnesses and Baha'is. Some religious minority are severely affected by the lack of legal recognition, including restrictions on their ability to license marriages, recognise their offspring as citizens, and engage in some religious practices. According to what was previously said, the Constitution grants those who practice "revealed religions" the freedom to build places of worship. In accordance with the provisions of Article 235 of the Constitution, which mandated that a legislation governing the construction and repair of churches be established during the first parliamentary term after the constitution's passage, the Church Construction legislation (Law No. 80 of 2016) was ratified in September 2016 (Buchanan, 2016).

According to the legislation, the church official who wants to build anything new or renovate what that exists must make a request to the governor of the relevant province. Within four months of reviewing the proposal, the governor must either grant it or refuse it; refusals must be supported by a 'justified' written conclusion. The governor's decision regarding the application may take into account the 'number and need of the citizens of the Christian denomination.' Furthermore, the legislation establishes a ministerial commission to examine requests for churches that had already been constructed without prior approval from the president or governor or before the law's ratification ('unlicensed churches'). This legal structure means that the legislation regulating the construction of Muslims' and Christians' respective places of worship are distinct and unequal. Religious minority who are not recognised are nevertheless unable to completely build houses of worship. Additionally, although belonging to a 'revealed religion,' Shi'a Muslims have not been permitted to build prayer spaces for their congregations (The Tahrir Institute for Middle East Policy, 2022).

Article 98(f) of the Egyptian Penal Code, which is the country's primary blasphemy statute, defines blasphemy as 'any use of religion to promote or advocate extremist ideologies... with a view to stirring up sedition, disparaging or showing contempt for any divinely revealed religion, or prejudicing national unity and social harmony' (Park, 2015). Different types of religious insult are addressed by other EPC rules. For instance, Article 160 criminalises impeding religious rituals as well as destroying, vandalising, or defiling religious structures, monuments, symbols, cemeteries, and graves. Article 161 makes it unlawful to publicly insult or ridicule religious rituals for the three religions recognised by the state (Islam, Christianity and Judaism). It also forbids the publishing and distribution of purposefully misrepresented religious literature (Report on International Religious Freedom in Egypt, 2022). Public provocation and treating a religious group with hostility or contempt are also prohibited by Article 176. Additionally, Article 178 imposes a maximum sentence of two years in jail for creating, distributing, or possessing papers that are against 'public morals,' albeit this word is not defined.

The rules against blasphemy and religious insults not only restrict core fundamental liberties like the freedom of speech, but also lack internal mechanisms to stop abuses that lead to additional restrictions on these liberties. For instance, they lack precise definitions for important concepts and are expressed in general terms. One writer claimed that Egyptian law is frequently reactive in character, whereby a statute is created to address a particular instance. The legislation is selective because of how it is created, and when it is tried to be more universal, it frequently becomes overly ambiguous (Report on International Religious Freedom in Egypt, 2022). The vague and imprecise wording in Article 98(f) of the EPC have made it a valuable instrument for resolving personal and political disputes, suppressing regime opponents, supporters of human rights, and opposition groups. In one instance, two human rights advocates who were working to protect the rights of Coptic Christians were arrested in August 2007 on charges of 'insulting a heavenly religion': Adel Fawzy Faltas and Peter Ezzat of the Canadian group Middle East Christian Association (MECA) (Spollen, 2007). The two guys visited the family members of a Coptic Christian who was reportedly slain by police in the days before their detention. Additionally, MECA was working to promote the controversial case of Mohammed Hegazy, a Christian convert, and had just filed a lawsuit against the Egyptian government in order to obtain restitution for the 2000 murder of 21 Copts in the hamlet of Kosheh in the north.

Despite the fact that the two men were subsequently released in November 2007 and that no formal charges were brought, the incident shows how Egypt's blasphemy and religious insult laws, along with the state's newly acquired authority thanks to the emergency law, are frequently used to violate rights and target particular people or groups) (Spollen, 2007). Any dissenting views of Islam are likewise prohibited by the blasphemy and religious insult statutes. Apostasy allegations or convictions can result from challenging Islam, which may be tried as blasphemy. Articles 98(f), 160, 161, 176 and 178 of the Penal Code are routinely applied against those who participate in civil religious discourse (Backet Fund for Religious Liberty, 2010).

Hisba is legally permitted in Egyptian courts as a result of the *Sharīʿah*-based foundation of the legal system, according to a 1966 decision of Egypt's highest court, the Court of Cassation (Johansen, 2003). Legal precedents allow the courts to use *hisba* cases to convict people of blasphemy and declare them apostates. According to Islamic law, the *hisba* principle enables a Muslim to file a lawsuit against another Muslim if he thinks the defendant is acting in a manner that is incompatible with Islamic principles. The idea is still broad, though, and practically any action might be considered an offence to Islam and subject to legal action. The International PEN Foundation claims that the process is allegedly abused for private gain or even extortion (Mostyn, 2007). Due to complaints from Egyptian attorneys, intellectuals, and certain media outlets over the aggressive use of *hisba* to punish academics and theological dissidents, the Egyptian parliament approved two laws to restrict its use in 1996. According to the first statute, *hisba* allegations cannot be brought before a judge before being approved by a prosecutor. Complainants must have a "personal interest" in the action, according to the second law. These protections aren't usually upheld in reality, though. Some *hisba* cases have reportedly been allowed by the courts despite improper prosecution due diligence (Arabic Network for Human Rights Information ANHRI, 2009).

Because it exclusively forbids blasphemy against one of any of the three 'heavenly' or 'divinely revealed' religions—Islam, Christianity, or Judaism—Article 98(f) is discriminatory. Unrecognised minority religious groups do not have protection and are adversely affected by the law, including the Baha'i and Ahmadiyya, a heterodox branch of Islam (Becket

Fund for Religious Liberty, 2010). Ahmadiyya and the Baha'i faiths do not have the same legal freedoms as Christians and Jews to practice. The Baha'i faith is really regarded as blasphemy. Law No. 263 of 1960 criminalises the faith, forbids Baha'i organisations and communal functions, and denies Baha'is any legal standing. Egypt's courts have upheld the government's claim that the legislation was passed to maintain "public order". The followers of the Baha'i faith in Egypt 'have faced several episodes of arrests, detentions, and imprisonment, the most recent being in 2001'. Baha'is continue to be closely monitored by the police. Periodically, their residences are searched. Baha'i books are removed and burned (U.S. House Committee on International Relations, 2006).

In Malaysia, Muslims are subject to limitations that do not hold true for other groups, most notably those that affect their freedom to practice another religion and their ability to have relationships with other people. In regards to their right to equal participation in cultural life, all Muslims who express opinions that are not recognised by recognised interpreters of Islam are subject to belief-based discrimination. As a result, Malaysia has been unable to balance its commitment to uphold the right to equality for adherents of all religions with its status as the official religion of Islam. Non-citizens experience discrimination in relation to their fundamental rights, with common patterns including assault, unfair detention and deportation, a lack of access to justice, the disruption of family life, and inadequate or nonexistent access to health care, education, and housing. Asylum seekers, refugees, and migrant workers—of which domestic workers are a particularly vulnerable subset—are just a few of the non-citizen populations who are impacted by discrimination against non-citizens. These groups all face disadvantages and discrimination in the determination of their refugee status and in the employment market. The Constitution's clauses that uphold the rights to equality and non-discrimination do not apply to non-citizens (ERT Country Report Series 2, 2012).

In accordance with Article 5 of the Federal Constitution, they also suffer disadvantages with regard to the criminal justice system, freedom of movement, and the rights to free expression, assembly, and association. Additionally, migrant workers face disadvantages due to discriminatory domestic laws, such as the Employment Act of 1955, which does not provide domestic workers with the same protections as other types of workers, and the Workmen's Compensation Act of 1952, which bars domestic workers from being entitled to compensation for injuries sustained at work and illnesses that occur at work. Finally, by enforcing stringent regulations on work permits, the Immigration Act of 1959–1960 makes it difficult for domestic employees to flee abusive situations. The legal system of Malaysia, which does not include the constitutional recognition of refugees, fails to provide migrant workers important rights under employment law, and, through its immigration regulations, places migrant workers in a position of extreme vulnerability, reflects the unprotected status of foreigners. Migrant workers are subject to prejudice in many facets of life as a consequence of this discrimination in the realm of law. Those who have been found guilty of immigration infractions, including asylum seekers, are held in horrific circumstances. In this regard, the actions of the Malaysian People's Volunteer Corps, or Ikatan Relawan Rakyat Malaysia (RELA), a voluntary group of citizens who enforce local security together with law enforcement agencies and support the Department of Immigration in the arrest of unauthorised immigrants and in the management of Immigration depots, as well as the circumstances as well as the treatment of immigrants in immigration detention facilities, are particularly troubling. Due to their condition of bonded servitude, certain migrant labourers are exposed to inhumane and humiliating treatment. Every non-citizen encounters impassable barriers to obtaining economic and social rights, as well as considerable limitations on their capacity to have a family life. Finally, because they do not have legal rights, noncitizens lack significant legal recourse (ERT Country Report Series 2, 2012).

Ever since Egypt's interaction with the West in the nineteenth century, the place of religion in the state has been one of the most pressing issues on the political agenda in Egypt. Egypt may have attained greater levels of modernization and Westernisation than any other Muslim nation outside of Turkey, but it has never forsaken the *sharīʿah's* supremacy in defining social standing or the long-standing basic Islamic unity of religion and state. An amendment to the Egyptian constitution that was approved by referendum as recently as 1980 acknowledged the *sharīʿah* as the main source of the nation's laws. After that, in 1985, the 1979 Law of Personal Status, which had strengthened women's rights in circumstances of divorce or child custody, was changed to placate Islamic organisations. The constitution's clauses 3 and 12 guarantee complete equality and religious freedom. Clause 13 declares that freedom of religion for all people of all faiths is protected "in accordance with the usages established in Egypt"; Clauses 23 and 24 define the people as the source of authority and grant the parliament full legislative authority; while Clause 149 declares Islam to be the official religion of the state without providing any further details. Allah is the ultimate source of authority and law, which corresponds to a *sharīʿah*-controlled state (Hatina, 2000, p. 37).

For a number of reasons, even though Clause 149 occurs towards the end of the constitution, it shouldn't be taken to mean that Islam has a little role to play in Egypt's new parliamentary system. First off, the public discussion over the legal status of religion in the state that erupted in the early 1920s was not resolved by Clause 149's more covert stance. Al-Azhar, on the other hand, regularly cited Clause 149 to buttress its hostility to criticism of Islam and its institutions. Second, the effectiveness of a written constitution depends on how it is put into practice, which is up to lawmakers and judges. Because of Islam's established role in Egyptian culture, especially in the 1920s and 1930s, these governmental branches tended to exhibit prudence and pragmatism on all matters involving religious regulations. Third, since the king had the right to oversee religious institutions and choose their managers (Clause 153), which increased his political clout, al-Azhar launched an effort to raise the monarch to the position of caliph. The inclusion of individuals holding conservative worldviews on the preliminary constitutional panel was largely responsible for the inherent uncertainty in the sections dealing to religion (Kedourie, 1968, p. 350). The former mufti of Egypt, Shaykh Muhammad Bakhit, was the most influential committee member. He led the unwavering opposition to the constitutional recognition of freedom of religion, arguing that it would encourage the growth of fringe ideologies that would jeopardise the standing of the monotheistic faiths. He suggested the phrase "absolute freedom of belief" (*hurriyyat al-iʿtiqad mutlaqa*) instead. Khakit responded, 'Belief is one thing and religion is another,' in response to a committee member's question on whether this encompassed freedom of religion. There are 73 distinct groupings of Muslims. Even though they all practice the same religion, each group has its own set of beliefs. He received the Coptic Patriarch Johannes' endorsement and the committee unanimously approved his plan after that. The constitution's numerous legal inconsistencies about how Islam should be treated in relation to the state, the monarchy, and the newly formed parliamentarian government made it clear that it was not the result of an evolutionary process but rather a governmental decree. This was evident to a number of Egyptian critics at the time, including Muhammad Husayn

Haykal, who noted that the constitution had been adopted at an inappropriate period in the course of Egypt's political evolution when speaking with a British official in 1926 (Hatina, 2000, p. 35). Indeed, rather than being a widely accepted doctrine, liberal nationalism was more popular in Egypt due to political factors. Although it was connected to the fight for independence, society's support for its core principles was lacking. Between the two world wars, this had the significant impact of restricting the intellectual discussion of religious issues in Egypt.

The 1930 Constitution initially made reference to Al-Azhar in article 142, which declared that the King selects his head (1930 Constitution). The Law 103 of 1961 was an ambitious attempt by the former president Nasser to restructure Al-Azhar (Aziz, 2013). Despite the fact that the 1971 constitution made no reference of it, Al-Azhar was given greater power and functions than ever before in the 2012 constitution, which's fourth article. The most contentious issue was using it for *Sharīʿah*-related issues. Al-Azhar protested to the Sukuk Law since no one had consulted it, yet the constitution demanded that (Aziz, 2013). He will be chosen in accordance with the legislation, which was previously hurriedly implemented by the military in January 2012. As a result, the Body's first membership will be entirely chosen by the present head of Al-Azhar, with any subsequent vacancies to be filled by the Body itself. Under the top leadership of Al-Azhar, the institution becomes a self-perpetuating entity that is exclusively responsible to itself, more so than even the police and similar to the Supreme Constitutional Court (Brown, 2014). The Al-Azhar Institute's position was made clearer by this change to the 2014 constitution. In 2012, in regard to other religious organisations. Furthermore, the Muslim Brotherhood insisted on having the power to organise endowments; nevertheless, Dr. Mohamed Emara said that the constitution should resuscitate this idea but that it should not have power until it is needed (Sayed, 2019). This topic was not covered in the 2014 constitution.

Both institutions came under growing fire from a sizable segment of the Egyptian people following the Azhar reorganisation and its apparent manipulation by the Egyptian government (Brown, 2014). A well-known Islamist speaker in Egypt and the Middle East named Shaykh 'Abd al-Hamid Kishk was a vocal opponent of the government's expanding interference with al-Azhar. Kishk, who had graduated from al-Azhar prior to the 1961 reorganisation, believed that government interference had compromised the school's standing and integrity. Kishk had asserted that 'ever since the reform [of 1961], the leadership of al-Azhar has ceased to render any service to Islam' (Kepel, 1985, p. 183). Kishk has called on the government to restore al-Azhar to its pre1961 position and, like many other Islamists, has denounced the government for its management of the institution. Al-Azhar has been criticised by Kishk for caving in to political intimidation and serving as a pawn for the authorities at the same time.

The rise of radical Islamist organisations like *Jihād, Takfir wa al-Hijra and al-Jamaa alIslamiyya*, which sought to overthrow the Egyptian government violently, were also likely a result of the government's expanding control over religious institutions (Kepel, 1985). One of the main causes of the growth in religious militancy, according to studies looking at the complaints and demands of Egypt's militant Islamist organisations, has been the growing subordination of religion to state interests (Bianchi, 1989, p. 179). In the words of Bianchi: 'the very success of corporatist policies has served to radicalize those who reject the right of state-appointed religious leaders to bend Islam to the needs of a secularizing regime' (Bianchi, 1989, p. 180). Further evidence that the growth of fundamentalism as a reaction to the state's stringent regulation of religion is not unique to Egypt comes from Ellis Goldberg's comparative study of extreme Islam and the Protestant movement. It implies that the same process may be expected to occur in circumstances that are comparable to Egypt's (Fandy, 1993, p. 25). Who has benefited more from the institutions' connection throughout time—the government or al-Azhar—is debatable. It is obvious that the government now has the ability to control al-Azhar if it so chooses thanks to its imposed changes. The government now has complete financial control and the authority to choose al-Azhar's top officials. The crucial question is whether using these levers as frequently as it has in the past serves the government's long-term objectives. Al-Azhar's incapacity to offer a convincing doctrinal defence, along with the emergence of militant Islam in the 1970s and again since 1992, raises the possibility that the government can only effectively manage al-Azhar at a high cost.

The Egyptian government's approach to religious institutions has come off as schizophrenic throughout time, as seen by the fact that it has alternated between dominating and cooperating with groups like the Muslim Brotherhood and al-Azhar. This contradictory link between governmental authority and societal control is what leads to these pendulum-like fluctuations in policy. Many emerging nations' major objectives are to uphold social control and fend off threats to the state. The achievement of this objective forces the government to pursue a strategy of dominance. The likelihood of the government exercising control over intermediate institutions increases when it has the ability to do so, especially over institutions that might represent challenges to the state. Inversely, state dominance harms both these institutions and the state's reputation in society. These influences compel the government to change course and form partnerships with social movements that share some of its objectives. Cooperative ties, however, are frequently tense when intermediary institutions start to push the government to pursue their own agenda, as the instance of al-Azhar demonstrates. The government is inclined to break up its cooperative partnership and restart a dominance approach as this pressure increases.

In Malaysia, with regard to the state and religion alliance, it is important to note how United Malays National organisation (UMNO) has held sway since the country's independence and has done so via forming coalition administrations. According to experts, UMNO adopted a more Islamic image in the early 1980s in response to a growing Islamic resurgence as well as the electoral danger posed by the opposition Islamic Party of Malaysia (PAS) (Saeed & Saeed, 2004). According to one scholar, UMNO, like every other political party, seeks to remain in power. Islamisation is a useful strategy for achieving this goal (Saeed & Saeed, 2004). Under the leadership of Prime Minister Mahathir Mohamed, who served as the nation's leader from 1981 to 2003, the government launched a number of initiatives and passed laws that significantly aided in the Islamisation of Malaysian institutions. JAKIM and *sharīʿah* were given more sway in the political process and judicial system.

Mahathir's initiatives also included the induction of Muslim religious leaders into government, the introduction of Islamic banking and insurance systems and the codification of *sharīʿah* at the state level through the adoption of laws creating *sharīʿah* courts (Smith, 2004, p. 357). JAKIM, founded in 1997, 'actively interprets and implements Islam in Malaysia and has widely been accepted as an appropriate authority' (Neo, 2003, p. 49). JAKIM is charged with creating policies to develop Islamic affairs, simplifying rules and regulations and enforcing mechanisms of laws and legal processes related to Islamic affairs (Saeed & Saeed, p. 160). It is also the organisation that creates definitions of 'deviancy,' keeps track of religious organisations and updates a list of forbidden sects.

Community tensions have increased as a result of UMNO's Islamisation agenda, which has also led to violent outbursts. The "1Malaysia" concept, which 'emphasises "acceptance" among the various races… so that they all live as the people of one nation,' has been adopted by UMNO in an effort to curb divisive rhetoric since the 2008 general elections, in which the coalition in power suffered significant losses to rival parties (Vasuvedan & Suparmaniam, 2009). Longstanding divisions within communities, however, are harder to reconcile, as was demonstrated in the beginning of 2010 when riots broke out in protest of a court decision allowing a Roman Catholic publication to refer to God as Allah. Additionally, regulations that penalise blasphemy and deviation are still in force and continue to undermine religious and ethnic harmony.

Both federal legislation and state-level *sharīʿah* laws outlaw blasphemy and disrespect to religion. The Malaysian Penal Code's Section XV (Articles 295-298A) deals with religious offences include desecrating a place of worship, interfering with a religious gathering, and trespassing on cemeteries (Penal Code of Malaysia, Act 574, 2006). In accordance with Articles 298 and 298A, it is forbidden to 'utter words, etc., with the deliberate intent to wound the religious feeling of any person' and to cause, etc., 'disharmony, disunity, or feelings of enmity, hatred or ill-will, or prejudicing, etc., the maintenance of harmony or unity, on grounds of religion' (Penal Code of Malaysia, 2023). Notably, Section XV's provisions do not mention any specific religion, meaning that all religions in Malaysia (except from those that JAKIM has prohibited) are theoretically protected against blasphemy or other forms of discrimination.

At the state level, blasphemy and insulting Islam in particular are forbidden. For instance, Section III of the Sharīʿah Criminal Offences Act 1997 (No. 559) of the Federal Territories states that anyone who—(a) insults or denigrates the religion of Islam; (b) derides, apes, or mocks Islamic practices or ceremonies; or (c) violates any law currently in effect in the Federal Territories that relates to the Islamic religion by demeaning it or holding it in contempt, is guilty of a crime, and upon conviction is subject to a fine of up to 3000 ringgit, a term of imprisonment of up to two years, or both. Anyone who disrespects the verses of the Al-Qur'ān or the Hadith by their words or actions is accused of a crime, and upon conviction they face a fine of up to 5000 ringgit, a maximum of three years in prison, or a combination of the two (Sharīʿah Criminal Offences-Federal Territories, Act 559, 1997). Similar clauses are found in various jurisdictions' *sharīʿah* criminal legislation, however the penalties and the severity of the law's execution vary. These laws have a wide range of applications and deal with a variety of additional *sharī'ah* infractions, some of which are classified as "insulting Islam."

The implementation of Malaysia's laws against blasphemy and other forms of religious insult essentially limits the right to practice any religion among its citizens. Non-Sunni Muslims are persecuted for their "deviant" views and JAKIM and the Islamic Religious Councils at the state level both monitor and target them. While this is going on, Sunni Muslims are compelled to adhere to the rigid restrictions set out by the government and its interpretation of Islam. Religious enforcement personnel, state and federal police and facilities where alleged *sharī'ah* breaches occur, such as pubs and nightclubs, are searched when someone are discovered to be in violation of these laws (Freedom House, 2010). According to JAKIM's list of deviant sects, distinct organisations fall within the federal definition of what defines deviant behaviour or belief, which state religious authorities often follow (International Religious Freedom Report, 2009). For instance, Nasrul Haq, a martial arts group, was founded in 1977 and had over 300,000 members by 1978 (Saeed & Saeed, 2004). The government attempted to exploit the organisation for this purpose, but when those attempts failed, it outlawed them on the grounds that they referenced Islam and Allah 'inappropriately,' employed Sufi chanting in their self-defense classes, and occasionally conducted meetings in mosques. It is unclear whether UMNO had considered the group as a potential counterweight to PAS, which was growing in popularity among Malay Muslims. Ashaari Muhammad founded Al-Arqam, a different organisation, in 1968. It was committed to advancing the Islamic way of life and by 1994 had a sizable following and wealth. In 1994, the government forbade the organisation because of concern that it had political aspirations. Ashaari was also detained under the ISA for deviating from the fundamental principles of Islam. He issued a formal apology and received a ten-year sentence (Mah & Reza, 2024).

3.6 Conclusion

This chapter examined the constitutional status of freedom of religion in Egypt and Malaysia, focusing on the legal provisions, practical implementation and challenges faced by religious minorities. Although the constitutions of both nations recognise the right to practice any religion, they differ in how much they actually do so. Egypt grants religious freedom to followers of Islam, Christianity and Judaism, although obstacles still exist in the form of social discrimination and limitations on non-Muslim practices. In Malaysia, the constitution guarantees religious freedom but also names Islam as the nation's official religion, which places restrictions on and causes disputes with religious minorities, particularly in regard to issues of personal status. Constitutional provisions, implementation and discrimination and tension are the three primary areas that may be used to analyse and debate the difficulties that come with the practical application of religious freedom (Ibrahim, 2021). These issues cover the challenges of securing the actualisation of religious freedom. The predominant religion in each nation has an impact on the constitutional provisions that provide freedom of religion in Egypt and Malaysia. The three Abrahamic religions—Islam, Christianity, and Judaism—are all recognised under Egypt's constitution as having the right to religious freedom even though Islam is the country's official religion. Although this acknowledgment is a step in the right direction, it is crucial to keep in mind that the influence of Islam as the official state religion may make it difficult for religious minorities to fully exercise their right to do so (Ibrahim, 2021). It might occasionally be more challenging for non-Muslim religious practices to be completely accepted and appreciated due to institutional prejudices brought on by Islam's dominating standing in Egypt's society. Similar to this, Malaysia's constitution recognises religious freedom but gives Islam a preference despite Islam being the country's official religion. In trying to balance the rights of the majority Muslim population with those of religious minorities, this dualism generates a difficult dynamic. The practice of nonMuslims' religious freedom may be constrained as a result of Islam's designation as the Federation's official religion, particularly on areas pertaining to one's identity as an individual, such as leaving Islam in favour of another faith (Report on International Religious Freedom in Malaysia, 2021).

Maintaining the rights of religious minorities while balancing the impact of the prevailing faith is a difficult undertaking. It necessitates making sure that constitutional clauses protecting the right to practice one's religion are understood and put into practice in a way that respects the rights and freedoms of all people, regardless of their religious views. Additionally, it calls for the development of a welcoming atmosphere that fosters communication, mutual respect, and tolerance across all religious communities. The rights of religious minorities should be protected, and efforts should be made to create a thorough legal system and strong institutional frameworks that guarantee their legal equality. This involves resolving stereotypes and discriminatory practices that prevent minorities from fully exercising their right to freedom of religion. A more inclusive society that respects and honours religious diversity may be achieved through enhancing education and awareness programmes to promote interfaith conversation and understanding. Additionally, doing comparative research and looking at best practices from nations that have successfully combined the influence of a dominant religion with the protection of religious freedom might give Egypt and Malaysia important insights.

The effective application of religious freedom is the second area where problems still exist. This includes the practical application and realisation of the values and protections related to religious freedom that are inscribed in laws and constitutions. Despite constitutional assurances, Egypt and Malaysia have major obstacles in implementing religious freedom in practice. NonMuslim religious practices in Egypt encounter administrative obstacles, mainly in connection with the building of churches. The capacity of religious minority to freely practice their beliefs may be hampered by these difficulties. In Egypt, acquiring licences for church building is one of the major problems. The administrative procedures needed to get these permissions are sometimes onerous and time-consuming. Construction and renovation of religious structures are subject to government clearance, which can cause delays and rejections, particularly for non-Muslim populations. This makes it difficult for religious minorities to start and grow their houses of worship, which restricts their freedom to practice their religion openly and freely. Additionally, there have been incidents of sectarian hostility and violence in Egypt, which makes the implementation of religious freedom even more challenging. These occurrences might lead to the desecration of places of worship or the targeting of religious minorities, creating an atmosphere of prejudice and fear. The country's ability to really implement religious freedom is threatened by the absence of solutions to these problems (Report on International Religious Freedom in Malaysia, 2021).

Similar problems with implementation are present in Malaysia, where *sharīʿah* courts have jurisdiction and there is a parallel legal system. In Malaysia, civil law and *sharīʿah* law coexist under a complicated legal system. This can lead to challenges, especially when it comes to conversion of religion and questions of personal standing. People who want to convert from Islam to another faith must consider the Sharīʿah Courts' jurisdiction in Malaysia. Such conversions frequently run into administrative and legal roadblocks, making it challenging for people to enjoy their right to freedom of religion. In instances involving people from Muslim backgrounds who desire to convert, *sharīʿah* courts may have a considerable impact, raising the possibility of conflicts between religious freedom and judicially maintained religious standards. The dual legal system in Malaysia also has an impact on issues related to personal status, including inheritance, divorce, and marriage. Different legal frameworks that are applied based on religious affiliation can result in inequities and discrepancies in how people from different religious origins are treated. This may make it difficult for people and families to manage their personal affairs, which might restrict their right to practice their religion (Bidin & Khan, 2022). The difficulties in putting religious freedom into practice reflect deeper socioeconomic and political problems in both Egypt and Malaysia. Governments, civil society organisations, and religious groups must work together to advance tolerance, inclusion, and respect for religious diversity in order to address these issues. Administrative procedures must be made more efficient, legal equality must be upheld, and religious minority must have sufficient protection. Additionally, promoting communication and understanding between various religious communities helps lessen sectarian tensions and establish a more welcoming climate where religious freedom can flourish.

The third area that significantly impacts the implementation of religious freedom is discrimination and tension. This relates to the experiences of religious minority who have to deal with prejudice and occasionally tense situations in the larger society. Religious minority encounter prejudice and sometimes violence in both nations. Minority religious minorities in Egypt, including Coptic Christians and other non-Muslim populations, have traditionally faced societal prejudice as well as sporadic violence. These groups frequently encounter societal prejudice, limited access to resources and opportunities, and discriminatory treatment in a variety of areas of life, including education, work, and public services, notwithstanding constitutional protections of religious freedom. Violence, including assaults on churches, religious groups, and individuals, has been a manifestation of discrimination against religious minorities in Egypt. These violent acts not only jeopardise the safety and well-being of religious minority populations, but they also damage the social cohesiveness and trust that are essential for the peaceful coexistence of various religious groups. Similar issues and challenges exist in Malaysia when non-Muslims try to get permission to construct houses of worship. The dual legal system and *shari'ah* court system that make up the country's legal system can make it difficult for religious minority to practice their religion freely and subject them to discrimination (Shuaib, 2012, p. 86).

In Malaysia, non-Muslim populations frequently encounter challenges and delays while trying to get permission to build or renovate houses of worship, particularly when it comes to non-Islamic religious structures. Permit application procedures can be laborious, bureaucratic, and prone to arbitrary judgements, which can result in rejections or protracted delays. These obstacles make it difficult for religious minorities to start and grow their houses of worship, which perpetuates a feeling of exclusion and inequity. Additionally, conflicts between religious groups can occasionally reach a point in Malaysia where they become violent or cause societal instability. While the country typically upholds a peaceful coexistence between various religious groups, rare incidents of religiously driven confrontations or acts of intolerance might happen, straining interfaith ties and hampering the implementation of religious freedom. Governments, civic society, and religious leaders must all work together to address prejudice and tension towards religious minorities in both Egypt and Malaysia. Governments must work proactively to prevent prejudice, advance interreligious understanding, and safeguard communities of religious minorities from harm and persecution. Campaigns for education and awareness may be extremely effective in advancing religious tolerance, encouraging understanding, and dispelling preconceptions and biases. Additionally, it is crucial to implement legislative and regulatory changes that end discriminatory practices and give all religious communities equal protection and access to opportunities (Shuaib, 2012, p. 87).

Making an inclusive and peaceful society requires developing trust and encouraging communication among various religious groups. It is possible to reduce tensions, improve understanding, and foster a culture of religious plurality by supporting interfaith projects, encouraging cooperation and collaboration, and providing forums for open and polite dialogue. In the end, ensuring the effective application of religious freedom necessitates a multifaceted strategy that addresses discriminatory practices, protects the rights of religious minorities, and promotes an atmosphere of respect and acceptance among all people, regardless of their religious beliefs.

References

Abdel Aziz, M. (2013, March 11). *AlShafei objects that instruments (Sukuk) law was not presented to AlAzhar*. Retrieved April 12, 2024, from www.masress.com/moheet/606867

Abdul Hak, N. (2012). Rights of a wife in the case of conversion to Islam under family law in Malaysia. *Arab Law Quarterly, 26*, 227–239.

Abdul Hamid, A. F. (2011). Malay racialism and the Sufi alternative. In M. Mohamad & S. M. K. Aljunied (Eds.), *Melayu: The politics, poetics and paradoxes of Malayness* (pp. 68–100). National University of Singapore Press.

Abdullah @Chew Li Hua, N. (2007, December). Legislating faith in Malaysia. *Singapore Journal of Legal Studies*. Retrieved April 4, from https://www.sjls.org/contents/upload/SJLS_Contents_V3%20No2%20Dec%2007.pdf#page=264

Ahmad Mohamed Ibrahim, T. S. D. (1996). Recent developments in the administration of Islamic law in Malaysia. *Yearbook of Islamic and Middle Eastern Law Online, 3*(1), 117–129.

Ahmad, S. S. S., & Rajasingham, R. R. (2001). *The Malaysian legal system, legal practice and legal education*. Institute of Developing Economies. Retrieved April 4, 2024, from http://www.ide.go.jp/English/Publish/Download/Als/pdf/04.pdf

Ahmad, W. A. B. W. (2006, June 6). *Human rights and freedom: A brief Islamic perspective*. Retrieved April 4, 2024, from https://www.ikim.gov.my/new-wp/index.php/2006/06/06/human-rights-andfreedom-a-brief-islamic-perspective/

Ali Mohamed, A. A., & Ahmad, M. H. (2021). British administration of Malay Peninsula and its impact on the status of Islamic law. In A. Trakic & H. H. A. Tajuddin (Eds.), *Islamic law in Malaysia: The challenges of implementation* (pp. 19–28). Routledge.

Allen, L. H., & Gledhill. (2016, June 16). *Malaysia: The federal constitution, Islamisation and the Malaysian Legal Order*. Retrieved April 4, 2024, from https://www.mondaq.com/constitutional-administrative-law/500882/the-federal-constitution-islamisation-and-the-malaysian-legal-order

Amnesty International. (2010). Egyptian blogger held despite completing prison sentence. Retrieved April 4, 2024, from www.amnesty.org/en/news-and-updates/egyptian-blogger-held-despitecompletingprison-sentence-2010-11-11

Arabic Network for Human Rights Information (ANHRI). (2009, January 10). Hesba cases cast away the civil state principles and citizenship rights, Egyptian government has to stop compromising. Retrieved April 4, 2024, from http://www.anhri.net/en/reports/2009/pr1001.shtml

Becket Fund for Religious Liberty. (2010). *United Nations Human Rights Council Universal Periodic Review: Egypt*. Retrieved April 4, 2024, from https://www.ohchr.org/sites/default/files/libdocs/HRBodies/UPR/Doc

uments/Session7/EG/BF_UPR_EGY_S07_2010_TheBecketFundforReligi ousLiberty.pdf

Berger, M. S. (2002). Conflicts law and public policy in Egyptian family law: Islamic law through the Backdoor. *American Journal of Comparative Law, 50*(3), 555–594.

Berger, M. S. (2003). Apostasy and public policy in contemporary Egypt: An evaluation of recent cases from Egypt's highest courts. *Human Rights Quarterly, 25*(3), 720–740.

Bianchi, R. (1989). *Unruly corporatism: Associational life in twentieth-Century Egypt*. Oxford University Press.

Bidin, A., & Khan, S. (2022). Compatibility analysis of Malaysian civil and Syariah laws to the international covenant on civil and political rights (ICCPR). Human Rights Commission of Malaysia (Suhakam).

Brown, N. J. (2014). Egypt's constitutional Cul-De-Sac. *Carnegie*. Retrieved April 4, 2024, from https://carnegieendowment.org/2014/03/31/egypt-s-constitutional-cul-de-sac-pub-55310

Brown, N. J., & Lombardi, C. B. (2006). The supreme constitutional court of Egypt on Islamic law, veiling and civil rights: an annotated translation of supreme constitutional court of Egypt case no. 8 of judicial year 17, May 18, 1996. Retrieved April 4, 2024, from www.researchgate.net/publication/.228135189_The_Supreme_Constitutional_Court_of_Egypt_on_Islamic_Law_Veiling_and_Civil_Rights_An_Annotated_Translation_of_Supreme_Constitutio nal_Court_of_Egypt_Case_No_8_of_Judicial_Year_17_May_18_1996

Buchanan, K. (2016, November 15). *Controversy over new Egyptian law that regulates the construction of churches*. Retrieved from https://blogs.loc.gov/law/2016/11/controversy-over-new-egyptian-lawthat-regulates-the-constr uction-of-churches/#:~:text=On%20September%2028%2C%202016%2C%20t he,gazette%20on%20the%20same%20day

Bureau of Democracy, Human Rights, and Labor. (2009). *Malaysia*. In *International Religious Freedom Report 2009*.

Cairo Institute for Human Rights Studies. (2013, August 7). Islamist groups must stop inciting to sectarian violence; Protection of Christians responsibility of the state.

Cheah Boon Kheng. (1998). *Sejarah Melayu: The Malay annals* (Transcribed by Abdur Rahman Ismail). Kuala Lumpur: The Malaysian Branch of the Royal Asiatic Society (MBRAS).

Choon, L. M. (1999). *Freedom of religion in Malaysia*. Kairos Research Centre.

Dass, D. (2019, June 9). Is equality a problem for Malaysia? Retrieved April 4, 2024, from https://www.malaysiakini.com/news/478935

Dupret, B. (2016). *The reference to sharia in Arab politics and constitutions. Constitutionalism, human rights and Islam after the Arab spring*. Retrieved April 4, 2024, from http://hal.archivesouvertes.fr/Hal01624579

Egypt's constitution of 2014. Retrieved April 4, 2024, from https://www.constituteproject.org/constitution/Egypt_2014.pdf

El Fegiery, M. A. (2013). Islamic law and freedom of religion: The case of apostasy and its legal implications in Egypt. *MWJHR, 10*(1), 1–26.

ERT Country Report Series: 2. (2012, November). *Washing the tigers addressing discrimination and inequality in Malaysia*. Retrieved April 4, 2024, from https://www.equalrightstrust.org/ertdocumentbank/Malaysia%20CR%201.pdf

Fandy, M. (1993). The tensions behind the violence in Egypt. *Middle East Policy, 2*(1), 25–34.

Faruqi, S. S. (2001). *The human rights and constitutional perspectives*. INSAF (Special Issues on Freedom of Religion).

Fernando, J. M. (2006). The position of Islam in the constitution of Malaysia. *Journal of Southeast Asian Studies, 37*(2), 253.

Feuer, S. (2020, August 20). New Egyptian legislation aims to reduce Al-Azhar's authority. Retrieved April 4, 2024, from https://www.washingtoninstitute.org/policy-analysis/new-egyptian-legislation-aimsreduce-al-azhars-authority

Freedom House. (2010, October 21). Policing belief: The impact of blasphemy laws on human rights—Malaysia. Retrieved April 4, 2024 from https://www.refworld.org/docid/4d5a700a2.html

Hamad, A. S. (1999). Legal plurality and legitimation of human rights abuses: A case study of state council rulings concerning the rights of apostate. In B. Dupret, M. Berger, & L. al-Zwaini (Eds.), *Legal Pluralism in the Arab World* (pp. 219–228). Kluwer Law International.

Hamzawy, A. (2014). On religion, politics and democracy legitimacy in Egypt, January 2011-June 2013. *Philosophy and Social Criticism, 40*(4–5), 402.

Hanna, M. W. (2015). Public order and Egypt's statist tradition. *The Review of Faith and International Affairs, 13*(1), 23–30.

Harding, A. (2012). Malaysia: Religious pluralism and the constitution in a contested polity. *Middle East Law and Governance, 4*(2–3), 356–385.

Hashish, A. (2013). The Egyptian second republic: The future of litigating Islam before the supreme constitutional court. *Berkeley Journal of Middle Eastern & Islamic Law, 5*(1), 120–163.

Hatina, M. (2000). On the margins of consensus: The call to separate religion and state in modern Egypt. *Middle Eastern Studies, 36*(1), 35–67.

Hillal, A. E. (2011). *Parliament Age in Egypt from Rise to Fall 1923–1952*. Egyptian Lebanese House.

Hirst, P. (1997). *From statism to pluralism*. UCL Press.

Hirst, P. (2000). Statism, pluralism, and social control. *The British Journal of Criminology, 40*(2), 279–295.

Hooker, M. B. (1984). *Islamic law in South-east Asia.* Oxford University Press.

Human Rights Commission of Malaysia. (2003). *Annual Report of the Human Rights Commission of Malaysia, 2003.* Percetakan Haji Jintan Sd. Bhd.

Human Rights Watch, & Egyptian Initiative for Personal Rights. (2007). *Prohibited identities: State interference with religious freedom.* Human Rights Watch.

Husina, W. N. W., & Ibrahim, H. (2016). Religious freedom, The Malaysian constitution and Islam: A critical analysis. *Procedia—Social and Behavioral Sciences, 217,* 1216–1224.

Ibrahim, A. M. (1997). *The administration of Islamic laws.* Institute of Islamic Understanding Malaysia.

Ibrahim, I. (2021, June 2). Egypt's officials don't see unrecognized religious minorities. Retrieved April 4, 2024, from https://timep.org/2021/06/02/egypts-officials-dont-see-unrecognized-religiousminorities/

International Religious Freedom Report. (2001). Retrieved November 28, 2024, from 2009-2017.state.govt/j/drl/rls/irf/2001/

International Religious Freedom Report. Egypt. (2016). Retrieved April 4, 2024, from https://www.state.gov/wp-content/uploads/2019/01/Egypt-3.pdf

Johansen, B. (2003). Apostasy as objective and depersonalized fact: Two recent Egyptian court judgments. *Social Research, 70*(3). Retrieved April 4, 2024, from http://findarticles.com/p/articles/mi_m2267/is_3_70/ai_110737774/pg_6/?tag=content;col1

Kedourie, E. (1968). The genesis of the Egyptian constitution of 1923. In P. M. Holt (Ed.), *Political and social change in modern Egypt* (pp. 350–352). Oxford University Press.

Kepel, G. (1985). *Muslim extremism in Egypt: The prophet and pharaoh.* University of California Press.

Koh Tong Ngee, P. (1987). *Freedom of religion in Malaysia—The legal dimension.* Graduates Christian Fellowship.

Liaw, Y. F. (1976). *Undang-undang Melaka (Malacca laws).* Martinus Nijhoff.

Mah, O., & Reza, D. R. (2024, October 8). Al-Arqam: Deviant sect or political threat? Retrieved November 28, 2024, from https://www.freemalaysiatoday.com/category/nation/2024/10/08/al-arqam-deviant-sect-or-political-threat/

Marican, P., & Adil, M. A. M. (2004). Apostasy and freedom of religion in Malaysia: Constitutional implications. *Yearbook of Islamic and Middle Eastern Law Online, 11*(1), 169–203.

Martinez, P. (2008). Muslims in Malaysia: Notions of human rights reform and their contexts. In S. Akbarzadeh & B. MacQueen (Eds.), *Islam and human rights in practice: Perspectives Across the Ummah* (pp. 119–141). Routledge.

Minority Rights Group International (MRG). (2019). *Justice denied, promises broken: The situation of Egypt's minorities since 2014*. Retrieved April 4, 2024, from https://minorityrights.org/wpcontent/uploads/2019/01/MRG_Rep_Egypt_EN_Jan19.pdf

Mohammad, M. N., & Kusrin, Z. M. (2017). Conversion out of Islam and its legal implications under the laws of Malaysia. *Ijtimā'iyya, 2*(2), 220–221.

Mohd Noor, N. F. (2020). Freedom of speech and the pandemic. *International Journal of Law, Government and Communication (IJLGC), 5*(21), 285–297.

Mostyn, T. (2007). *Defamation in Egypt today*. International PEN Foundation. http://www.internationalpen.org.uk/files/dmfile/defamationegypt.pdf

Moustafa, T. (2010). The Islamist trend in Egyptian law. *Politics and Religion, 3*, 610–630.

Musa, M. F. (2022). *Freedom of religion in Malaysia: The situation and attitudes of "deviant" Muslim groups*. ISEAS – Yusof Ishak Institute, Issue No. 16, 1–47.

Neo, J. L. (2003). Anti-God, anti-Islam, anti-Qur'an: Expanding the range of participants and parameters over women's Rights and Islam in Malaysia. *UCLA Pacific Basin Law Journal, 21*, 49.

Neo, J. L. (2018). Definitional imbroglios: A critique of the definition of religion and essential practice tests in religious freedom adjudication. *International Journal of Constitutional Law, 16*(2), 574–595.

Nor, M. R. M., Abdullah, A. T., & Ali, A. K. (2016). From Undang-undang Melaka to federal constitution: The dynamics of multicultural Malaysia. *Springerplus, 5*(1683), 1–8.

Nor, M. R. M., Ibrahim, A. Z. B., & Hamid, F. A. F. A. (2012). Ibn Khaldun's theory of 'Asabiyyah and its application in modern Muslim society. *Middle-East Journal of Scientific Research, 11*(9), 1232–1237.

O'Sullivan, D. (2003). Egyptian cases of blasphemy and apostasy against Islam: Takfir al-Muslim. *The International Journal of Human Rights, 7*(2), 97–137.

Office of International Religious Freedom. (2021). *Report on International Religious Freedom: Egypt*, June 2, 2022. Retrieved April 3, 2024, from https://www.state.gov/reports/2021-report-on-internationalreligious-freedom/egypt/

Park, J. (2015, November 3). Blasphemy law in Egypt: The intersection of sharī'a and state control over public morals. Retrieved April 4, 2024, from https://islamiclaw.blog/2015/11/03/blasphemy-lawin-egypt-the-intersection-of-sharia-and-state-control-over-public-morals/

Penal Code of Malaysia. (2023). Retrieved November 28, 2024, from sprm.gov.my/admin/files/sprm/assets/pdf/penguatkuasaan/Akta_574_(31.5.2023)_BI.pdf

Report on International Religious Freedom: Egypt. (2022). Retrieved April, 4, 2024, from https://eg.usembassy.gov/2022-report-on-international-religious-freedom-egypt/

Report on International Religious Freedom: Malaysia. (2021). Retrieved April, 4, 2024, from https://www.state.gov/reports/2021-report-on-international-religious-freedom/malaysia/

Rieffer-Flanagan, B. A. (2016). Statism, tolerance and religious freedom in Egypt. *Muslim World Journal of Human Rights, 13*(1), 1–24.

Risley, D. E. (2017). Freedom of religion and the constitution in Egypt: The distinction between belief and practice and protecting religion and government from each other. In A. Ferrari & J. Toronto (Eds.), *Religions and constitutional transitions in the Muslim Mediterranean: The pluralistic moment* (pp. 170–183). Routledge.

Rutherford, B. (2008). *Egypt After Mubarak.* Princeton University Press.

Saeed, A., & Saeed, H. (2004). *Freedom of religion, apostasy and Islam.* Ashgate.

Sayed, E. S. (2019). Constitutions and religion in Egypt: A comparative study. *Review of Economics and Political Science.* Retrieved April 4, 2024, from https://www.emerald.com/insight/content/doi/10.1108/REPS-06-2019-0081/full/pdf?title=constitutions-and-religion-in-egypt-a-comparative-study

Sayed, E. S. (2020). Constitutions and religion in Egypt: A comparative study. *Review of Economics and Political Science.* Retrieved April 4, 2024, from https://www.emerald.com/insight/content/doi/10.1108/REPS-06-2019-0081/full/pdf?title=constitutions-and-religion-in-egypt-a-comparative-study

Scott, R. M. (2014). Managing religion and renegotiating the secular: The Muslim Brotherhood and defining the religious sphere. *Politics and Religion, 7*(1), 63.

Shah Haneef, S. S. (2010). Discourse on Hudud in Malaysia. *Journal of Islam Law and Culture, 12*(2), 131144.

Shah, T. S. (2021). Institutional religious freedom in full: What the liberty of religious organizations really is and why it is an "essential service" to the common good. *Religions, 12*(6), 1–24.

Shah, D. A. H., & Mohd, M. A. S. (2011). Freedom of religion in Malaysia: A tangled web of legal, political, and social issues. *North Carolina Journal of International Law, 36*(3), 648–673.

Shariah Criminal Offences (Federal Territories) Act 559. (1997). Incorporating all amendments through January 1, 2006. Retrieved April 4, 2024, from http://www.mylawyer.com.my/law/syariah_Criminal_Offences_Federal_Territories_Act.php

Shuaib, F. S. (2008). Strengthening administrative institutions of Islamic Law in Malaysia: An overview. *Shariah Journal, 16*, 443–464.

Shuaib, F. S. (2012). The Islamic legal system in Malaysia. *Pacific Rim Law & Policy Journal, 21*(1), 86113.

Smith, P. (2004). Speak no evil: Apostasy, blasphemy and heresy in Malaysian Syariah law. *UC Davis Journal of International Law and Policy, 10*(2), 357.

Spollen, J. (2007, August 11). MECA director rejects claims of insulting prophet Mohamed. *Daily News (Egypt)*. Retrieved April 4, 2024, from http://www.dailystaregypt.com/article.aspx?ArticleID=8731

Tan, K. Y. L., & Thio, L.-A. (1997). *Constitutional law in Malaysia and Singapore*. Butterworth Asia.

The Tahrir Institute for Middle East Policy, Egypt's religious minorities: The legal framework. (2022, January 6). Retrieved April 4, 2024, from https://timep.org/2022/01/06/egypts-religiousminorities-the-legal-framework/

U.S. House Committee on International Relations. (2006, June 30). The plight of religious minorities: Can religious pluralism survive? *Hearing before the subcommittee on Africa, global human rights and international operations, 109th Cong. 2nd sess.* Retrieved April 4, 2024, from http://commdocs.house.gov/committees/intlrel/hfa28430.000/hfa28430_0f.htm

UN Human Rights Committee (HRC). (1993, July 30). CCPR general comment No. 22: Article 18 (Freedom of thought, conscience or religion). CCPR/C/21/Rev.1/Add.4. Retrieved April 4, 2024, from https://www.refworld.org/docid/453883fb22.html

United States Commission on International Religious Freedom Annual Report. (2013). Commission on International Religious Freedom.

Vasuvedan, V., & Suparmaniam, S. (2009, June 16). Najib: 1Malaysia idea for everyone. *New Straits Times (Malaysia)*.

Zemni, S., & Bogaert, K. (2009). Egyptian Muslim Brotherhood and competitive politics. In M. A. Mohamed Salih (Ed.), *Interpreting Islamic political parties* (pp. 149–166). Palgrave Macmillan.

CHAPTER 4

From Constitutional Guarantees to Practical Challenges: The Divergence of Freedom of Speech and Expression in Egypt

4.1 Introduction

The right of freedom of speech and expression confers upon individuals the unassailable prerogative to freely disseminate their intellectual ruminations, opinions and ideas thereby fostering an intellectual milieu that thrives on unrestrained dialogue, uninhibited public deliberation and the unrestricted diffusion of knowledge (Bakircioglu, 2008, p. 13). In the democratic context, freedom of speech and expression assumes paramount significance, as it engenders a milieu conducive to the functioning of an emancipated and pluralistic society, empowering citizens to actively partake in the governance process, hold their leaders accountable and substantively contribute to the formulation of public policies. The salience of these rights is particularly conspicuous during episodes of dissent and epochal political metamorphosis. Within the democratic paradigm, the legitimacy of peaceful protests and demonstrations is unequivocal, representing legitimate conduits for citizens to vociferously ventilate their grievances and ardently advocate for transformative change. In this regard, freedom of expression, as a potent enabler, bestows upon dissatisfied voices the profound resonance required for facilitating peaceful conflict resolution while obviating the ominous specter of potential discord (Smet, 2011, p. 184).

A. Mohiuddin, *Human Rights Law in Egypt and Malaysia: Freedom of Religion and Expression, Volume 1*, Political Economy of Islam,
https://doi.org/10.1007/978-3-031-63859-6_4

Moreover, these rights act as a bulwark against proclivities towards authoritarianism and instances of governmental misuse of authority. A liberated press and unrestricted media channels substantiate the notion that those occupying positions of power are held answerable for their actions. In this context, the role of investigative journalism and incisive reportage acquires a momentous stature, as it assumes the onus of exposing instances of corruption, violations of human rights, and other transgressions, thereby buttressing the indispensable system of checks and balances intrinsic to the functioning of a democratic framework. Nevertheless, the comprehensive realisation of freedom of speech and expression confronts formidable challenges across diverse contexts. The proliferation of ambiguous legislation, selective enforcement practices, and a disregard for upholding international human rights standards has given rise to constraints and curtailments on these cardinal rights. Resolving these predicaments necessitates an unwavering commitment on the part of governments to espouse democratic principles and human rights, while concurrently relying upon the robust advocacy efforts of a strong civil society devoted to the advocacy of free expression and relentless pursuit of constructive transformation (Mazzanti, 2013).

In Egypt, Article 65 stands as testament to the acknowledgement of the pivotal role played by these freedoms in nurturing an enlightened and actively engaged citizenry (Barker, 2022). Ostensibly fortified by such constitutional assurances, the protection of individuals' rights to articulate their viewpoints, scrutinise governmental actions and partake in open public deliberations should, in theory, be securely safeguarded. Notwithstanding the theoretical underpinnings of constitutional guarantees, the practical implementation of freedom of speech and expression in the country has emerged as a subject of apprehension. In spite of the constitutional protections, Egypt has come under scrutiny and censure for the constraints and restraints that have been placed upon the actual exercise of these rights in practice.

This chapter focuses on analysing the constitutional status of freedom of speech and expression in Egypt. It is evident that the country is dedicated to upholding these standards since it has signed the Universal Declaration of Human Rights (UDHR) and the International Covenant on Civil and Political Rights (ICCPR). The successful realisation and maintenance of these fundamental rights have, nevertheless, faced major challenges in each national context. To facilitate a comprehensive exploration, the historical context delves into the nuanced trajectory of Egypt illuminating the intricate influence of colonial legacies, independence movements and democratisation struggles on the evolutionary trajectory of freedom of speech and expression within each country. Drawing upon legal precedents and judicial interpretations, the analysis investigates the role of the judiciary in preserving and adjudicating issues related to freedom of speech and expression.

4.2 Power Dynamics and Freedom of Speech in Egypt's Past

In ancient Egypt, the belief in divine kingship occupied a central position, profoundly influencing the formulation of societal norms and values. At the heart of this belief system stood the pharaoh, exalted as a living embodiment of divinity, commanding supreme dominion over religious, political, and social realms. The perpetuation of the pharaoh's divine persona stood as an imperative, as any dissent or criticism challenging the monarch's legitimacy or celestial status posed an ominous threat to the kingdom's stability and harmony. In conjunction with the pharaoh's exalted role, the priestly class assumed a formidable position, intimately interwoven with the pharaoh's rule. As intermediaries between the celestial pantheon and the populace, they enjoyed privileged access to sacred wisdom and rituals, endowing them with significant influence over religious beliefs and practices. As such, the priestly class played a pivotal role in promulgating sanctioned religious narratives while subduing any alternative interpretations or dissenting perspectives that could undermine their authority or contest the pharaoh's divine mandate. The symbiotic relationship between the divine kingship and the priestly class shaped the contours of Egypt's ancient societal fabric and entrenched a hierarchical structure that reinforced the prevailing religious orthodoxy.

The dissemination of written communication in ancient Egypt primarily transpired through hieroglyphic inscriptions, an art form wielded with notable control by the ruling elite. These inscriptions served as potent instruments to propagate political propaganda and reinforce the state's hegemonic authority. Adorning prominent edifices such as temples, monuments, and tombs, these inscriptions assumed the role of conveying messages glorifying the pharaoh's grandeur and his purported divine affiliations. Although certain inscriptions recounted historical events, they were often tailored to present a narrative that celebrated the pharaoh's accomplishments while downplaying any instances of fallibility. In this context, the sphere of public discourse was subjected to rigorous regulation, impeding the prevalence of open debates or critical evaluations of the ruling powers. Conformity to prevailing societal norms and allegiance to established religious and political ideologies were fervently expected from individuals. Divergence from the established order was perilous, bearing the risk of severe repercussions, including imprisonment, exile, or even capital punishment (Frankfort, 1978).

In antiquity, the notion of freedom of speech, as a fundamental human right, remained conspicuously absent within the societal framework of ancient Egypt. Instead, paramount importance was attached to the preservation of social order and the steadfast maintenance of state stability, overshadowing considerations for individual expressions of dissent or divergent viewpoints. The authoritarian character of the ancient Egyptian society, coupled with the pervasive dominance of religious authorities, synergistically conspired to stifle the unfurling of unbridled intellectual inquiry and precluded the prospect of open discourse concerning political or social matters (Frankfort, 1978).

The period of Ottoman rule in Egypt spanning the sixteenth to the nineteenth centuries presented a host of formidable challenges to the very notion of freedom of speech, engendered primarily by the centralized and authoritarian configuration of the Ottoman Empire. Situated at the pinnacle of authority, the Sultan in Istanbul wielded unassailable power, and his jurisdiction reverberated through a hierarchically structured administrative apparatus, wherein provincial governors were appointed to enforce his edicts across various regions, including Egypt. This centralized system of governance left scant leeway for dissenting voices or critiques that could impinge upon the established order of the ruling establishment. The Ottoman rulers maintained control over the diffusion of information as an instrumental means to assert and perpetuate their dominion over the region. Employing a well-honed stratagem, the ruling elite, including provincial governors and local functionaries, assumed an authoritative monopoly over the generation and dissemination of knowledge. They maintained surveillance over educational institutions and religious establishments, ensuring strict alignment with the official Ottoman narrative, which fervently upheld the Sultan's supremacy and validated the state's legitimacy. Religion assumed an integral role in the overarching framework of Ottoman governance, with the Sultan simultaneously assuming the exalted mantle of the Caliph, thereby presiding as the ultimate religious authority within the Sunni

Islam domain. This intrinsic fusion of religion and state rendered any critique directed towards religious authorities or contesting prevailing religious interpretations tantamount to challenging the very legitimacy of the Sultan's rule. Consequently, religious dissent was sternly suppressed, thereby safeguarding religious orthodoxy and fostering unwavering allegiance to the state. Access to education was predominantly channeled through religious institutions, relegating the privilege of acquiring knowledge to an exclusive cadre of scholars and religious luminaries. This stark limitation in educational accessibility engendered a dearth of widespread education, suffocating the cultivation of critical thinking and intellectual discourse among the broader populace. The constricted conduit to educational enlightenment obstructed the rise of a wellinformed and erudite public capable of partaking in open deliberations or voicing dissenting perspectives (Behrens-Abouseif, 1994).

The Ottoman authorities adroitly employed stringent censorship mechanisms to stifle the dissemination of dissident ideas or opinions that could potentially undermine the state's authoritative rule. Writers, intellectuals, and scholars who dared to voice ideas perceived as threats to the state confronted the dire prospect of encountering severe persecution, imprisonment, or even execution. The specter of harsh retribution effectively deterred individuals from publicly expressing their opinions or venturing to challenge the established order. To bolster their grip on power, the Ottoman rulers ingeniously relied on a network of informants to surveil the populace meticulously, vigilantly reporting any manifestations of dissent or subversion. This pervasive atmosphere of surveillance spawned a climate of fear and suspicion, compelling individuals to restrain from candidly voicing their genuine opinions lest they be subject to reporting and subsequent repercussions by the authorities (Behrens-Abouseif, 1994).

Arbitrary repressive measures were unreservedly employed to suppress even the faintest semblance of political dissent or insurrection. Suspected individuals found plotting against the state incurred severe and harsh punishments, exemplifying in a grim and unequivocal manner the inexorable consequences awaiting those who dared to challenge the unyielding dominion of the Ottoman regime. The restrictions on freedom of speech during the Ottoman rule in Egypt left a lasting impact on the country's political and social landscape. Even after the decline of the Ottoman Empire and Egypt's quest for independence in the twentieth century, the remnants of limited expression continued to profoundly shape the course of free speech in the nation's subsequent history. Realising a paradigm shift towards facilitating more open dialogues and acknowledging freedom of speech as an inherent human right necessitated substantial political and social transformations in the twentieth and twenty-first centuries.

In the nineteenth century, under the leadership of Muhammad Ali Pasha, Egypt underwent a momentous phase of modernisation, seeking to restructure the nation's economic, military, and administrative frameworks. As a pivotal component of this transformative process, the advent of newspapers and periodicals wielded a profound influence in shaping public sentiment and fostering intellectual exchanges. The introduction of the printing press represented a significant milestone in Egypt's media landscape, facilitating the mass production and widespread dissemination of written materials. During this epoch, newspapers assumed a paramount role as conduits of communication and purveyors of information. Nevertheless, despite their proliferation, the press operated under stringent state supervision, reflecting Muhammad Ali's government's intention to harness media as an instrument to consolidate power and advance its agendas. Newspapers and publications were frequently subjected to state control, thereby constraining their ability to openly scrutinise the government or challenge the prevailing ruling establishment (Winter, 1982).

Muhammad Ali's transformative era of modernisation heralded a seminal phase in Egypt's media landscape, instigating the burgeoning development of the press. The advent of the printing press and the concomitant proliferation of newspapers served as seminal catalysts, galvanizing a trajectory of growth and expansion within the country's journalistic milieu. Concurrently, this epoch bore profound implications for the rise of Egyptian nationalism, as the press emerged as a potent vehicle for nurturing a collective sense of identity and heightened social consciousness among the Egyptian populace, sowing the seeds of a nascent national movement that would find fertile ground in the subsequent decades. Amidst the British occupation of Egypt, the nationalist press assumed an influential role, adroitly articulating the soaring aspirations and deep-seated grievances of the Egyptian people. Notably, the pivotal contributions of Ahmed Lutfi al-Sayed, a prominent nationalist intellectual and journalist, reverberated through the establishment of independent newspapers, notably 'Al-Jarida' and 'Al-Ahram,' formidable bastions of the nascent nationalist ethos (Reid, 2002). These influential platforms not only served as conduits for the dissemination of stirring nationalist ideals but also engendered a profound sense of unity and solidarity among Egyptians, vehemently championing the nation's inalienable right to self-determination and emancipation from foreign yoke. The nationalist press adroitly deployed a multifaceted arsenal of strategic measures to mobilise public support for the burgeoning independence movement. Through a plethora of resolute articles and incisive editorials, they artfully illuminated the historical grandeur of Egyptian civilisation, adroitly underscoring the nation's illustrious past and its inherent potential to reclaim its sovereign standing on the world stage. Harnessing the potency of the written word, journalists sought to inculcate an overwhelming sentiment of collective pride and unyielding nationalism, fostering an unwavering spirit of defiance and resistance against the shackles of foreign subjugation.

Furthermore, the press played a pivotal and indispensable role in disseminating crucial information concerning the oppressive policies and egregious injustices enforced by the British colonial authorities. The widespread circulation of reports exposing British atrocities, exploitative economic practices, and repressive political measures served to unveil the stark realities of colonial dominion, consequently fomenting public indignation and fervor. By illuminating the plight and suffering endured by the Egyptian populace, the nationalist press significantly contributed to the burgeoning discontent and fervent yearning for independence. Cognisant of the press's potent impact on cultivating nationalist sentiments, the British colonial authorities adroitly wielded their power to impose rigorous censorship and enact stringent press laws, exerting meticulous control over the flow of information. In a bid to stifle the resonating voice of the nationalist press, they resorted to severe measures, such as the closure of newspapers, apprehension of journalists, and the ruthless suppression of any content perceived as subversive or seditious. Notwithstanding these relentless endeavors to silence the nationalist press, its tenacity prevailed as it ingeniously devised novel means to disseminate its resolute message, often resorting to clandestine underground publications and employing coded language to elude the clutches of censorship.In response to the repressive measures imposed by British colonial authorities, the nationalist press adopted an indomitable and unwavering stance, as journalists and intellectuals exhibited exceptional courage by willingly sacrificing their personal freedom in their relentless pursuit of independence. Esteemed figures such as Mustafa Kamil and Saad Zaghloul emerged as eminent leaders of the nationalist movement, skillfully harnessing the power of the press to mobilise the masses, galvanize support and kindle the flames of resistance against the shackles of colonial dominion (Reid, 2002).

The nationalist press played an indispensable and multifaceted role in fostering a profound sense of cohesion and unity across divergent strata of Egyptian society, adroitly transcending the constraints of regional, religious, and socio-economic disparities. Through its adept facilitation of an inclusive and emancipatory platform, the press engendered a collective consciousness, forging a potent sense of shared identity that bound Egyptians together under the banner of national independence. By endowing the hitherto marginalised and silenced voices of the populace with an empowering and amplified platform, the press catalysed the formation of a cohesive national narrative, a shared vision that fervently yearned for a liberated Egypt. The climax of the nationalist movement was realized in the historic Egyptian Revolution of 1919, commonly acclaimed as the '1919 Revolution' or the 'Great Revolution' (Sugita, 2023, p. 76). This momentous event not only signified a resolute stand against the dominion of British colonial power but also heralded the advent of a sweeping wave of independence resonating throughout the Arab world. In this epochal era of transformation and upheaval, the nationalist press assumed a multifaceted role, serving as an unassailable fortress of impassioned nationalist fervor while concurrently functioning as a profound source of illumination and inspiration, galvanizing the masses into dynamic and decisive action. It is noteworthy that the foundations of the nationalist press were firmly laid in Egypt's intellectual and political milieu prior to the watershed events of the revolution. Its origins could be traced back to earlier pioneering endeavors during the late nineteenth century, when it first emerged as an articulate and fervent platform, disseminating potent nationalistic ideals and articulating poignant critiques of the British occupation. The advent of newspapers and periodicals engendered a seismic shift, bestowing upon Egypt's erudite intelligentsia an empowering and resonant channel to actively participate in dynamic public discourse, subsequently capturing the imagination and passion of an ever-expanding and increasingly diverse cross-section of the populace.

Led by eminent figures like Saad Zaghloul, Mustafa Kamil, and other prominent voices, the nationalist press actively endeavored to rouse the collective national consciousness of the Egyptian populace. These newspapers played an integral role in articulating a shared identity and instilling a collective sense of pride in Egypt's illustrious historical heritage. Emphatically, they underscored the nation's cultural and civilisational richness, staunchly asserting its inherent entitlement to selfdetermination and sovereignty, effectively unifying diverse social and regional factions under a common banner. Throughout the unfolding of the revolution, the press emerged as an indispensable linchpin in mobilizing widespread public support and disseminating vital information regarding the unfolding events. Through the compelling narratives etched on their pages, newspapers vigorously advocated for strategic initiatives such as strikes, civil disobedience, and non-violent protests, thereby exerting substantial pressure on the British colonial administration. Moreover, they diligently chronicled the progression of the protests, disseminating news of the movement's triumphs, and thereby fervently fanning the flames of revolutionary ardor among the masses. Beyond its domestic role, the nationalist press assumed a pivotal diplomatic function, wielding its influence not only within Egypt but also on the international stage. Diligently forging alliances and seeking global support for Egypt's cherished quest for independence, the press employed its reporting and editorials to bring to the fore the egregious injustices perpetrated by the colonial regime, evoking widespread sympathy and solidarity from disparate quarters across the globe. However, this period was fraught with substantial challenges for the press. Faced with the ironclad grip of the British colonial authorities, the press encountered a barrage of stringent censorship measures and suffocating press restrictions engineered to suppress the burgeoning sentiments of revolution and preserve the status quo. The closure of numerous newspapers and the arrest and detention of journalists and activists posed formidable obstacles. Despite these adversities, the nationalist press exuded remarkable resilience, adaptability, and an unwavering commitment to the noble cause of independence (Sugita, 2023, p. 77).

The 1919 Revolution achieved its ultimate objective of compelling the British government to heed the legitimate demands of the Egyptian populace. Subsequently, the political landscape of Egypt underwent significant transformations. The fruits of the revolution culminated in the partial attainment of independence, and the nationalist movement charted the path towards the establishment of the Kingdom of Egypt in 1922.The enduring legacy of the 1919 Revolution continues to resonate within Egypt's historical tapestry and collective memory. The epochal significance of the press during this transformative period reverberates across Egypt's historical landscape, leaving an indelible mark on the nation's yearning for the cherished ideals of freedom of speech and expression. The press, serving as an influential agent of unparalleled potency, showcased its formidable capacity in galvanizing public sentiment, contesting the yoke of colonial dominion, and shaping the course of the nation's destiny. The seeds of press freedom, diligently sown during this tumultuous epoch, have endured the test of time, exercising a profound and lasting impact on Egypt's evolutionary path towards democratic governance and the protection of its bedrock principles of fundamental rights and liberties.

In 1923, Egypt indeed achieved a measure of independence from British rule, marking a pivotal moment in the country's constitutional evolution. The inauguration of Egypt's first constitution in the same year laid the groundwork for subsequent constitutional advancements. This foundational document established Egypt as a constitutional monarchy, delineating a parliamentary system of governance. To this end, it instituted a bicameral legislature, comprising the People's Assembly (lower house) and the Senate (upper house). While the monarch, initially Sultan Fuad I, later succeeded by King Farouk I, wielded substantial powers, the constitution also prescribed the role of the parliament, thereby imposing certain constraints on the ruler's authority (Tignor, 1976, p. 43). A prominent and noteworthy aspect characterising the early Egyptian constitutions was the judicious inclusion of meticulously crafted provisions designed to serve as bulwarks, guarding and ensuring the inviolability of fundamental rights and freedoms. Embedded intricately within the constitutional framework, the rights to freedom of speech and freedom of the press were etched indelibly, embodying unequivocal symbols of the nation's commitment to revering and safeguarding the fundamental pillars of civil liberties. This purposive assimilation of constitutional safeguards stands as a testament to the acumen of the framers of the constitution, conferring upon the Egyptian populace an ennobling agency that bestows upon them a formidable prowess to artfully articulate their well-reasoned perspectives, ardently participate in the realm of public discourse and actively contribute to the nation's democratic ethos. Nonetheless, the pragmatic realisation of these rights often encountered impediments through governmental censorship and restraints, particularly during episodes of political instability or upheaval. Governments, both prior to and following the revolutionary tide that led to Egypt's independence, frequently wielded their authority to curtail freedom of expression and quash dissenting voices.

During periods characterised by sociopolitical turbulence or perceived threats to the established government's stability, the Egyptian authorities deployed stringent measures of regulatory scrutiny to curtail media discourse, restrict public assemblies and detain dissidents who dared to vocalize their dissenting views against the prevailing ruling regime. The ostensible justification behind such measures lay in the imperative of maintaining public order or safeguarding the nation's security integrity. Throughout Egypt's history, significant events have led to constitutional changes, marking crucial moments that resonated across the nation's political scene. Notably, the year of 1952 witnessed a paradigm-shifting event when the country experienced a military coup spearheaded by the Free Officers Movement, culminating in the subversion of the erstwhile monarchy and the establishment of a republican order (Gordon, 2017). In the aftermath, an epoch-defining constitution was promulgated in 1956, anointing the nascent Arab Republic of Egypt as the embodiment of the nation's newly crystallized identity. In subsequent iterations of constitutional documents, the tenets of fundamental rights and freedoms were enshrined; nevertheless, these rights remained susceptible to the vicissitudes of governmental restrictions and restraints, most pronouncedly during epochs characterized by autocratic rule.

After assuming leadership in the wake of the 1952 Revolution that toppled the monarchy, Gamal Abdel Nasser became a prominent and revered figure within the Free Officers Movement, a pioneering entity instrumental in Egypt's momentous political metamorphosis. Nasser's rise to power accentuated the centrality of Arab nationalism in his policy agenda, characterized by a fervent dedication to forge unity among Arab nations and liberate them from Western dominance. Concurrently, Nasser's ascendancy was also marked by the impetus of socialist paradigms, underpinning the nationalization of pivotal industries and the implementation of sweeping agrarian reforms aimed at effectuating land redistribution among the peasantry. Driven by the aspiration of forging an equitable social order and eradicating the hegemony of the privileged stratum, Nasser's tenure evinced a semblance of political openness and a milieu of relative liberty in the domain of expression. Opposition factions were accorded the latitude to partake in the political process and the media landscape bore witness to a semblance of pluralistic discourse, encompassing a diverse spectrum of opinions.

During Nasser's tenure as a leader, his regime exhibited a nuanced metamorphosis, gradually veering towards authoritarian tendencies that curbed dissenting voices, particularly those offering critical evaluations of the regime and its policies. The gradual course of development witnessed a simultaneous marginalisation of political dissenters and the imposition of rigorous restrictions on the unhampered manifestation of freedom of speech. This transformative progression additionally involved the solidification of state authority over the media landscape, reaching its culmination in the establishment of government-endorsed newspapers and broadcasting networks. These government-sanctioned media platforms facilitated the manipulation of information dissemination and the shaping of public sentiment, effectively restricting the profusion of diverse viewpoints accessible to the Egyptian citizenry. Notwithstanding Nasser's widespread popularity among numerous Egyptians and across the broader Arab world, his regime encountered palpable censure and opposition due to the abridgment of political liberties and the consolidation of executive authority (Osman, 2011).

Following Nasser's demise in 1970, Anwar Sadat ascended to the presidency of Egypt, marking the dawn of a new era characterised by a pronounced shift in economic policy under the banner of the 'Infitah' or 'Open Door' policy (Weinbaum, 1985, p. 210). This strategic maneuver entailed a concerted effort to liberalise Egypt's economic landscape by encouraging foreign investments and gradually extricating the state from the grip of substantial intervention in key sectors. While this wave of economic liberalisation engendered certain favorable changes, political freedoms lingered fettered, and the machinations of censorship endured with unfaltering persistence. Concurrently, the government tenaciously persevered in its quest to suppress opposition voices, inescapably relegating the ambit of freedom of expression to constricting confines. Notable during Sadat's reign was the epochal occurrence of the 'Corrective Revolution' in 1971, the aftermath of which witnessed the apprehension and confinement of myriad political dissidents and critics, a seismic event that solidified Sadat's grip on executive power while concurrently accentuating the stringent clampdown on dissenting voices (Baker, 1981, p. 378).

Hosni Mubarak's assumption of the presidency following Sadat's assassination in 1981 set the stage for a continuation of prevailing trends. Despite initial optimism for political reforms and advancements in human rights, Mubarak's regime perpetuated and even intensified repressive measures. The government increasingly tightened its grip on the media, exercising stringent control over freedom of expression. Dissent and opposition voices were systematically suppressed, and censorship mechanisms were pervasive, deterring independent media outlets and opposition figures from functioning without facing dire consequences. Throughout Mubarak's nearly threedecade rule, political dissidents and critics of the regime experienced a climate of suppression, encountering harassment, imprisonment, or forced exile. This overarching control over the media and opposition entities provided Mubarak's government with a means to consolidate its power and maintain an ironclad grip on authority. Nonetheless, this centralisation of control bred mounting discontent and disillusionment among the populace. Echoing patterns observed under Sadat's administration, the era was marked by a juxtaposition of limited political openness and escalating control over the media, accentuated by punitive actions against those challenging the status quo. Although some economic reforms were implemented, the lack of genuine political freedom and persistent human rights abuses fostered a simmering cauldron of grievances (Acemoglu et al., 2018, p. 25).

During the 2011 Arab Spring uprisings in Egypt, a tumultuous chapter unfolded. Emanating as a series of popular movements in January 2011, these uprisings were galvanised by deeply entrenched grievances against the autocratic rule of Hosni Mubarak. Fuelled by the impassioned quest for sweeping political reforms, an end to systemic corruption and the protection of fundamental human rights and civil liberties, the demonstrations gained momentum and solidarity (Acemoglu et al., 2018, p. 25). As the fervor escalated, the iconic Tahrir Square in Cairo served as a powerful emblem of collective resolve, symbolising the populace's relentless struggle for emancipation from oppressive governance. Enduring an arduous 18-day test of will, characterised by escalating pressures, Mubarak ultimately succumbed to the overwhelming public outcry and tendered his resignation from the presidency in February 2011. This pivotal turning point symbolised a monumental victory for the Egyptian populace, illuminating a promising path towards a future defined by enhanced freedoms and democratic governance. The repercussions of the transformative effects of the Arab Spring continue to resonate deeply within the collective consciousness of Egypt, embodying the determination of its people and their steadfast pursuit of a more inclusive, equitable and democratic societal structure.

In the aftermath of Mubarak's resignation, Egypt experienced a phase marked by political instability and uncertainty. The reins of power were temporarily assumed by the military, ushering in a transitional period. Despite endeavors to conduct democratic elections, apprehensions emerged concerning the ascent of Islamist factions and the potential consolidation of power. In 2012, Mohamed Morsi, affiliated with the Muslim Brotherhood, secured election as Egypt's inaugural civilian president. However, his tenure encountered obstacles, with mounting reservations regarding his administration's allegiance to democratic ideals and inclusiveness. This climate of political polarization further fragmented Egyptian society, delineating a spectrum of support for Morsi's policies juxtaposed with oppositional stances (Jumet, 2017, p. 152).

After the military intervention in July 2013, El-Sisi assumed the presidency, engendering an era of heightened repression. The government enacted a clampdown on opposition factions, encompassing the Muslim Brotherhood and liberal activists. Freedom of expression was curtailed, independent media outlets were shuttered, and divergent voices were suppressed. This resurgence of military rule and the ensuing tightening of media and political avenues engendered additional constraints on freedom of expression and political pluralism. Egypt regressed into an epoch of authoritarianism, prioritizing stability and control while compromising essential freedoms. Presently, Egypt grapples with persistent challenges concerning human rights, political liberties, and democratic governance. The aftermath of the Arab Spring in Egypt stands as a complex reminder of the intricacies inherent in transitioning from an authoritarian paradigm to a more allencompassing and democratic framework. The nation's expedition toward authentic democratic reforms and the veneration of human rights continues to represent a principal preoccupation for its populace and the international community.

4.3 Egypt's Constitutional Evolution and Press Autonomy

The evolutionary trajectory of constitutional development in Egypt finds its historical roots in the nation's arduous struggle for independence and emancipation. The first Egyptian constitution dates back to 1882, albeit it was the constitution introduced on April 19, 1923, that holds profound significance among legal scholars (Hamad, 2012, p. 53). This pivotal constitutional enactment closely followed the Egyptian government's declaration of the abolishment of the British Protectorate in Egypt on February 28, 1922. Commensurate with the stipulations of the 1923 constitution, a fresh parliamentary body was democratically elected, and its inaugural session convened in 1924. The continuity of this constitution persisted until October 22, 1930, when its implementation was temporarily suspended by the government, only to be subsequently reinstated in 1931, remaining functional until the advent of a military coup in July 1952 (Morsy, 1995, p. 310). Since that transformative juncture, Egypt has borne witness to a succession of constitutional developments, delineating a compelling narrative of evolution and transformation.

The introduction of the 'Constitutional Declaration' on December 10, 1952, marked a pivotal moment, leading to the abrogation of the 1923 Constitution. In its wake, a specialised committee was established to conceptualise a new constitution founded on what the government deemed as exalted constitutional principles. Subsequently, on January 16, 1956, yet another constitutional declaration was promulgated, garnering public endorsement through a referendum on June 23, 1956. This marked the advent of the first constitution of the Republic of Egypt following the dissolution of the Monarchy (Morsy, 1995, p. 310). Subsequently, the unity between Egypt and Syria on February 22, 1958, engendered the introduction of a new Unity Constitution in March 1958, christened the Constitution of the United Arab Republic. However, a further constitutional transformation ensued on March 25, 1964, wherein the United Arab Republic constitution was supplanted after the separation of the two countries in September 1961. On September 11, 1971, another constitutional charter was established, ultimately ratified by a public referendum in 2005. Following the Egyptian revolution of 2011, a novel constitution was issued in 2012.

As it stands, Egypt's present Constitution, promulgated in 2014, bears a striking resemblance to the Constitution initially crafted in 1971 (Brown, 2014). In the midst of ongoing changes, the current constitution holds a variety of rights for citizens. Key articles such as 41, 42, 45, 47, 48, 54, and 57 emphasize the importance of protecting individual rights and freedoms. These articles focus on privacy, freedom of expression, and the right to liberty and security, reflecting the constitution's commitment to the people's diverse aspirations.

In the gradual evolution of successive constitutional frameworks, the comprehensive consideration of topics concerning human rights emerges as a pivotal theme, reflecting an earnest exploration of the principles enshrined in human rights and fundamental freedoms. This profound introspection further substantiates Egypt's commitment to adhering to internationally recognised and regional human rights standards, as exemplified by the Universal Declaration of Human Rights endorsed by the United Nations, thereby imposing a solemn obligation to uphold and embrace the rights and duties outlined therein. Such an unwavering dedication to human rights principles and fundamental freedoms is underscored by the imperative to translate these principles into legally binding norms at the domestic legislative level. Notably, Egypt's accession to the UN Covenant on Civil and Political Rights (CCPR) in 1982 exemplifies the nation's acknowledgement of Articles 18 and 19 of the Covenant, which unambiguously underscore the critical significance of safeguarding freedom of opinion and expression, imposing a looming responsibility (Ahram Online, 2023).

In accordance with Article 47, the Egyptian Constitution unequivocally ensures the entitlement to freedom of opinion, affirming that every individual possesses the unassailable right to freely express their perspectives, whether orally, in writing, or through alternative means, within the confines prescribed by law (Youssef, 2012). This acknowledgment extends to encompass the value of self-criticism and constructive criticism, which are hailed as guardians of the national structure's integrity, affirming their paramountcy in nurturing a secure and resilient sociopolitical fabric. Subsequently, Article 48 goes on to enshrine the guarantee of freedom of the press, printing, publication, and media, denouncing any form of newspaper censorship and prohibiting their suspension through administrative edicts during times of emergency or war (Youssef, 2012). However, it does permit limited censorship in specific contexts such as matters pertaining to public safety or national security, but strictly in compliance with the stipulations laid out by the law.

Moving forward, Article 49 upholds the state's responsibility to safeguard the freedom of scientific research, as well as literary, artistic and cultural innovation, further mandating the provision of requisite resources to actualise these endeavors. Furthermore, a significant point of interest lies in the Egyptian Constitution's allocation of a dedicated section labeled 'the sovereignty of the press,' housing six distinct articles (206, 207, 208, 209, 210, and 211). This section delves into the nuanced dynamics governing press authority, its independence, and the explicit proscription of both censorship and confiscation. Such provisions distinctly attest to the Constitution's commitment to safeguarding journalistic autonomy and unimpeded access to information by journalists.

The multifaceted landscape of press freedom in Egypt is characterised by a complex interplay of constitutional provisions and legislative constraints. While Articles 206 to 210 of the Egyptian constitution undeniably assert the principles of press freedom, emphasizing its vital role as a public instrument bound by the Constitution and the law, practical realities reveal a more intricate picture. The press is granted the fundamental rights of freedom of expression and the autonomy to serve society within the confines of the societal framework. Notably, Article 208 explicitly safeguards press freedom, prohibiting censorship of newspapers and shielding journalists from executive warnings, suspensions, or revocations. This constitutional affirmation seeks to foster an environment conducive to open and independent journalism. Moreover, the Constitution ensures the unimpeded publication of newspapers and allows ownership by various legal entities, including public, private, or political entities. Journalists are granted the right to access news and information according to legal stipulations, and their work is not subject to censorship (Salam, 2017).

Complementing these constitutional provisions, Article 211 establishes the Higher Council of the Press, entrusted with a pivotal role in delineating the Council's mandate and its relationship with the state. The Council's objectives revolve around bolstering press freedom and safeguarding the fundamental elements of society, such as national unity and social harmony, in alignment with the Constitution and the law. However, in practice, the realm of press freedom in Egypt contends with various legal restrictions. The Egyptian Press Law No. 96/1996, for instance, grants the government-appointed Supreme Press Council exclusive authority over the issuance of newspaper licenses. This concentration of licensing power raises legitimate concerns over media independence, with potential implications for media pluralism and objectivity.

In Egypt's media landscape, the interplay of regulations and constraints continues to cast a profound impact on the exercise of freedom of the press and expression, evoking a plethora of challenges and considerations. The exclusive right bestowed upon political parties and public legal entities to issue newspapers, contingent upon stipulated conditions, inevitably perpetuates constraints on media diversity and ownership, thereby entrenching certain perspectives and limiting the multiplicity of voices that could otherwise enrich public discourse. Concomitantly, the extensive powers vested in the Supreme Press Council, enabling it to wield censorship and oversight over journalists and press institutions, ostensibly in pursuit of societal interests, introduces an inherent tension between the noble objectives of safeguarding public welfare and the potential impingement upon the sacrosanct principles of journalistic independence and unrestricted expression.

The Council's authority in matters such as pricing and exclusive control over the distribution of printing materials, while possibly intended to streamline media operations and maintain economic stability, can inadvertently skew the media landscape, determining the scale and viability of media participation and potentially disadvantaging smaller players in the realm of media ownership. Moreover, the discretionary powers of the Supreme Press Council to ban publications, whether originating from domestic or foreign sources, evoke palpable apprehensions about the availability and diversity of information accessible to the public. The specter of information asymmetry looms large, threatening to encroach upon the democratic ideals of transparency and plurality, as the flow of diverse viewpoints may be inadvertently stifled or regulated.

Within the folds of Egypt's penal code, a multitude of articles addressing press-related offenses, ranging from accusations of defaming the state to disseminating unverified information, adds further layers of complexity to the media landscape. These legal provisions, ostensibly conceived to safeguard national interests and societal cohesion, can inadvertently foster a climate of fear and intimidation among journalists and media organisations, exerting a chilling effect that may impede the pursuit of bold and audacious journalism on matters of public interest. Nurturing a media ecosystem that upholds democratic principles of media pluralism and unhindered expression demands a delicate and nuanced approach. Striking a harmonious balance between the preservation of state interests and the promotion of vibrant journalistic integrity requires concerted efforts to engender a space where the press can thrive as a fearless watchdog, illuminating truth, and empowering the public with informed perspectives. Embracing an ethos that cherishes diverse voices and celebrates robust public discourse remains the path forward to nurture an inclusive and resilient media environment in Egypt (Salam, 2017).

Amidst the complex web of Egypt's post-revolutionary political metamorphosis, a dynamic and multifaceted interplay of legislative authority ensued, delineating a complex and at times convoluted landscape. Triggered by the 2011 revolution and the consequential ousting of President Mubarak, a series of consequential shifts in the locus of legislative power unfolded. This entailed a transfer of authority to the Supreme Council of the Armed Forces (SCAF), followed by a brief stint of an elected parliament, which regrettably encountered dissolution through constitutional court intervention. Subsequently, the reins of legislative control reverted back to SCAF until 2012, when President Mohamed Morsi's ascension to power marked a pivotal juncture. The abrogation of SCAF's constitutional declaration during Morsi's tenure led to the restoration of legislative power to the Consultative Council, concurrently coinciding with the adoption of the 2012 (then new) constitution (Fathy, 2018, p. 102).

Nonetheless, the political landscape remained dynamic and transformative, as the year 2014 witnessed yet another consequential phase, featuring Morsi's ouster, the dissolution of the Consultative Council, and amendments to the constitution. In the aftermath of these events, Abdel.

Fattah El-Sisi's rise to the presidency ensued, with the establishment of a new council postponed until 2015, thereby prolonging a period where legislative authority predominantly remained concentrated in El-Sisi's hands. Throughout this complex transition, an array of laws, including the new constitution, emerged, exerting significant impact on fundamental rights, most notably freedom of expression. However, the right to freedom of expression found itself ensnared within a labyrinthine legal framework, comprising a mosaic of antiquated legislation, vestiges of laws from the former autocratic regime and newly drafted regulations, all of which surfaced during a delicate interim period, characterised by parliamentary dissolution. This complex legal landscape posed formidable challenges to the unfettered exercise of freedom of expression, as its manifestation encountered notable constraints and limitations.

Furthermore, in tandem with the 2014 Egyptian constitution, the prevailing legal framework pertaining to freedom of expression encompasses an intricate amalgamation of legislative instruments. Notably, the 1936 publications law, the 1937 penal code, the 1996 press law, the 2002 intellectual property law, and the 2003 telecommunication regulation law form a complex mosaic of regulations governing the contours of expression within the country. Within this intricate legal landscape, the press law ostensibly endeavors to strike a delicate balance between upholding a notion of 'responsible' freedom of expression and averting the imposition of censorship or the closure of newspapers. Despite its efforts to preserve a semblance of liberty, the same press law prescribes penalties for a spectrum of offenses related to publication, thus introducing a nuanced interplay between the assertion of rights and the imposition of restrictions. Intersecting with the press law, the penal code introduces further constraints on the exercise of freedom of expression. The penal code's provisions pertaining to speech delineate stringent sanctions for a myriad of offenses, spanning incitement to disorder, acts of military disobedience, and instances of religious discrimination (Articles 171–177). Additionally, the dissemination or publication of materials deemed contrary to public morals (Article 178) and the defamation of prominent figures such as the head of state, foreign dignitaries, public officials, and judges (Articles 179–187) are met with stringent punitive measures. Furthermore, the propagation of false news and rumors (Article 188) is subject to penal repercussions. The confluence of these legal provisions engenders a nuanced legal landscape, wherein expressions of freedom are carefully delimited by stipulations designed to maintain societal order and safeguard reputations (Egypt: News Websites and Alternative Voices, 2014).

As a signatory to both the Universal Declaration of Human Rights (UDHR) and the International Covenant on Civil and Political Rights (ICCPR), Egypt's commitment to international human rights standards is underscored. Ratifying the ICCPR in 1982 reinforced Egypt's dedication to upholding fundamental freedoms, including freedom of expression (Fathy, 2018, p. 103). The 2014 Egyptian constitution aligns with these international conventions, prominently articulating the right to freedom of expression through various provisions. Article 57 guarantees citizens' entitlement to avail themselves of all forms of public means of communication, while Article 68 ensures access to information and official documents. Moreover, Article 72 safeguards the independence of press institutions and media outlets, fostering an environment conducive to unfettered journalistic practices. Expounding further, Article 65 staunchly upholds freedom of thought, firmly asserting that every individual possesses the right to express opinions through verbal, written, visual, or any other mode of expression and publication. As a collective whole, these constitutional tenets aim to promote a democratic milieu wherein freedom of expression thrives while adhering to the broader imperatives of social cohesion and national stability.

Despite the apparent constitutional assurance of upholding fundamental liberties, a comprehensive examination of the provisions pertaining to freedom of expression reveals inherent shortcomings that markedly deviate from the rigorous standards set forth in Article 19 of the International Covenant on Civil and Political Rights (ICCPR) (Taylor,

2020, p. 538). Article 65 ostensibly purports to enshrine an unequivocal entitlement to freedom of thought and opinion, yet a closer analysis uncovers its conspicuously limited purview. Specifically, the article glaringly excludes crucial forms of expression, including but not limited to political discourse, commentary on public affairs, discussions relating to human rights, journalism, cultural and artistic expressions, pedagogy, religious discourse, commercial advertising, and any form of expression that might be deemed deeply offensive. This marked limitation stands in direct contravention of the quintessential essence of Article 19 of the ICCPR, which unequivocally upholds the inalienable right of individuals to seek, receive, and impart information without any discriminatory boundaries, transcending geographical frontiers.

Within the realm of freedom of the press and publication, Article 70 seeks to enshrine these liberties, ostensibly conferring upon each Egyptian the privilege of engaging in multifarious press-related activities encompassing the domains of press, printing, paper, visual, audio, and electronic publication (Fathy, 2018, p. 104). Concurrently, the article affirms the entitlement of individuals to own and establish newspapers, as well as visual, audio, and digital media outlets. However, upon scrutinizing the finer nuances, an evident discriminatory bias comes to the fore, as non-Egyptians face restrictive impediments on their right to ownership and issuance of online publications. Furthermore, the same article subjects online publications to onerous legal and bureaucratic exigencies, subjecting them to regulatory requirements analogous to their printed counterparts, and necessitating governmental endorsement for their inception and operation.

The Egyptian Constitution, while upholding freedom of expression and the legitimacy of all publications, paradoxically includes provisions that allow for censorship, confiscation, and suspension of Egyptian websites and media outlets during times of war or general mobilization. Moreover, Article 31 enables security authorities to prosecute and intimidate digital activists and citizens based on vague national security grounds related to their online activities. This ambivalent stance on freedom of expression is further compounded by the constitution's broadly defined restrictions concerning "crimes related to the incitement of violence, discrimination between citizens, or impingement of individual honor" (Article 71), leaving ample room for potential abuse by authorities.

The Telecommunication Regulation Law 10/2003, the primary regulatory instrument governing the telecommunications sector, aims to enhance telecommunication services while protecting users' rights. However, it also mandates the National Telecommunications Regulatory Authority (NTRA) to prioritize national security concerns, and the presence of security authorities on the NTRA's board of directors raises concerns about its independence and objectivity. Additionally, the NTRA's funding from the state's general budget, along with the prime minister's determination of the executive management's remuneration, casts doubt on the regulatory body's autonomy from government influence. Such arrangements contradict international standards that demand an impartial and independent media and communications regulatory authority (Fathy, 2018, p. 105).

The law includes provisions that infringe upon freedom of expression under the pretext of national security, a departure from internationally recognized human rights standards. Articles 64 to 69 vaguely define national security, making references to the presidency, armed forces, and other competent authorities, thus falling short of articulating precise and well-defined boundaries for legitimate national security concerns. Additionally, the law grants competent authorities the power to assume control over telecommunication services in the event of natural disasters or declared periods of general mobilization (Article 67) (Fathy, 2018, p. 104). This particular provision was used to justify the internet shutdown during the 2011 revolution, a measure deemed unnecessary and repressive, as it sought to quell public demonstrations, a legitimate expression of opinion.

Concerns regarding privacy and encryption are similarly heightened in relation to national security matters. Article 64 prohibits telecom operators, service providers, and users from employing encryption software without prior consent from the National Telecommunications Regulatory Authority (NTRA) and security authorities. The article further mandates that service operators and providers grant the armed forces and national security entities access to their technical resources, including equipment, systems, software, and communication, to execute their powers within the confines of the law. Such provisions contravene international legal norms as they allow authorities to monitor users without the necessity of a judicial warrant (AlAshry, 2022, 10). Furthermore, telecommunication service providers and operators are permitted to collect information and data details of users without prior consent (Article 64), presenting a grave threat to user privacy, particularly in the absence of a comprehensive legal framework regulating privacy and data protection in Egypt.

4.4 The Supreme Constitutional Court (SCC) and Freedom of Expression Under the Constitution

In the context of constitutional governance, the adjudication and implementation of provisions concerning freedom of speech and expression by the judiciary play a pivotal role in shaping the tangible realisation of these rights. In Egypt, the courts have consistently embraced an expansive approach when construing the limitations on freedom of expression, resulting in a constriction of the space available for dissenting voices and the flourishing of diverse perspectives. Central to the framework of the Egyptian judicial system lies the indispensable position of the esteemed Supreme Constitutional Court (SCC). Underpinning the significance of the SCC, the Egyptian Constitution (EC) explicitly enunciates in Article 192 that the SCC enjoys exclusive jurisdiction to render verdicts on the constitutionality of laws and regulations and to provide authoritative interpretations of legislative texts. Functioning as an autonomous and sovereign entity, the SCC's decisions bear binding authority over all other state organs, thus endowing it with profound responsibility in safeguarding the fundamental rights of individuals and perpetuating a "living Constitution" where the expansive principles are adroitly applied to intricate and evolving circumstances (The Constitution of Egypt, 2014).

The Supreme Constitutional Court (SCC) assumes a paramount role in ensuring the high efficacy of the constitutional edifice. Notably, if the SCC ascertains that a law promulgated by Parliament or a state legislature encroaches upon, or poses a threat to, the fundamental rights of citizens, it possesses the authority to render such legislation unlawful or unconstitutional. Consequently, any legislation that diverges from the essence or letter of the constitutional charter, or transgresses the prescribed legal boundaries of the government, falls within the purview of the SCC's prerogative to invalidate. This critical function of the SCC assumes a pivotal stance in fostering constitutional democracy and safeguarding the cherished rights and liberties of individuals. Through the practice of judicial review, the SCC stands as a vanguard, upholding the supremacy of the people's will as enshrined in the constitutional framework and ensuring the preservation of freedom of expression (Fahmi, 2012). In fulfilling this mission, the SCC has displayed its distinctive prowess in dismantling antiquated common law institutions that once constricted freedom of expression in the grip of political power and has resolutely reconstructed the legal landscape on new and more justifiable foundations.

In Egypt, the fundamental right of freedom of speech and expression exists in an ambiguous state, entrenched in all Egyptian Constitutions from the 1923 Constitution to Article 65 of the 2014 Constitution. The latter articulates, "[a]ll individuals have the right to express their opinions through speech, writing, imagery, or any other means of publication." Despite this explicit guarantee, the Constitution expounds on the diverse manifestations of this right, encompassing various modes of communication (The Constitution of Egypt, 2014). For instance, in Case 44, the Supreme Constitutional Court (SCC) elucidated that freedom of expression comprises multiple rights, entitling individuals to freely convey their thoughts through speech, writing, or artistic expression, as long as they do not infringe upon the law or the rights of others.

Modes of speech and expression can manifest conventionally or unconventionally. Conventional methods entail communication through writing, spoken words, or artistic forms. Conversely, unconventional expression allows individuals to convey their ideas through any medium, including activities such as demonstrations, where people voice their opinions through placards or symbolic acts like flag burning. In Case 160, the SCC upheld the right of demonstrations as a form of freedom of expression. Notably, the Constitution also protects nonverbal forms of expression, such as remaining silent or displaying no emotion. Strikes, too, are considered a form of expression, as one commentator argues that they convey messages in a nonverbal manner and deserve similar protection to verbal speech. Article 15 of the Constitution explicitly guarantees the right to peaceful strikes, organized by law. Workers, therefore, have the right to voice their grievances by abstaining from work and maintaining silence before governmental departments to protest work policies or other concerns (Alsubaie, 2019).

The complex domain of freedom of speech and expression in Egypt extends its purview to encompass the essential realm of freedom of the press. Within the realm of constitutional discourse, diverse labels such as 'freedom of speech,' 'freedom of expression,' and 'freedom of the press' find usage; however, their essence converges on the significance of bestowing individuals with the fundamental right to articulate their thoughts and beliefs. Professor Emad contends that even aesthetic nonverbal expressions warrant constitutional protection, provided they do not jeopardize national security, public morals, or the rights of others

(Alsubaie, 2019). This perspective accentuates the comprehensive ambit of protected forms of expression enshrined in the Egyptian Constitution.

Within this context, the press and publishers assume a pivotal role, embracing diverse forms of freedom of expression through publications, filmmaking, artistic endeavors, and musical expressions. The principles articulated by the Supreme Constitutional Court (SCC) regarding freedom of speech seamlessly extend to the domain of freedom of the press, and vice versa, forging an inseparable connection. The Egyptian Constitution bears witness to the multifaceted nature of freedom of expression, embracing a comprehensive array of speech forms. An examination of these myriad means of free speech reveals a general consensus, affirming their status as protected speech under free speech laws. Notably, the Egyptian Constitution, among other free speech laws in the Arab world, explicitly embraces the various types of speech without rigid classification. In legal cases involving communicative conduct, the Egyptian Courts adopt a broader approach, focusing on overarching principles rather than limited, case-specific analyses.

This broader perspective enhances the robustness of the constitutional protection accorded to the cherished freedom of expression in Egypt.

4.5 The Supreme Constitutional Court's Approach to Islamic Legal Interpretation

After achieving independence in 1979, Egypt's Supreme Constitutional Court (SCC) has assumed diverse responsibilities, among which interpreting legislative texts holds particular significance. A key aspect of its mandate involves offering an authoritative elucidation of Article 2 in the Egyptian Constitution, which declares, "Islam is the state's religion, and the Arabic language is its official language. The principles of Islamic law serve as the primary source of legislation (El-Morr et al., 1996, p. 37). Contrary to enforcing a strict separation between the State and religion, the SCC is envisioned as an instrument to harmonise constitutional jurisprudence with Islamic norms. Given the abstract and open-ended nature of Article 2, the Court assumes a pivotal and consequential role in adapting Islamic principles to align with modernity (El-Morr et al., 1996, p. 38). This endeavor has been ongoing since the establishment of the Court, with endeavors made to incorporate Islamic Law into Egypt's judicial framework. As such, the SCC's jurisprudential contributions in this regard carry significant weight and impact on the evolving legal landscape of the nation.

In 1993, the Supreme Constitutional Court (SCC) undertook a comprehensive examination of past judgments, seeking those that fulfill two essential criteria. Firstly, the SCC aimed to identify rulings grounded in a direct and unequivocal text from either the Qur'ān or the few authenticated Sunnah. Secondly, the SCC sought assurance that these rules were not contingent on specific circumstances, emphasizing the necessity for legislation to be unambiguously certain in their authenticity and meaning. This approach allowed the SCC to establish a comprehensive principle with broad consensus, thus gaining acceptance from Islamic scholars.

Although the SCC did not explicitly delineate a particular approach for incorporating *sharīʿah* into legislation, it becomes evident, as we delve into their decisions, that the Court relies on the Qur'ān, Sunnah and *Ijtihād* as fundamental pillars shaping their judgments. Despite the broad applicability of these principles, the SCC has adopted a stringent methodology to construct a comprehensive theory regarding the interpretation of *sharīʿah* or the identification of legislation as Islamic. To discern the application of these principles in specific cases, it is essential to grasp the functioning of Islamic principles. By adhering to this rigorous framework, the SCC endeavors to ensure a coherent and principled approach to the integration of Islamic norms into the legal landscape.

The Qur'ān and Sunnah hold a position of paramount importance as primary sources of *sharīʿah*. According to the Supreme Constitutional Court (SCC), they stand as ultimate laws governing all aspects of human life. The language and messages contained within the Qur'ān and Sunnah often give rise to debates and varying viewpoints. Certain passages may lack explicit meanings, inviting diverse interpretations. To address such complexities, scholars and jurists have formulated linguistic rules to derive specific meanings from metaphorical language and general expressions found in these sacred texts.

A notable instance, Case No. 8 of Judicial Year 17, exemplifies how these intricate interpretive processes come into play. The SCC was confronted with a written complaint from a father advocating for his two daughters, who faced an educational restriction imposed by the Minister of Education due to their adherence to veiling practices, particularly the *niqāb*—a full-face veil prevalent in Egypt. In navigating such cases, the SCC's role becomes critical in striking a harmonious balance between religious principles and practical application in contemporary society (Supreme Constitutional Court, Case No 7 of Judicial Year 8, 1993). This particular form is characterized not as a mere source but rather as an ongoing activity and endeavor to uncover the law from primary texts and apply it to fresh circumstances. Although certain historical Muslim scholars have minimised the right to practice *ijtihad*, the SCC has taken a more permissive stance, granting judges wider latitude in its exercise. The SCC strives to adhere to the principles of faith while upholding morality and justice in a contemporary context. The SCC's mixed approach to textual interpretation raises intriguing questions: How will the Court interpret *sharīʿah*? And how will the SCC employ these interpretations to uphold human rights?

To provide answers to these questions, it is vital at this juncture to comprehend that the primary objectives of *sharīʿah* were primarily focused on safeguarding religion, self-preservation, reason, honor, and property. In its 1993 opinion, the SCC clarified that the scope of ijtihad should not be boundless: 'Ijtihad must occur within the framework of the universal foundations of Islamic *sharīʿah* (*al-usul al-kulliyya li-ʾl shari'a al-Islamiyya*) …formulating practical judgments and basing them on the justice of Shari'a, with the expectation that they will reflect the general goals of *sharīʿah* (*al-maqasid al-ʿamma li-ʾl Shari'a*), including the protection of religion, life, reason, honor, and property' (Supreme Constitutional Court, Case No 7 of Judicial Year 8, 1993).

The central focus of all Islamic legislative theories is to ensure the highest level of protection for human rights, which is closely associated with *sharīʿah's* five fundamental necessities known as '*maqasid al-sharīʿah*'. A commentator describes this potential benefit as something that jurists perceived could be achieved through the process of induction from scriptural sources. This involves promoting certain benefits (*maslaha*) or preventing harmful outcomes (*darar*). Understanding the broader objectives and *maqasid* as a form of utilitarian reasoning helps the justices interpret *sharīʿah* in a manner consistent with modernity and diverse cases. Professor Qaraḍāwī asserts that embracing the doctrine of *maqasid al-sharīʿah* is the most appropriate approach to comprehend Islam in practical terms (Kamali, 2012). He highlights that utilising *maqasid al-shariʿah* not only protects individual rights but also serves the collective interests of the entire community. The SCC could achieve these objectives by employing the process of induction from various sources to advance benefits and prevent harm.

The Court's extensive authority to interpret *sharī'ah* has played a significant role in shaping the diverse array of sources considered by the SCC concerning matters of public interest. According to Lombardi and Brown, the Court has displayed creativity in utilising tradition to establish a fresh approach to Islamic legal thinking within the context of constitutional thought (Lombardi & Brown, 2005, p. 379). The SCC perceives this as evidence that *sharī'ah* is not confined to rigid principles and can be flexibly applied whenever potential benefits arise, whether for individuals or the community. Illustratively, in a 1995 ruling, the SCC highlighted that Muslims should always bear in mind that whatever God prohibits is likely to lead to harm, while what is required or permitted is certainly beneficial. This indicates that Islamic teachings are consistently geared towards promoting benefits and preventing harm. Moreover, this perspective implies that *sharī'ah* safeguards people's freedom, including freedom of expression, whenever there is an optional benefit for them. However, the SCC does not interpret this as a license for unrestrained behavior. Rather, they assert that *sharī'ah* protects freedom of expression unless it causes harm to others (Lombardi & Brown, 2005, p. 379).

The preceding examination reveals that even within its relatively short existence, the SCC has made a notable impact by expanding the interpretation of the Islamic judicial concept. Despite criticisms regarding the wide discretion given to judges in interpreting *sharī'ah*, the discussion presented above demonstrates the SCC's triumph in formulating a *sharī'ah* theory that resonates with widely-accepted beliefs about its fundamental nature. An extensive analysis of the purpose and historical application of *sharī'ah* suggests that its principles retain relevance across all time periods and geographical locations, as long as the actions are aimed at expressing a specific viewpoint.

The implementation of *ijtihād* paved the way for the SCC to adopt a distinct approach in addressing various matters, including cases concerning human rights. This approach soon came to be known as "*new-ijtihād*." The adoption of "*new-ijtihād*" is considered modern, diverging from the old perspective of seeking specific rules that all *mujtahids* had historically articulated and upheld as binding. The focal point of the debate lies in whether the SCC's approach is an addition to Islamic norms or merely adheres to Islamic principles. To be deemed modern, an approach must be applicable across all times and places, rather than aligning solely with the views of old mujtahids or the practice of *taqlid* (emulation). In essence, the SCC does not align with the old mujtahid views in terms of its own values (Alsubaie, 2019). A closer examination of the SCC reveals that its approach aims to address problems from a modern standpoint. According to a commentator, over the past two decades, the SCC has developed a creative new theory of Islamic law. Utilizing this method, the Court has interpreted *sharīʿah* norms in line with international human rights standards and liberal economic policies. Indeed, the new approach introduced by the SCC, which is compatible with changing circumstances and new contexts, demonstrates the Court's uniqueness. It should come as no surprise that the SCC has earned a reputation as the most powerful court in the Arab world and has, at times, garnered global attention for the boldness of its rulings.

4.6 The SCC and Freedom of Expression: Safeguarding Against State and Society

The establishment of the SCC had a paramount objective: to ensure unfettered access to justice and effectively manage the intricate relationship between individuals and state authorities. Armed with supervisory authority, the SCC possesses the formidable capacity to meticulously scrutinize the alignment of laws governing freedom of expression with the tenets of the Constitution. Any law found to be incongruous with the constitutional principles is rendered unconstitutional by the SCC, thereby compelling all future court cases involving such legislation to dutifully adhere to the SCC's authoritative pronouncement. Hence, the SCC shoulders a momentous responsibility to exercise the rule of law with unswerving fairness and without any semblance of bias, while steadfastly shielding human rights from the clutches of unconstitutional actions. Elevated as the supreme adjudicator on constitutional matters in Egypt, the SCC is bestowed with empowering authority that positions it to zealously champion human rights vis-à-vis other institutions, thereby standing as a vanguard of justice and liberty (Lombardi, 2008, p. 235).

Embarking on a comprehensive exploration of the SCC's cardinal role in safeguarding the cherished right to freedom of expression, a compelling case surfaces, exemplifying situations wherein public authorities endeavor to impose stringent restrictions, potentially curtailing the precious freedom to organize marches and demonstrations. A particularly illuminating instance unfolds in the context of Case No. 160, Year 36 (December 3, 2016), wherein an applicant ardently sought the right to organize a peaceful march, as unequivocally granted by EC (Mohie,

2016). However, regrettably, the police obdurately denied the applicant's earnest plea, invoking Article 10(1) as the persuasive legal instrument empowering them to cogently regulate meetings, marches and demonstrations. In this intricate legal labyrinth, the SCC's adjudicative prowess becomes manifest, as it embarks upon the daunting task of deftly navigating and unraveling the web of intricacies that beset the contours of freedom of expression.

The SCC underscored the paramount importance of freedom of expression, viewing it as a fundamental principle that safeguards an individual's right to exchange ideas, experiences, and knowledge without any governmental interference. The SCC firmly maintained that even a highly improbable yet severe threat does not justify curtailing speech. According to the SCC's perspective, advocating lawlessness without any direct intent to incite or engage in such actions should remain unregulated. Individuals, in the SCC's view, have the liberty to take abstract positions on specific issues without constraint. The SCC deemed it essential to expand the scope for practicing freedom of speech. By doing so, the SCC sought to prevent unwarranted interventions by public authorities that could severely impact people's right to express themselves freely. Simultaneously, the SCC aimed to provide broader protection for the exercise of freedom of expression. The SCC posited that the constitution aimed to secure freedom of expression, shielding the innermost expressions of life from the imposition of guardianship by public authorities, thereby preserving the integrity of the collective mind. This landmark judgment of the SCC reiterates the critical role of freedom of expression in upholding democratic order and underscores its profound significance as a cornerstone of society, ensuring a vibrant exchange of ideas and opinions.

In a momentous ruling, referred to as Case No 234, Year 36 (3 Dec 2016), the SCC delved into the multifaceted nature of freedom of expression (Alsubaie, 2019). While the SCC firmly upholds the importance of this fundamental right, it also recognizes that there are legitimate circumstances wherein the government may justifiably curtail it, particularly when it involves matters of paramount national security or the potential infliction of harm upon others. The case in question centered around an applicant facing charges due to their active participation in a demonstration that not only disrupted people's interests but also posed an ominous threat to the very fabric of national security. In an impassioned plea, the applicant argued that Article 107/2013 was in clear violation of constitutional tenets, fervently seeking to have their conviction overturned.

However, the SCC staunchly dismissed the applicant's plea, asserting that while freedom of expression remains a foundational right, it is not an untrammeled entitlement. The SCC clarified that this right does not grant individuals unrestrained liberty to freely express their thoughts or ideas without regard for consequences, regardless of time or place. Instead, the SCC elucidated that in exceptional circumstances, where compelling concerns of national security and broader public interest are at stake, judicious and measured restrictions on freedom of expression may be deemed necessary.

The SCC astutely underscored the weighty responsibility borne by judges in such instances, recognizing the delicate task of adroitly balancing competing interests. When freedom of speech intersects with other fundamental rights, the SCC emphasized the need for a scrupulous and conscientious evaluation to ascertain the rightful precedence that should be accorded to each right. This seminal pronouncement rendered by the SCC provides an incisive and multifaceted elucidation of the intricate dynamics at play when safeguarding the treasured freedom of expression while concurrently ensuring the overall well-being and stability of the nation. The ruling serves as a resolute testament to the SCC's devotion to the pursuit of justice, deftly navigating the complex terrain of balancing individual rights with the collective welfare of society. It stands as an embodiment of the SCC's unwavering dedication to preserving the delicate equilibrium between unfettered expression and the greater public interest, cementing its position as a stalwart guardian of constitutional principles and societal harmony (Supreme Constitutional Court, Case No 195 of Judical Year 19).

The decision rendered by the SCC served as a resounding affirmation of the importance of exercising freedom of expression within the bounds of the law. In a pivotal and illustrative case, identified as Case No 160, the SCC took a definitive stance by nullifying Article 42/2002, which pertained to civic associations and foundations. This particular article had vested government authorities with powers to restrict the functioning and activities of these associations, going so far as to grant them the authority to completely halt their operations (El-Din & El-Mahdawy, 2016). In the fulfillment of its constitutional mandate to assess the constitutionality of laws and regulations, the SCC astutely discerned that Article 42/2002 had unequivocally encroached upon multiple constitutional rights. Foremost among these was the right of assembly, expressly enshrined in Article

75 of the EC, which envisions that citizens possess the right to establish non-governmental organisations and institutions based on democratic principles. Furthermore, these organisations are entitled to engage in their activities freely, invulnerable to any interference from administrative agencies (The Constitution of Egypt, 2014).

Notably, the SCC was keenly aware that Article 42/2002 infringed upon the right to freedom of expression and the exchange of ideas, protected under Article 65 of the EC. The SCC emphasised that this transgression not only violated the core essence of the EC but also contravened the principles espoused in various international charters, most notably Article 20 of the Universal Declaration of Human Rights. In striking down Article 42/2002, the SCC upheld constitutional rights and preserved democratic principles. This ruling further solidified the SCC's position as a defender of justice and human rights, ensuring that freedom of expression remains a cornerstone of a democratic society.

Henceforth, the SCC rendered Article 42/2002 null and void, underlining the vital role of such actions in upholding democratic principles. This landmark case exemplified the imperative need to safeguard civic associations as an expression of freedom, impervious to lawless acts. In essence, the SCC's judgment emphasised that freedom of assembly stands as an irreplaceable element within a democratic society, essential for fostering pluralism, tolerance and open-mindedness. The SCC went on to assert that civil society organisations function as the vital bridge connecting individuals and the state, empowering societal growth through the dissemination of knowledge, raising awareness and promoting a thriving public culture. In a similar vein, another ruling addressing lawless decisions emerged in Case No 44, Judicial Year 7 (decided on 7 May 1988). The SCC examined Article 4(7) of the Political Parties System, which imposed a ban on party leaders or members from affiliating with any organisation advocating the undermining of the peace treaty between Egypt and Israel. Exercising its constitutional duty to assess the validity of laws and regulations, the SCC nullified Article 4(7) and reinstated the political rights of the opposition. In its 1988 ruling, the SCC declared that Article 4(7) of Law 40/1977 of the Law of Political Parties encroached upon the rights of political participation and freedom of expression, contravening Article 47 (pertaining to freedom of speech) and Article 62 (addressing political rights) of the EC. This further underscored the SCC's belief in the special protection of political participation and freedom of expression, recognising their pivotal role as foundational pillars of any robust and progressive system (Supreme Constitutional Court of Egypt Case No. 44 of Judicial Year 7, 1988).

4.7 Analysing the Legal Framework for Limitations on Freedom of Speech

Freedom of Speech and Expression is guaranteed in both the 1971 and 2014 Constitutions of Egypt, with the latter's Article 65 leaving no room for ambiguity thereby elevating the status of individuals as eloquent orators who wield the power of expression through multifarious conduits, encompassing speech, writing, imagery, and all conceivable forms of communication and dissemination (Alsubaie, 2019). Yet, it is incumbent upon discerning minds to acknowledge that within the purview of Egyptian law, a measured set of constraints on freedom of expression has been carefully carved. One such embodiment is Article 12 of the 1971 Constitution, which solemnly pledges society's commitment to preserving moral virtues and authentic Egyptian traditions, while Article 53 of the 2014 Constitution leaves no doubt about its stance against discrimination and the inflammatory provocation of hatred, categorically classifying these as reprehensible offenses, subject to legal retribution. The Supreme Constitutional Court (SCC) has been consistent in its clarion call, echoing the dictum that freedom of expression must only find its expression within the parameters of the law. Implicitly validating the authority of the government, it reserves the prerogative to regulate or even penalize expressions imbued with contentious content or relating to sensitive subject matter, yet unequivocally emphasising that such measures must be undergirded by irrefutable justification (The Constitution of Egypt, 1971).

Kameel advocates that freedom of expression should align with the country's values and laws as written in the statutes. While this right is guaranteed, it is not absolute, as certain limits protect individuals, groups, and society from harm. The Supreme Constitutional Court consistently stresses that freedom of speech has its limits. Justice Salman asserts that this freedom does not allow unrestricted speech without consequences (Kameel, 2016). The legal principle of freedoms, including the right to express oneself, requires any limitations to be governed by the law. To ensure clarity, restrictions on freedom of expression must be explicit and published in laws, guiding people on what is permissible and prohibited. This prevents undue burden on individuals' rights. Importantly, any restrictions on freedom of speech must be justified by necessity, and any misuse of power to suppress speech would violate the Constitution.

4.8 The Complex Struggle between Free Speech and the Protection of the Reputation of Others

The protection of others' reputations provides a valid basis for limiting freedom of expression. Defamation is recognised as a legitimate reason to restrict speech. In Egypt, the reputation of individuals is highly esteemed and well-guarded. Whether true or false, making defamatory statements that harm someone's reputation in the eyes of respected segments of society, through spoken words, visual representations like photographs or cartoons, or symbolic gestures, constitutes a punishable offense. Egypt's highest non-constitutional court for civil and criminal justice, the Cassation Court, emphasises the importance of respecting citizens' private lives and refraining from attacking their honor and reputations.

4.9 Egyptian Slander Law: A Threefold Lens on Attribution, Publicness and Intent

In the context of Egypt's legal framework, slander is defined under Article 302/1 of the Egyptian Penal Code as attributing certain matters to another person using methods described in Article 171(Alsubaie, 2019). If the attributed matters were true, they would lead to legal penalties or cause the person to be despised among patriots and fellow citizens. Egyptian law considers slander to encompass any meanings that lead to the disparagement of dignity (Alqsas, 2014). Analysing alleged slander cases, it becomes evident that the Egyptian Penal Code employs three criteria to assess whether a statement qualifies as slander, focusing on attribution, publicness, and criminal intent.

Regarding attribution, a statement is deemed slanderous when it specifically targets an individual, whether directly or indirectly and attempts to tarnish their character, reputation, or family standing, resulting in social rejection or avoidance. Therefore, speech that does not lead to the person's despisal among their community members is not considered slander. For instance, statements indicating a person's lack of sports skills or less famous family background would not be classified as slander, as per a commentator, as it does not concern 'honor and dignity'

(Alqsas, 2014). Additionally, the law does not differentiate between direct or indirect, true or false, or rumors spread by third parties (Alsubaie, 2019). According to Egyptian law, when slanderous statements directly target a living person, using defamatory names and adjectives commonly understood as slanderous, they become punishable offenses.

The highest court within the ordinary judicial system, known as the Court of Cassation, has defined slander as a state of mind that can be conveyed not only through direct speech but also through surrounding circumstances. For instance, when an expression, either in words or gestures, indirectly attacks the family of the person involved, such as saying, 'your mother is rich because she sleeps outside the home' (Alsubaie, 2019). It is important to highlight that directing slander without attributing it to a specific individual is not considered a crime. In such cases, the situation differs significantly from statements aimed at specific individuals, families, or society (Alsubaie, 2019). The absence of specific names or titles means there are no facts or information to prove the veracity of the hurtful speech, and thus, no slander exists (Alsubaie, 2019)

Secondly, publicness plays a crucial role in determining slander as per Egypt's law. Article 171 of the Penal Code asserts that slanderous acts must occur in a public place, whether through speaking, shouting, writing, or any other form of speech that can be understood by others (Freedom House, 2010). This includes abuse that is visible on television and social media, reaching a wide audience (Freedom House, 2010). Notably, Egypt's law does not accommodate slander under the umbrella of freedom of speech when it comes to publicness. The impact of abuse in magazines is even more significant than abuse in public places due to its widespread influence. However, publicness in abuse cases is exempt from legal restriction when it occurs in certain government departments, such as complaint cases. As per Article 309, abuse is exempted when it occurs during the verbal or written defense before the court, with each litigant imputing to the other (Freedom House, 2010). In Case No. 8439 of Year 70 (8 Dec 2003), the Court of Cassation emphasised that permissible criticism should still safeguard the reputation and dignity of others. It is worth noting that abuse can also occur in private settings, such as during gatherings of friends. However, in certain cases, telephone abuse is the only form that can be criminalized in private situations, mainly due to its obvious criminal intent. Thirdly, criminal intent plays a crucial role in slander cases, as Egyptian law presumes the defendant not guilty unless criminal intent can be proven. Criminal intent is determined by two elements: firstly, the perpetrator's knowledge that their slander, if true, would harm the target's reputation within the local community. Secondly, there is the intention of publicizing the abuse through media platforms like TV, social media and newspapers.

However, criminal intent can be excluded from slander when the abuse is not attributed to a specific person or group. The intention to protect the public interest is considered sufficient evidence to avoid criminal prosecution. In many slander cases, criminal intent becomes the cornerstone of proving the crime, but when the abuse targets public employees, intention can be utilised to validate the truthfulness of the slander, provided it is based on valid intentions. For instance, it is not permissible to falsely accuse public employees of crimes like corruption, bribery, or theft. The determination of criminal intent falls under the court's interpretation, and in cases where slanderous words hold dual meanings, the court evaluates the meaning to decide on the presence of criminal intent.

4.10 The Intersection of Freedom of Expression and Dignity in Egyptian Law

Insult is an area that directly impacts the freedom of expression in Egypt. It refers to cursing at someone in a manner that diminishes their honor or dignity, whether through spoken, written, or other forms of speech (Alsubaie, 2019). There are three principles established in Egyptian law for insult to be punishable: the outrage of honor or dignity, publicness, and criminal intention. Firstly, outrage of honor or dignity is the key distinguishing factor between insult and slander. Insult involves insulting individuals either directly or indirectly in a way that injures their dignity or lowers their standing in society. For instance, the attribution in an insult should not be directed towards general matters like accusing someone of rigging company documents, while slander should not be directed towards specific matters, such as calling someone a criminal or a hustler (Alsubaie, 2019). If it is unclear whether an expression constitutes slander or insult, the judge can refer to surrounding circumstances to understand the meaning. Secondly, publicness is a critical element in insulting cases. Insults made in public places, where a group of people may have heard it, are considered restricted speech and a violation of freedom of expression. This includes insults on social media, TV, or during public meetings. However, the presence of the victim while the insult occurs is not a requirement for it to be considered a crime. Thirdly, criminal intent plays a crucial role in determining whether speech qualifies as insult. It cannot be criminalised unless the insulting party has the knowledge and intention to widely publish the insult. If the insult happens in a private place or is not intended for public exposure, it would not be considered a public crime. Similarly, there would be no sufficient insult or crime if someone inadvertently mentions insulting words to another, not intending to insult those who speak foreign languages (Alsubaie, 2019).

4.11 Freedom of Expression and the Moral Imperatives of Society

Protection of public morals is a valid reason for limiting freedom of expression. Public morals are not subjective; rather, they are derived from heavenly principles that distinguish one community from another. In Egypt, safeguarding public morals is a top priority of the Constitution. It aims to preserve the community's principles and values from any speech or actions that may threaten them. Article 178 of the Criminal Code lays down stringent regulations on situations where public morals are violated. It pertains to printed matter, images, or other subjects that go against public morals and aims to protect Egypt's moral fabric and cultural identity. Criminalising the violation of public morals is primarily to shield the community from corruption and perversion in various forms. Obscene or pornographic materials pose a genuine threat to public morality, leading Egyptian law to combat both their existence and the behaviors that promote them. The Court of Cassation has ruled that facilitating the incitement of obscene or indecent behavior is a punishable offense. Pornography, in its broadest sense, encompasses all forms of expression with a significant impact on individuals, including books, films, photographs, and other images (Alsubaie, 2019). Therefore, the restrictions on such material extend to cover both conventional and unconventional forms of speech.

Certain forms of publishing face restrictions due to their involvement in creating obscene and indecent content. The Court of Cassation ruled that books portraying women and girls as objects for sexual exploitation and promoting pornography were criminal offenses that posed a genuine threat to community values. Similarly, the Administrative Court invalidated government decisions that did not cooperate in suspending sexual websites. The court deemed these websites a real threat to Egyptian values and principles, justifying the bans for the protection of public morals. It is crucial to distinguish cases involving publicness in adultery and indecency from private and genuine cases. They should not be conflated. The Court of Cassation clarified that immoral acts could be excluded from Article 171 of the Penal Code if publicness was absent. Furthermore, the North Cairo Court held that publishing books or stories referencing public morals was not a crime if done in good faith. For example, educational institutions may display images of naked individuals for educational purposes. As previously mentioned, Egyptian law is highly committed to protecting public morals, particularly in cases marked by publicness and intentions to undermine community values, presenting real threats (Fahmi, 2012).

The vigilant monitoring of publications containing indecent materials yields tangible benefits for society. Undoubtedly, the dissemination of such indecent content has a detrimental impact on public morals. Furthermore, when the publication and distribution of such materials adhere to prescribed limits, many negative phenomena, such as harassment and immoral acts, diminish significantly. Therefore, restricting the circulation of such material is not only essential to safeguard public morals but also presents a valuable opportunity to promote respectable publications that embrace and preserve community values. This perspective posits that the issue of pornography centers on its harmful repercussions at both individual and collective levels.

4.12 The Interplay Between Freedom of Expression and National Security

National security stands as a compelling exception to the cherished freedom of expression in Egypt, often seen as a crucial safeguard against potential threats to society's safety. Nevertheless, it must be emphasised that the protection of this vital national interest should never serve as a carte blanche for undue restrictions on free speech (Fahmi, 2012). While Article 47 of the Egyptian Constitution upholds the right to express opinions, it underscores the importance of exercising this right within the bounds of the law, thus preserving room for constructive criticism that bolsters the nation. Moreover, in extraordinary circumstances such as a state of emergency or war, the Constitution acknowledges that limited censorship may be imposed, solely for reasons of public safety or safeguarding national security (The Constitution of Egypt, 1971).

According to Egyptian law, decisions pertaining to national security possess a considerable level of discretion, presumably owing to the government's expertise in handling intricate security issues. Nonetheless, the government bears the responsibility of furnishing a convincing rationale for any limitations imposed on freedom of expression that purportedly aim to safeguard national security. Such restrictions must not only align with the explicit provisions of Egyptian law but also demonstrate their essential role in preserving national security, adhering to the principles articulated in Article 47 and 48 of the Egyptian Constitution (Awad, 2011). A telling case, exemplifying this precarious balance between national security concerns and constitutional rights, is Case 7741 of Year 57 (February 4, 2003). Here, the Court unreservedly refuted the Ministry of the Interior's contention that a peaceful demonstration might pose an insidious threat to national security. In an intricate display of judicial scrutiny, the Court methodically assessed the Ministry's failure to substantiate the necessity of restraining the demonstration to protect national security interests, thereby bolstering the constitutional sanctity of freedom of expression for all citizens and demonstrators (Administrative Court Case 7741, 2003).

While delving into a comprehensive analysis of cases involving the protection of national security, an array of conclusions springs forth. Principally, the formulation of legally restricting freedom of expression within the context of national security defies any standardised blueprint; rather, the multiplicity of cases necessitates scrupulous consideration of specific situational factors and the meticulous interplay of manifold considerations. Secondly, the sway of freedom of expression may be confined in situations where its unbridled exercise substantively poses palpable threats to national security, justifying prudent limitations. Thirdly, the onus rests squarely on the Egyptian government to furnish cogent justifications for any curtailments it seeks to impose on speech, thereby steering clear of arbitrary restrictions that might encroach upon constitutional liberties. Lastly, Egyptian Courts exhibit an unwavering commitment to the essence and substance of the expression being restricted, transcending mere formalities and adeptly distinguishing between benign, peaceable speech and language steeped in incitement or advocacy of nefarious terrorist activities. Overarching this intricate discourse on the limitations of freedom of expression vis-à-vis national security lies the unequivocal constitutional commitment of Egypt to the preservation and protection of this fundamental right.

4.13 Freedom of Speech, Public Demonstrations and the Rule of Law

Freedom of expression in Egypt goes beyond conventional speech and also encompasses processions and protests, which play a significant role in public discourse. Nevertheless, this right is not absolute, and restrictions may apply when such demonstrations pose genuine risks to national security or human safety. These demonstrations serve as potent vehicles for public opinions and sentiments, wherein individuals gather to voice their dissent or support for particular causes, employing various means of expression, including direct speech like spoken words and written messages, as well as symbolic acts like gestures and signs. The democratic ethos embedded within the Egyptian Constitution has consistently underscored the significance of allowing citizens to organize and engage in peaceful public meetings and gatherings, a principle evident from the earliest iterations of the constitution in 1923 (The Constitution of Egypt, 2014). Even the more recent 2014 Constitution firmly reiterates the people's entitlement to partake in public events, marches, demonstrations, and other forms of peaceful protests, firmly stipulating the prohibition of carrying weapons during such activities. In parallel, this legal framework places constraints on the intervention of security forces, expressly forbidding them from monitoring, attending, or eavesdropping on these gatherings, thereby reinforcing the value of an open and participatory public sphere.

The intrinsic value of allowing unfettered public demonstrations and processions in a society that cherishes democratic principles cannot be overstated. Such freedoms enable citizens to assert their viewpoints, participate actively in societal discourse, and hold public authorities accountable. Consequently, any endeavors to suppress or curtail these avenues of peaceful expression would inherently infringe upon the foundational right to freedom of speech. Emphasising the weight of this right, Egyptian law accords substantial protection to processions and protests, meticulously defining their scope and purpose (Egypt Law No.107, 2013). The present study endeavors to unravel the nuanced jurisprudential approach embraced by Egyptian law in navigating the intricate terrain between safeguarding free speech and acknowledging the sacrosanctity of the right to engage in peaceful protests and processions.

The Supreme Constitutional Court acknowledges the significance of citizens expressing their opinions freely, provided it falls within the boundaries defined by the law (Supreme Constitutional Court, Case No 37 of Judicial Year 11, 1993). However, when such expression endangers the rights, reputation of others, or threatens national security and public order, the SCC considers it a violation of Article 73 of the Constitution. The court argues that restrictions in such cases are necessary to safeguard national security and uphold the judiciary's authority. This analysis delves into the potential restrictions on processions and protests under Egyptian law. Case No 232 of Judicial Year 36 (decided on 7 May 2017) is illustrative, where the applicant participated in an unlawful demonstration that posed threats to public interests. The applicant and others were charged and sentenced to imprisonment and fines under the Presidential Law No 107/2013 for organizing peaceful public meetings and processions. The SCC upheld the conviction, asserting that it was justified to protect national security and public interest (Supreme Constitutional Court, Case No 232 of Judicial Year 36, 2017). The court's decision underscores the importance of practicing free expression within legal limits.

A similar scenario involved the 6 Oct group, charged with unlawful procession leading to attacks on police and destruction of property, resulting in a three-year prison sentence. The applicants appealed, highlighting the importance of the right to freedom of expression and engagement in processions and demonstrations. Nonetheless, the Court of Cassation ruled in favor of the punishment, as the actions of the demonstrators genuinely threatened national security and public interests, in line with Article 7 of the Law 107/2013. The court thereby reaffirmed the authority of public institutions to restrict freedom of expression when it surpasses its permissible boundaries, ultimately dismissing the appeal.

The Court of Cassation found itself entangled in a web of appeals, wherein individuals had been accused by the administrative authority under Article 32 of the Punishment Law for engaging in unlawful demonstrations that posed a palpable threat to national security and public interests. Undeterred by the complexity of the cases before it, the Court embarked on a rigorous analysis, steadfastly embracing the rule of law as its guiding principle. With a commitment to justice, the Court discerned that the pertinent judgment harmoniously met the stringent criteria governing the restriction of demonstrations. The Court adroitly invoked the margin of appreciation, conclusively determining that the reasons underpinning the punitive measures were equitable, fitting the contours of proportionality. The Court saw the restrictions and penalties as vital protections for public interests and national security, crucial for supporting democratic ideals. With firm conviction, the Court decisively rejected the appeals (Supreme Constitutional Court, Case No 232 of Judicial Year 36, 2017).

These cases highlight the legal protection afforded to processions and protests. However, this fundamental right is not unrestricted, as limitations may be imposed to safeguard interests related to national security and public or private property. Achieving a delicate balance in a democratic society requires that any restrictions be reasonable, crafted with proportionality and necessity in mind. SCC Case No. 86 of Judicial Year 18, decided on 6 December 1997, serves as a guiding light, emphasising that governmental regulations must carefully balance the infringement on the right of association with the legitimacy, potency, and urgency of governmental interests and the means used to pursue those interests (Supreme Constitutional Court, Case No 86 of Judicial Year 18, 1997). Amidst this harmonious interplay of rights and restrictions, the right to free speech remains vigilant, protecting against slanderous accusations and insults while also safeguarding criticism aimed at public figures. Similarly, the right to protest stands firm, offering refuge only to peaceful gatherings that aim to express democratic ideals. In this intricate balance, the protection of processions and protests finds its foundation in reasoned deliberation, where restrictions, as demonstrated by the aforementioned cases, are justified and steadfast (Alsubaie, 2019).

4.14 Government Practices and Freedom of Speech in Egypt

The constitution guarantees freedom of expression, encompassing the press and other media members, with the exception of limited censorship during wartime or public mobilisation. However, this right is often disregarded by the government. Those advocating for human rights, journalists, activists and similar individuals regularly encounter legal action on charges believed to be a response to their government criticisms. As per the regulations, newspapers are mandated to produce their copies at approved printing facilities endorsed by the Supreme Council for Media Regulation. Online news websites are required to host their servers within the country's borders. Newspapers must furnish 20 copies of each printed edition to the council, while news websites and TV channels must maintain online copies of all published or broadcast materials for one year, submitting a monthly copy of their content to the council. The law also prohibits recording, filming, or conducting interviews in public areas with the intent to air them on a media platform without a permit granted by the council (Egypt Human Rights Report, 2022).

In the grim realm of violence and harassment, media reports and accounts from local and international human rights groups revealed a disturbing pattern of authorities employing intimidation tactics against journalists. In January 2022, banners were callously torn down, and employees were forcibly evicted from the Cairo Book Fair, following the closure of the Cairo and Alexandria libraries affiliated with the Arab Network for Research and Publishing. The chairman of the board for the network cited a litany of harassment, security restrictions, repeated visits by state security officers, detention of employees, and seizure of book shipments as reasons for the closure. In another distressing incident, journalist Mohamed Salah spent an alarming 29 months in detention without trial or formal charges before finally being released in April 2022. These individuals have endured harrowing abuse while in detention, reflecting the perils faced by journalists who endeavor to exercise their right to free expression (Egypt Human Rights Report, 2022). Such occurrences emphasise the imperative of vigilance and advocacy in safeguarding press freedom and freedom of expression within Egypt's media landscape.

Amidst the multifaceted realm of independent media, an intricate web of divergent perspectives emerged, yet their growth was persistently hindered by the formidable constraints imposed and the authoritative hand of censorship that occasionally descended.

Enshrined within the constitutional fabric, the penal code, and the media and publications law lay a labyrinthine set of guidelines that guided the conduct of media entities, often relegating them to dance within the boundaries of permissible discourse. Tightly gripped by the governmental reins, the licensing process for newspapers, even those privately owned, remained under stringent control, while the printing and distribution of most newspapers fell under the watchful gaze of state oversight, casting an overcast shadow upon the landscape of media independence.

On the thirtieth page, the narrative unveils the presence of the Supreme Council for Media Regulation (SCMR), an institution established according to the president's design, with members handpicked by him, granting it significant authority to influence the media landscape. The SCMR controls the issuance of licenses to favored media outlets and websites, while also blocking access to digital platforms, asserting control over the flow of information online. Moreover, it closely monitors media funding and scrutinises the content of media productions. State-owned media entities play a crucial role in echoing official government policies, acting as steadfast supporters of the government's agenda. The National Press Authority guides the editorial direction of stateowned print publications, while the Egyptian Radio and Television Union oversees programming on state-owned radio and television channels, exerting considerable influence over the narrative presented to the public. Despite occasional glimpses of criticism against government policies in both state-owned and private media, dissenting voices often struggle to be heard amidst a prevailing narrative that overwhelmingly endorses the president and his initiatives (Reuters Staff, 2018).

Throughout history, numerous rights groups and independent media advocates have emerged as staunch defenders of truth, unyielding in their pursuit of unmasking the shadowy specter of censorship that loomed large. In a report released in March 2022 by a local human rights group, the SCMR emerged as a formidable adversary, obstinate in its refusal to heed the pleas of privatelyowned news websites seeking the coveted licenses. Astonishingly, these websites had knocked at the SCMR's door, beseeching for recognition through license applications submitted more than three years prior, only to languish in a perpetual state of bureaucratic limbo. In April, the SCMR did grant licenses to several state-owned and privately-owned news websites. However, these actions seemed to be marred by political favoritism, where the appearance of transparency masked a darker reality. The licensing process, supposedly fair and transparent, was criticized as a mere facade meant to disadvantage opposition and independent websites, leaving them vulnerable without legal protections. Amidst these regulatory complexities, the struggle for free expression continued unabated. The media faced a daunting landscape, navigating through a maze of power dynamics and control mechanisms (Egypt Human Rights Report, 2022).

In May 2022, local media sources disseminated accounts of the United Media Services Company, a pro-government entity and the parent organisation of numerous media channels, orchestrating a rigid mandate. This directive castigated newspaper and television content managers, strictly forbidding any dissemination of news pertaining to the 'civil democratic movement' (CDM) in the run-up to the national dialogue. A distinguished cadre of opposition luminaries, led by the likes of Hamdeen Sabahi, a former contender for the presidency, Mohamed Anwar al-Sadat, at the helm of the Reform and Development Party, Ahmed al-Tantawi, guiding the al-Karama Party, and Akmal Kurtam, at the forefront of the Conservative Party, coalesced to form the very core of the CDM (Egypt Human Rights Report, 2022).

Subsequently, in June, Reporters Without Borders (RSF) unleashed a scathing exposé, unmasking a series of calculated maneuvers carried out by pro-government television personalities and media outlets under state jurisdiction. These parties stood accused of engineering and amplifying insidious 'smear campaigns' directed at journalists daring to critique the government. Such campaigns, it was disclosed, implicated pro-government presenters in casting aspersions upon journalists critical of official policy, accusing them of 'plotting against Egypt' and 'fomenting animosity towards the military'. The repercussions of these campaigns were manifold, instilling self-censorship and instilling trepidation amongst independent journalists, who harbored fears of arrest on nebulous charges such as 'traitors to the nation' or 'agents of chaos.'

Throughout the course of the year, law enforcement authorities apprehended a multitude of journalists, ensnaring them in the meshes of politically sensitive topics. While certain individuals were granted reprieve through subsequent releases, others remained ensconced in detention as the year reached its denouement. Notably, in the month of September, the spotlight fell upon three reporters affiliated with the independent news outlet Mada Masr. These journalists were slapped with grave accusations of 'spreading false news,' misusing social media, and vilifying members of the pro-government Nation's Future Party. Their predicament stemmed from an article that levied corruption allegations against party members, thereby entangling them in the legal web. Furthermore, the editor in chief of Mada Masr, Lina Attalah, faced the additional burden of operating a website without a license. Astonishingly, Mada Masr had applied for a license on several occasions since 2018, only to be met with resounding silence from the government. The outlet defended its journalistic endeavors by substantiating the information gleaned from multiple credible sources. Despite the defendants securing bail, the initiation of trials remained conspicuously absent as the year drew to a close. In a disconcerting case, the photojournalist, Hamdy al-Zaeem, languished in pretrial detention for 700 days, as his family persistently protested the paucity of evidence supporting his detention. Alarming echoes of the past reverberated, with authorities repeating the charges in a new case, following a similar ordeal he endured in 2016. A protracted period of pretrial detention persisted until 2018, only for him to be subjected to further precautionary measures, tethering him to regular reporting at a police station. However, his rearrest in 2021 marked an inescapable descent into the abyss of protracted detention, ensnared by unresolved charges of 'spreading false news,' misuse of social media, and promulgating the agenda of a terrorist organization. Persevering under the weight of these draconian charges, al-Zaeem's confinement remained unyielding at year's end, standing testament to the poignant struggle for justice and the urgent call for a fair and impartial adjudication (Agence France Presse, 2021).

In a judicial proceeding held in absentia, journalist Ahmed Taha, known to be associated with al-Jazeera, received a harsh sentence of 15 years behind bars and found his name added to Egypt's register of suspected terrorists. The charges levied against Taha included the dissemination of false information, endangerment of national interests, and compromising public safety and security. These allegations were rooted in an interview Taha conducted with a prominent opposition figure and former presidential candidate back in 2018. The verdict triggered widespread condemnation from seven human rights organisations, who voiced strong apprehensions about the fairness of not only Taha's trial but also those of the 23 other co-defendants entangled in the same case. Throughout the year, the government executed stringent measures, leading to the blockage of numerous websites, with over 129 news-related platforms, including notable ones like *Mada Masr*, *al-Manassa*, and *Daarb*. *Mada Masr*, in particular, took the matter to court in 2017, endeavoring to ascertain the rationale behind the censorship, but the case languished in the Justice Ministry's Authority of Experts for technical review since 2018, ultimately resulting in the continued inaccessibility of the website within Egypt.

The authorities resorted to blocking al-Manassa's website inside the country on multiple occasions, a distressing action undertaken no less than 13 times since 2017. In response to the latest incident, 28 local and international organisations joined forces to release a joint plea, urging the authorities to lift the ban on the news site. Regrettably, despite their united appeal, the website persisted in its inaccessible state throughout the year. During Egypt's hosting of the UN Climate Change Conference (COP27) in Sharm el-Sheikh, a temporary unblocking of some NGO and media websites took place, yet this brief reprieve was soon followed by reports of re-blocking shortly after the conclusion of the conference (Suliman & Francis, 2022).

Under the purview of the law, websites and social media accounts boasting a considerable following of 5000 or more subscribers were officially recognized as media outlets, thereby subjecting them to licensing fees and granting the Supreme Council for Media Regulation (SCMR) the extensive authority to oversee and block their content at will. In April, the SCMR wielded its power by issuing a series of 12 decisions to shut down and block various online platforms, encompassing websites, social media accounts, YouTube channels and applications. The grounds cited for these decisions ranged from alleged violations of media codes and standards to perceived deficiencies in licensing, all in accordance with a law from 2018 that governs the press and media. Among the allegations, the dissemination of false news, incitement to violence and hatred, and insulting individuals or religious beliefs featured prominently.

The climate of arrests connected to media activities and social media postings left a chilling effect on online expression. Activists and journalists candidly admitted to engaging in selfcensorship, consciously refraining from criticizing the government or expressing any semblance of sympathy towards banned entities like the Muslim Brotherhood due to the prevailing progovernment media atmosphere. Moreover, publishers exercised caution in releasing works that might incur criticism toward religious institutions, most notably al-Azhar, or pose challenges to Islamic doctrine. The looming specter of reprisals, ranging from prosecution to detention, loomed large over online journalists, prompting them to avoid broaching sensitive subject matters altogether.

Within the legal framework, libel, slander and defamation constituted criminal offenses, leading to strong accusations from rights campaigners that government authorities weaponized these laws to muzzle survivors of gender-based violence and their allies, with journalist Rasha Azab serving as a poignant illustration. Azab faced the daunting prospect of imprisonment and fines for her supportive social media posts standing in solidarity with women who accused film director Islam Azazi of sexual assault. However, the economic court in Cairo moved to quash these charges and the civil suit, effectively exonerating her in April. Within the borders of this nation, the act of voicing criticism towards religious beliefs stands as a grave offense, met with the harsh repercussions of severe punishment (Smith, 2022).

Several human rights organisations, both national and global in scope, have extensively documented a diverse array of occurrences where individuals have confronted allegations, endured legal procedures, and ultimately faced convictions under the much-debated blasphemy law. Although the bulk of these accusations have been targeted at Christians, it is not infrequent for Muslims to be ensnared in analogous charges. A striking instance revolves around one Marco Gerges, condemned to endure a five-year prison sentence under laborious conditions. This ruling, reinforced by the Appeals Chamber of Misdemeanors of the Economic Court in Cairo, found Gerges guilty of displaying contempt for Islam, transgressing against time-honored Egyptian family values, and, most significantly, propagating extremist ideologies under the guise of religious discourse. However, the defense adamantly argued that the evidence marshaled against Gerges, encompassing private messages replete with explicit imagery and religious comments on his phone, bore no substantive connection to the charges at hand. Their plea emphasised that none of this content was ever intended for public consumption, further contending that the entire investigation and subsequent prosecution were instigated through an unlawful and intrusive search (Egyptian Initiative for Personal Rights, 2022).

Meanwhile, the country's governing authorities have firmly asserted their control over matters of national security, notably empowered by laws that enable government censors to obstruct the flow of intelligence-related information. To bolster their efforts, the establishment of hotlines has expedited the reporting of instances deemed to constitute 'false news,' ostensibly representing a menacing threat to the state's security. The specter of penalties looms large for those found culpable of deliberately disseminating such information, potentially incurring hefty fines ranging from 5000 to 20,000 Egyptian pounds.

Amidst this environment of restriction, human rights organisations and legal advocates have resolutely spoken out against the government's cynical deployment of terrorism charges, an ostensibly potent tool to silence dissenters and curtail freedom of expression. Individuals daring to engage in open discussions on various media platforms, daring to broach subjects as seemingly innocuous as the Grand Ethiopian Renaissance Dam or venturing to share satirical content on TikTok, have all too often found themselves summarily accused of affiliating with terrorist groups or spreading spurious information. The predictable outcome entails swift arrests, long-term detentions, and a sense of stifled creativity and expression that blights once-promising careers.

Efforts to control the flow of information extend to strategic issuance of restraining orders, preventing media coverage of court cases that may carry even the faintest hint of sensitivity regarding national security matters. Nonetheless, such measures have consistently incurred criticism from rights groups, alleging that they are often strategically misused to shield government, police, and military officials from the prying eyes of public scrutiny. The purported reasoning, often dressed in the garb of safety and security concerns, selectively restricts media access to certain regions, with North Sinai being a hotbed for such tactics, where reports of widespread abuses and stifling repression abound.

4.15 Internet Freedom

The constitution unequivocally safeguards citizens from arbitrary interference with their internet communications, forbidding the government from interrupting, disconnecting, or depriving them of access to online platforms without due cause. Telecommunications services and internet providers are subject to regulation under the telecommunication regulation law, overseen by the National Telecommunications Regulatory Authority. However, concerns arise as this regulatory body lacks independence from government influence. As a result, the authorities maintain a tight grip over the internet infrastructure and fiber-optic cables, endowing them with the power to control user access, censor online content, and even surveil social media accounts and internet usage. Law enforcement agencies exhibit a willingness to limit individuals' internet access, with potential investigation and prosecution awaiting those who dare to post content considered objectionable (Country Reports on Human Rights Practices in Egypt, 2020).

To combat the menace of terrorism, the nation has introduced a counterterrorism law that deems the use of the internet to promote terrorist acts or disseminate deceptive information related to terrorism cases as criminal offenses. This legislation empowers the public prosecutor and investigators to monitor and record online communications among terrorism suspects for a period of 30 days, renewable indefinitely, without any specified maximum duration. The government has also enacted a cybercrime law that bestows broad authority upon investigating authorities to order the blocking of any website they deem to harbor criminal content or present a threat to national security or the country's economic interests. In its efforts to disrupt terrorist communication networks, the government resorts to cutting mobile services, internet connections, and sometimes landlines. This approach, however, has the unintended consequence of also severing civilian communication channels in the affected areas.

The unfolding saga of digital liberties in this nation paints a stark picture, illustrating the tight constraints imposed on internet users. A network of website blockades, content removals, punitive measures, intimidation and surveillance has created an environment of self-censorship, stifling expression within Egyptian cyberspace. At the center of this complex digital terrain, the case of TikTok influencer Haneen Hossam symbolizes the government's relentless scrutiny. Initially sentenced to a decade-long imprisonment on charges of human trafficking, her penalty was subsequently reduced to three years, accompanied by a substantial fine of EGP 200,000 ($8060) (MEE Staff, 2022). Her offense involves the encouragement of young women to embark on video content creation as a means of livelihood. This contentious ruling has ignited a debate among local and international advocates, yet her appeal before the Court of Cassation remains ensnared in a web of uncertainty.

In tandem with this narrative, another legal saga unfolds with TikTok personalities Sherifa Rifaat and her daughter Zumoroda, affectionately known as 'Sherry Hanim.' Accused of 'inciting impropriety' and 'propagating indecency' through their expressive dance videos on social media, they were initially burdened with an onerous six-year sentence, later ameliorated to five years. Their appeal before the Court of Cassation faced jurisdictional hurdles, making their quest for justice an uphill battle. Within the intricate fabric of the digital world, unsettling stories emerge, revealing authorities' tactics to monitor social media and dating platforms. These encounters often result in arrests, leaving the possibility of prosecution uncertain. Section 6 of the detailed report delves into acts of violence, criminalisation and other abuses, shedding light on victimisation based on sexual orientation, gender identity, expression, or sex characteristics. Additionally, the government's influence extends to internet messaging apps, with intermittent control measures like temporarily blocking features such as WhatsApp's calling functionality (Country Report on Human Rights Practices in Egypt, 2021).

Against this backdrop of digital controls, a coalition of media rights organisations raised their voices on the government's persistent campaign to block hundreds of websites, including 129 news outlets. This blanket censorship extends its reach to international NGOs, local human rights defenders and various virtual private network services. Clearly, these restrictions are aimed at curbing critical government coverage or stifling antigovernment political activities and demonstrations. Though some websites experienced fleeting liberation during the COP27 event in November, they were promptly ensnared again once the conference concluded, leaving the landscape of internet access fraught with uncertainty.

As per information reported by local media, the Supreme Council for Media Regulation granted a significant number of licenses in June to certain media platforms believed by many to be aligned with the government's perspectives. However, numerous independent websites and news platforms are still waiting for their licenses, enduring prolonged delays that can extend for years. Turning our attention to academic freedom and cultural events, there have been accounts of the government imposing restrictions. Notably, authorities have taken measures to erase any mention of the country's transformative 2011 and 2013 revolutions from high school history curricula, aligning their actions with a decree issued by the Ministry of Education and Technical Education in 2017.

According to reports from media outlets and local rights groups, academics have been practicing self-censorship akin to that observed among nonacademic commentators, especially when engaging in public discourse about politically and socioeconomically sensitive matters. This culture of cautiousness has even extended to university faculty members and Ministry of Education employees, who now need to seek approval from security agencies before traveling abroad for academic or professional purposes. Similarly, faculty and officials associated with public universities and research centers must obtain explicit permission from the Ministry of Foreign Affairs for any international travel, irrespective of the purpose.

In certain public educational institutions, access for foreign speakers or delegations to campus was subject to restrictions, while delegations of university students traveling abroad were required to have faculty chaperones. Academic professionals and scholars outside the country, together with rights groups, issued a series of statements and reports highlighting the numerous challenges faced by academics in Egypt and those conducting research on sensitive subjects from abroad. A comprehensive report by a local rights group in January investigated the plight of academics studying and working overseas, revealing the array of pressures they encountered, including the threat of arrest, convictions, and travel bans imposed on researchers, along with the added burden of family members being targeted in the country or abroad. An alarming July 2021 statement from the minister of immigration underscored the perceived danger posed by students abroad, due to their purported exposure to false ideologies propagated by hostile entities against the nation (Country Reports on Human Rights Practices in Egypt, 2020).

The Middle East Studies Association expressed deep concern over the consistent assault on academic freedom. It brought attention to the situation where some detained academics remained in pretrial detention, while others faced trial on what were deemed 'baseless' charges. Authorities further imposed travel bans and curtailed the movements of academic researchers within the country, even after court proceedings were concluded. In a notable case, the Cairo Criminal Court issued a suspended sentence of one year of hard labor and imposed a fine of EGP 20,000 ($725) on Cairo University media professor Ayman Mansour Nada for charges of insulting a member of the SCMR. Nada's initial arrest in September 2021 was a result of his critical remarks concerning the government-appointed president of Cairo University and government-aligned media professionals. However, he was later released in November of the same year, and the court dismissed other charges against him, including allegations of 'spreading false news.'

In September 2021, the Supreme Administrative Court dismissed an appeal requesting the reinstatement of Mona Prince, a faculty member at Suez University. Reports from the media indicate that the university terminated her employment in 2018 after she shared video clips of herself dancing and encouraging her students to do the same. The court justified its decision by stating that such videos undermined the prestige of a university professor. Additionally, the court cited Prince's deviation from the approved curriculum and her failure to adhere to accepted religious doctrines while teaching John Milton's 'Paradise Lost.' It asserted that her teaching methods contradicted religious principles and consequently restricted academic freedom. Cultural events also faced censorship. As per a decree by the Prime Minister, it became unlawful to organise a special event or festival without obtaining prior permission from the Ministry of Culture and liaising with relevant state entities. This requirement added to the existing regulations that necessitated organizations to obtain permits from the Ministry of Culture's Censorship Board, as well as permits from the Interior Ministry and the respective artists' union for concerts, performances and other cultural activities. The Ministry of Culture was granted the authority to approve all scripts and final productions of plays and films. It exercised censorship over foreign films to be screened in theaters, but interestingly, the same films were not subjected to censorship when sold as DVDs.

In relation to the arts, the Musicians Syndicate, which has close ties to the government, prohibited non-member artists from performing in the country. However, on January 17, the syndicate reversed a decision from 2021 that had banned singers of Mahraganat music, a popular genre previously considered objectionable for allegedly promoting sex, drugs, and 'depravity,' according to media reports. Amidst the grandeur of the 53rd Cairo International Book Fair, an unexpected turn of events unfolded for the *Asir al-Kutub* publishing house. Without any explicit reason or justification, the management of the book fair rejected their participation, as the firm asserted. Media allegations had surfaced, insinuating that the publishing house was involved in releasing books and materials authored by Islamists (MEE Staff, 2021).

In response to this unfavorable development, the publishing house took swift action. Company officials reviewed all their religious heritage publications, leaving no stone unturned. Their aim was to ensure the absence of any content that could be construed as endorsing 'religious extremism.' Taking a proactive approach, they promptly removed a significant number of books from their electronic platform in an attempt to rectify any potential misconceptions. However, the repercussions of this situation extended beyond *Asir al-Kutub*. Six days after the commencement of the book fair, the River Nile Center for Publishing, a fellow participant, announced its unexpected withdrawal from the event (El-Naggar, 2022). The firm stated that authorities provided no reason or documentation to justify their removal from the exhibition. Meanwhile, in March, an Alexandria Economic Court delivered a verdict against two renowned singers, Hamo Beeka and Omar Kamal. The court found them culpable of violating family values and profiting from a video that featured dancing and singing alongside a Brazilian belly dancer. The artists were sentenced to one year in prison and an EGP 10,000 ($403) fine each. Interestingly, the court offered an alternative to suspend the prison sentences if they agreed to pay an additional EGP 10,000 ($403) fee (Egypt Today Staff, 2022).

4.16 The Exercise of Freedom of Expression Online in Egypt

The digital landscape in Egypt witnessed a profound transformation with the emergence of blogs and social media. On one hand, these platforms offered a newfound sense of freedom and security for self-expression, leading to a significant rise in blog visitors (Abdulla, 2013). A considerable percentage of Egyptian blogs attracted substantial traffic, drawing attention to the absence of censorship in the blogosphere. However, this newfound liberty also caught the state's eye, leading to concerns about unregulated content. Despite these challenges, social media became a potent tool for dissenters, enabling them to expose government corruption, police brutality, and injustices. The role of social media in mobilising and coordinating the 2011 revolution cannot be underestimated. Even after the revolution, online activism in Egypt remained vibrant, with the internet serving as a crucial platform to publish and document human rights violations (Abdulla, 2014). Mosireen and Kazeboon are prominent examples of digital activism platforms, with the former documenting protests and police/army brutality, while the latter organized public screenings of Mosireen's videos (Abdulla, 2014).

Furthermore, news websites emerged as significant channels for freedom of expression amid the post-revolution polarisation. Unlike social media, news websites faced less regulation and censorship, offering an alternative to the state-controlled print and broadcast media (Abdulla, 2014). However, despite the strides made in digital expression, the Freedom House's 'Freedom on the Net' report rated Egypt's internet freedom as "not free" between 2014 and 2017, with a notable increase in violations of users' rights during 2012 to 2017. While social media and political content remained unblocked between 2011 and 2014, reports of arrests and prosecutions of bloggers, human rights activists and internet users for alleged offenses were rampant.

4.17 Internet Filtering, Censorship and Surveillance

In May 2017, in response to terrorist attacks, Egypt implemented a state of emergency, granting presidential powers to monitor private communications and social media without any judicial oversight. This move marked a significant shift in online censorship in the country (Information and Decision Support Center-IDSC, 2008). Several news websites critical of the government, including Mada Masr, Al-Jazeera and Huffington Post's Arabic websites, were suddenly blocked, accusing them of spreading false news and supporting terrorism, without any official statement. By September 2017, the number of blocked websites surged to 432, even including news agencies and human rights organizations (Fathy, 2018, p. 97). During the aftermath, the UN Special Rapporteurs raised red flags about the opacity surrounding the blocking procedure and the dearth of substantiating evidence, asserting that these actions ran afoul of internationally recognised human rights norms. The Human Rights Council's 36th session also became a platform to denounce Egypt's predicament, with Zeid Ra'ad al-Hussein painting a somber picture of human rights in the country and 40 other nations, using terms like 'dark and dangerous.' Regarding internet surveillance in Egypt, Citizen Lab at the University of Toronto reported the installation of Blue Coat ProxySG on public and government networks in January 2013. This device is known for filtering, censorship and surveillance, raising serious concerns about potential violations of basic human rights.

4.18 Egypt's Human Rights Spectrum: Global Recognition and Local Realities

Egypt's commitment to human rights is prominently displayed through its ratification of not just one, but an impressive total of eight fundamental international human rights conventions. This firm dedication serves as a clear demonstration of the nation's comprehensive and allencompassing acceptance of human rights principles on a global level, surpassing mere symbolic gestures and affirming a profound determination to safeguard and defend these essential rights. Moreover, Egypt's fervent and impassioned engagement extends well beyond mere acceding to conventions. The nation's proactive involvement in the establishment and reinforcement of international human rights mechanisms within the esteemed forum of the United Nations further amplifies its role as a dedicated and influential advocate for human rights causes. As a recurrent participant in the esteemed Human Rights Council and through the election of a significant number of Egyptian experts to influential human rights treaty bodies, Egypt assumes a pivotal role in fortifying the efficacy of these bodies and championing the relentless advancement of human rights advocacy. Such unwavering dedication is a testament to Egypt's enduring commitment to the noble cause of safeguarding human rights and upholding the inherent dignity and freedom of every individual worldwide. Not confining its efforts solely to the global arena, Egypt has extended its human rights endeavors to the regional level. By actively joining conventions within the Arab and African human rights systems, Egypt has reinforced its commitment to safeguarding human rights within its own regional sphere. Its proactive and influential role within the framework of joint international action underscores its determination to address crucial human rights issues that affect not only Egypt but also other developing nations. These issues include the urgent challenges posed by racism, xenophobia, and other pressing concerns that impact the collective well-being of nations (State Information Service, 2022).

The United Nations laid the foundation for the protection and promotion of human rights. The creation of the UN Charter, which included multiple texts highlighting the significance of human rights, marked a significant milestone for human rights groups and activists. The 'Universal Declaration of Human Rights' in 1948 was widely praised and endorsed by 48 nations, including Egypt. This declaration underscored the fundamental rights of individuals and marked a new era in global acknowledgment of human rights. Another notable development took place with the introduction of 'The two International Covenants on Human Rights of 1966.' One covenant, the 'International Covenant on Civil and Political Rights,' focused on protecting civil liberties, while the other, the 'International Covenant on Economic, Cultural, and Social Rights,' aimed to support economic, cultural, and social well-being. Egypt has demonstrated a strong commitment to preserving human rights by actively participating in numerous international and regional conventions dedicated to this cause. The nation has also played a key role in shaping the 'Universal Declaration of Human Rights' and remains engaged in international human rights law (Cairo Declaration on Human Rights in Islam, 1990).

Throughout history, Egypt has consistently made formal promises to uphold human rights and has demonstrated its endorsement by signing various international conventions and declarations that champion the principles of freedom of expression. Nevertheless, the actual implementation of these rights often falls short of the ideals propagated on the global stage. A notable concern revolves around the existence of ambiguous and vague laws that grant authorities extensive powers to restrict freedom of expression under the pretext of preserving national security and public order. These laws have been selectively wielded to target dissenters and individuals voicing critical opinions, thereby fostering an atmosphere of fear and self-censorship among journalists, activists, and ordinary citizens. The anti-terrorism laws in Egypt have encountered substantial criticism attributable to their perplexing and convoluted phrasing (United Nations Human Rights, 2020). This ambiguity leaves room for authorities to potentially exploit the pretext of counterterrorism efforts as a cloak to target individuals and organizations expressing disapproval or opposition to the government. As a consequence of this lack of clarity, profound inquiries have emerged concerning the underlying motives driving the establishment of these laws, particularly in light of their misuse to suppress political dissent and impose restraint on critics. Consequently, a prevailing sentiment has emerged, questioning whether these laws are genuinely directed at safeguarding national security or if they are rather wielded as a mechanism to curb dissenting voices and impede the free exercise of speech.

As a result, Egypt's genuine dedication to preserving freedom of expression and safeguarding individual rights has been subjected to close examination. While bold proclamations may resonate on the global platform, the actual situation presents a contrasting landscape, characterised by a lack of substantial actions to protect these core liberties. This conspicuous divergence between rhetoric and implementation raises doubts about the authenticity of Egypt's commitment to human rights and its true inclination to foster an environment where diverse voices can thrive freely and without fear of retribution (Abdelmonsef, 2018).

Media control presents a significant and prevailing concern in Egypt's context. The ownership or control of major media outlets by government-linked entities curtails the diversity of perspectives, instigating an environment of self-censorship among journalists. This stifles their capacity to report critically on sensitive subjects and government affairs. Furthermore, internet freedom and social media platforms have not remained exempt from constraints. The government has imposed restrictions on online content, blocking websites that critique the administration and prosecuting individuals expressing dissenting views in the virtual realm. The Cybercrime Law in Egypt empowers authorities to regulate online content perceived as jeopardizing national security or public order. In spite of the lack of precise delineations regarding the parameters of a perceived threat, Egypt has resorted to targeting journalists, activists and social media users who dare to express opposing viewpoints on digital platforms. Moreover, the employment of Egypt's defamation laws as instruments to repress criticism and dissent has culminated in the imposition of legal repercussions upon individuals who dare to articulate their perspectives on matters pertaining to public figures or governmental policies. The vague language in these laws allows authorities to construe any form of criticism as defamatory, thereby inducing self-censorship among journalists and media outlets.

In Egypt, defamation laws have been employed to target individuals who dare to express critical views concerning public figures, including government officials and politicians. The opacity surrounding the precise definition of defamation enables authorities to construe expressions of criticism as assaults on the reputation of public figures, subsequently instigating legal actions against journalists or activists who voice dissenting opinions (Amnesty International, 2010). Online users have not been exempt from the reach of defamation laws in Egypt, with social media users facing similar charges for their expressed views. The ambiguous language in these laws empowers authorities to interpret online posts or comments as defamatory, resulting in arrests or prosecutions. Moreover, independent media outlets that adopt a critical stance against the government or influential entities may find themselves entangled in defamation lawsuits, posing a potential deterrent to investigative reporting and media freedom. The elusive nature of the laws empowers authorities to utilize defamation charges as tools to coerce media outlets and journalists into exercising self-censorship. It is important to note that Egypt's defamation laws are not solely restricted to cases involving public figures, as they can be applied to instances involving nonpublic figures, enabling individuals to face legal repercussions for articulating critical opinions about private individuals or entities. The language employed in these defamation laws lacks precision and lucidity, leaving ample room for subjective interpretations and selective enforcement. The terms "insult," "defamation," and "damaging reputation" remain ill-defined, granting authorities wide-ranging latitude in their application and implementation.

The enactment of the Protest Law in Egypt in 2013 has engendered a protracted and contentious debate, casting a disquieting pallor over the realm of freedom of expression and the right to peaceful assembly (Hamzawy, 2016). This legislation imposes stringent constraints on public gatherings and demonstrations by mandating that organisers first secure official authorisation from the authorities prior to orchestrating any protest. Such a precondition has not been immune to sharp criticism, with detractors vehemently decrying the onerous bureaucratic impediments it introduces, raising fears that it confers upon the government an unfettered discretion to withhold permission for peaceful protests at its own behest. Moreover, the Protest Law further exacerbates apprehensions by endowing the authorities with discretionary prerogatives to prohibit or disperse protests based on a labyrinthine mélange of nebulous and ill-defined criteria, such as the specter of 'threatening public order' or 'disrupting traffic.' This prolix language in the legislation permits a broad array of interpretations, affording the authorities an undue license to construe even the nonviolent demonstrations as a menacing threat to public order, thereby affording them the pretext to employ forceful tactics to disband protesters. Regrettably, these heavy-handed measures have, on numerous occasions, culminated in lamentable clashes and untoward arrests.

The opaque nature of the criteria for dispersing protests has engendered a profoundly stifling and chilling impact on the right to peaceful assembly. A climate of trepidation has taken root among activists and protesters, fraught with anxiety that their gatherings might inadvertently be deemed illegal, potentially precipitating their apprehension and the levying of charges against them. Consequently, this chilling effect has resulted in a worrisome and alarming hesitancy among individuals and groups, discouraging them from unreservedly exercising their cherished right to free expression and peaceably articulating their grievances. On numerous occasions, peaceful demonstrations encompassing diverse advocacies, ranging from human rights and social justice to political reform, have encountered dispersion at the hands of security forces, ostensibly under the guise of preserving public order. Curiously, the peaceful nature of these gatherings notwithstanding, authorities have perceived them through the prism of potential sources of social upheaval and, in response, wielded force as a tool for their dispersal. Somewhat disconcertingly, within the purview of the nebulous criterion of "disrupting traffic," protesters have found themselves enmeshed in arrests and charged, even when their actions bore no semblance of actual endangerment to public safety. The astonishingly pliant construal of this term bestows upon authorities the capability to quash demonstrations that possess the capacity to garner public attention, even if their impact on society is insubstantial.

It is imperative to underscore that the arm of the Protest Law has extended its reach to encompass the domain of online protests and virtual gatherings, wherein activists and social media users voicing dissenting views or orchestrating online campaigns have found themselves ensnared in legal quagmires by dint of the loosely defined criterion of 'disrupting public order.' As an egregious illustration, individuals sharing posts or images critical of the government have found themselves subjected to arrest and legal prosecution. Intriguingly, the prerequisite of obtaining authorities' imprimatur before holding a protest endows them with discretionary leeway to imperiously repudiate permits at their own whim. The dearth of definitive guidelines for granting permits has created a conducive milieu for arbitrary denials, even when the tenor of the demonstration aspires towards peaceable and lawful conduct. Conspicuously, demonstrations countenancing opposition to specific governmental policies or actions have faced draconian reprisals in the form of forceful dispersal and resultant arrests, all premised upon the indistinct and elastic criterion of 'threatening public order.' Evidently, this has engendered a most chilling and inhibitory impact, one that impels citizens to refrain from openly articulating dissenting views and partaking in public demonstrations (Hamzawy, 2016).

Within the matrix of such ambiguous criteria, there have been disquieting instances wherein peaceful protests have been met with forceful dispersion and protesters have been ensnared in the clutches of arrests and legal entanglements, even when their aspirations espoused peace and goodwill. The dearth of clearly delineated boundaries endows the government with the prerogative to construe any manifestation of dissent or critique as an ominous peril to public order, thereby occasioning a disheartening curtailment of the right to peaceful assembly and the hallowed mantle of freedom of expression. The nebulous nature of the criteria within Egypt's legal framework gives rise to impediments in accountability and transparency during the enforcement of the law. With the absence of unequivocal standards, oversight and legal scrutiny of the government's actions in dispersing protests remain limited. This opacity in the process can precipitate abuses of power and human rights violations, as authorities seize the opportunity to exploit the imprecise language for stifling dissent and opposition (Michaelson, 2018).

Furthermore, the ambiguity inherent in the criteria engenders a climate of trepidation and intimidation among citizens, dissuading them from partaking in public demonstrations out of fear of repercussions for exercising their sacrosanct right to free expression. This prevailing atmosphere of uncertainty discourages individuals and groups from engaging in peaceable protests, thereby restricting avenues for civic engagement and impeding the vibrant democratic discourse essential for a participatory and flourishing society. Under the pretext of national security, Egypt's legal landscape harbors ill-defined provisions that have been wielded as tools to target government critics or those dissenting against its policies. The dearth of precise definitions and discernible criteria pertaining to what indeed constitutes a threat to national security furnishes authorities with considerable latitude to subjectively construe and apply the law, leading to capricious arrests, detentions, and prosecutions. The litany of vague provisions includes charges of "spreading false news," "inciting violence," and "undermining national unity," lacking perspicuous boundaries that enable authorities to interpret them in a sweeping manner to encompass a wide array of dissenting activities, ranging from peaceable protests and social media posts to critical reportage.

The Cybercrime Law grapples with a challenging conundrum—the criminalisation of disseminating 'false news' online sans a coherent and definitive demarcation, resulting in a shifting provision (Egypt Today Staff, 2022). This clause has metamorphosed into an all-pervasive tool wielded by the authorities to scrutinize, stigmatize and apprehend journalists and individuals audacious enough to voice dissenting perspectives on social media platforms, engendering an alarming surge of arrests and detentions. Similarly, the Cybercrime Law's proscription on inciting violence bears the indelible imprint of ambiguity, rendering it susceptible to diverse and expansive interpretations. The inherent lack of precision has bestowed upon the authorities the latitude to exploit this amorphous terrain, leading to the apprehension of activists and ordinary citizens for merely articulating criticisms of governmental policies.

Simultaneously, the imprecise charge of 'undermining national unity' has been adroitly wielded as a cudgel against political adversaries and government critics, capitalising on the law's veritable dearth of lucidity. This inherent deficiency has engendered a fertile ground for subjective interpretations, thus empowering the authorities to effectuate the arrest and detention of individuals for simply exercising their constitutionally enshrined right to express opinions on sensitive matters. Given the multifaceted repercussions arising from the Cybercrime Law's complex provisions, the indomitable spirits of journalists, activists and human rights defenders, fortified by their resolve to challenge government policies and lay bare human rights violations, have invariably become entangled in the intricate threads of legal retribution, besieged by allegations of jeopardizing national security. The implementation of these vague clauses has sent ripples of anxiety resonating throughout the social fabric, enveloping freedom of speech and expression in uncertainty. This environment has, in turn, sown seeds of pervasive self-censorship, instilling a profound trepidation among citizens who now tread cautiously, dreading the potential repercussions that might befall them for daring to openly articulate their perspectives (Egypt Today Staff, 2022a).

Furthermore, the opaqueness surrounding the utilisation of these regulations has enabled the authorities to quell political dissent and muzzle dissenting voices without adequate substantiation. The imprecise nature of the allegations places individuals in a precarious position, hampering their ability to mount a defense against accusations, given the nebulous bounds of acceptable discourse, which lie open to the authorities' subjective interpretation. Moreover, the pretext of safeguarding national security has been wielded to rationalise prolonged periods of pre-trial detention, the denial of access to legal counsel and the orchestration of secretive judicial proceedings, thereby stripping individuals of their entitlement to due process and a just trial. These actions have ignited substantial apprehensions over potential human rights violations and the gradual erosion of the foundations of justice within Egypt's legal infrastructure.

The misapplication of these loosely defined stipulations in the context of the national security pretext has garnered substantial rebuke from international human rights entities and foreign governments. Such actors have vocalised grave concern over the constriction of space for uninhibited expression and the curtailment of political opposition in Egypt. This has led to an urgent and collective plea for a more explicit delineation of what constitutes threats to national security, as well as a resolute endeavor to ensure that these statutes are not exploited to curb authentic dissent and constructive criticism of the government's actions and policies.

4.19 Conclusion

Egypt's constitution guarantees the right to freedom of speech and expression, but there are also differences in how these rights are upheld and exercised. Despite having signed international human rights treaties, Egypt not has been able to fully implement the promise of these rights in its own society. A number of confusing and sweeping legislation, like the Protest Law and the Defamation Law, have been used to restrict the freedom of speech and the right to peaceful assembly, which has caused journalists, activists, and individuals to self-censor and feel afraid. Concerns over arbitrary arrests and the limitation of freedom of expression have been exacerbated by the use of national security as a cover to target opposing voices (Hamzawy, 2016). These concerns necessitate urgent attention, prompting both nations to adopt resolute measures that nurture and protect the realm of freedom of speech and expression. For the cultivation of an environment conducive to open and unrestrained public dialogue, it might be prudent to embark on a journey of reform, reimagining convoluted and vague statutes while also revisiting, altering, or even nullifying repressive legislations. A paramount stride towards ensuring unbiased and equitable legal interpretations of fundamental liberties entails bolstering the autonomy and impartiality of the judiciary.

A flourishing democratic fabric demands nurturing, entailing the cultivation of a culture characterised by tolerance and reverence for divergent perspectives. To incubate an environment that cherishes spirited public discourse and the exchange of ideas, it becomes imperative for the government of Egypt to actively forge partnerships with journalists, activists, and civil society entities. Through collaborative efforts, a crucible of support can be forged, fostering an atmosphere that embraces the vigorous exchange of thoughts while safeguarding the integrity of these fundamental freedoms. Fostering improvements in the realm of freedom of speech and expression within Egypt necessitates comprehensive endeavors involving both governmental bodies and civil society groups. The complexities of this issue demand a holistic approach rather than a segmented one. A fundamental transformation can be attained through a series of strategic actions, applicable to both nations. One of the pivotal steps involves a thorough overhaul of the legal framework. Harmonizing domestic laws with globally recognised human rights standards becomes paramount. This involves rectifying the imprecise and overly broad regulations such as the Sedition Act and the Protest Law in Egypt. The objective should center on the formulation of laws that distinctly define offenses while simultaneously safeguarding the unimpeded exercise of freedom of expression.

Central to this transformation is the establishment of an impartial judiciary. This guarantees the impartial interpretation and application of laws pertaining to freedom of speech and expression. The insulation of judges from political pressures is indispensable in guaranteeing individuals' capacity to articulate their viewpoints without apprehension of reprisal. In tandem, nurturing an environment conducive to freedom of the press emerges as a priority. This entails dismantling censorship mechanisms and relinquishing undue influence over media channels, thus granting journalists the leeway to scrutinize critically and hold authorities accountable (Mohd Sani, 2008, p. 69). Furthermore, provisions must be in place to shield journalists from intimidation and threats. Educating the populace on the value of free expression assumes significance in this discourse. Public awareness initiatives, promoted by the government, serve to illuminate citizens about their entitlements and the pivotal role played by open discourse within a democratic framework. This engenders a culture of inclusive dialogue and tolerance for divergent perspectives. Collaborative engagement with international human rights organizations is another crucial avenue. Interaction with these entities aids in addressing specific concerns related to freedom of expression and implementing their recommendations. This external partnership can contribute significantly to enhancing human rights practices. The endorsement and safeguarding of civil society organizations, human rights advocates, and activists is essential. Rather than stifling dissent, governments should facilitate an atmosphere that nurtures candid debates and permits civil society to actively promote human rights and democratic ideals.

References

Abdelmonsef, A. (2018, June 11). *Egypt's position on human rights conventions.* Retrieved April 5, 2024, from https://en.eipss-eg.org/egypts-position-on-human-rights-conventions/

Abdulla, R. (2013). *Mapping digital media: Egypt.* Open Society Foundations. Retrieved April 5, 2024, from http://www.opensocietyfoundations.org/reports/mapping-digital-media-egypt

Abdulla, R. (2014). *Egypt's media in the midst of revolution.* Carnegie Endowment for International Peace.

Acemoglu, D., Hassan, T. A., & Tahoun, A. (2018). The power of the street: Evidence from Egypt's Arab spring. *The Review of Financial Studies, 31*(1), 1–42.

Administrative Court, case 7741, Year 57 (4 Feb 2003). Retrieved April 5, 2024, from http://qadaya.net/?p=4478.

Agence France Presse. (2021, January 21). Egypt 'disappeared' two journalists: Press freedom group. *Barron's*. https://www.barrons.com/news/egypt-disappeared-two-journalists-press-freedom-group01611250504

Ahram Online. (2023, March 1). Egypt building integrated system for promoting human rights: Justice minister to HRC. https://english.ahram.org.eg/News/489941.aspx

AlAshry, M. S. (2022). A critical assessment of the impact of Egyptian laws on information access and dissemination by journalists. *Cogent Arts & Humanities, 9*(1), 1–17.

Alqsas, Y. (2014). *Aldawabit aljinayiyuh lahuriyat alraay waltaebir* (Drasih Maqarinah). Dar aljamieuh aljadiduh.

Alsubaie, S. (2019). *The limitations of freedom of expression in theory and practice (Between the First Amendment of the U.S. Constitution and Egyptian Law)* [Ph.D. thesis, University of Stirling]. Retrieved April 5, 2024, from https://dspace.stir.ac.uk/bitstream/1893/30387/1/Final%20Copy3.pdf

Amnesty International. (2010, May 25). Egypt using defamation laws to prosecute dissenting voices. Retrieved April 4, 2024, from https://www.refworld.org/docid/4c0367ac1a.html

Awad, R. (2011). *Alquyud alwaridah alaa huriyat altaebir fi qanun aleuqubat walqawanin almukmilah lah (Derasah Muqarinah)*. Dar alnahdah alearabiuh.

Baker, R. W. (1981). Sadat's open door: Opposition from within. *Social Problems, 28*(4), 378–384.

Bakircioglu, O. (2008). Freedom of expression and hate speech. *Tulsa Journal of Comparative & International Law, 16*(1), 1–51.

Barker, C. (2022, November 13). COP27 shines light on civil liberties in Egypt, but it'll take work to achieve real freedom. *The Conversation*. Retrieved April 5, 2024, from https://theconversation.com/cop27shines-light-on-civil-liberties-in-egypt-but-itll-take-work-to-achieve-real-freedom-194407

Behrens-Abouseif, D. (1994). *Egypt's adjustment to Ottoman rule: Institutions, Waqf and architecture in Cairo: 16th & 17th Centuries*. Brill.

Brown, N. J. (2014, March 31). Egypt's constitutional cul-de-sac. Retrieved April 5, 2024, from https://carnegieendowment.org/2014/03/31/egypt-s-constitutional-cul-de-sac-pub-55310

Cairo Declaration on Human Rights in Islam. (1990, August 5). U.N. GAOR, World Conf. on Hum. Rts., 4th Sess., Agenda Item 5, U.N. Doc. A/CONF.157/PC/62/Add.18 [English translation]. Retrieved April 5, 2024, from http://hrlibrary.umn.edu/instree/cairodeclaration.html

Country Report on Human Rights Practices: Egypt. (2021). Retrieved April 5, 2024, from https://www.ecoi.net/en/document/2071155.html

Country Reports on Human Rights Practices: Egypt. (2020). *Bureau of Democracy, Human Rights, and Labor*. March 30, 2021. Retrieved April 4, 2024, from https://eg.usembassy.gov/2020-country-reports-onhuman-rights-practices-egypt/

Egypt Human Rights Report. (2022). *Country reports on human rights practices for 2022.* United States Department of State, Bureau of Democracy, Human Rights and Labor. Retrieved April 5, 2024, from https://eg.usembassy.gov/egypt-2022-human-rights-report/

Egypt Today Staff. (2022, March 28). Hamo Bika, Omar Kamal sentenced over 'Enti Ma'lema' clip with belly dancer Lurdiana. *Egypt Today.* Online at: https://www.egypttoday.com/Article/4/114279/HamoBika-Omar-Kamal-sentenced-over-Enti-Ma-lema-clip

Egypt Today Staff. (2022a, February 26). Egypt's cybercrimes law: Imprisonment and fine up to 200K over attacking website, email of legal person. *Egypt Today.* Retrieved April 5, 2024, from https://www.egypttoday.com/Article/1/113254/Egypt-s-cybercrimes-law-Imprisonment-and-fine-up-to200K#:~:text=Article%2018%20of%20the%20law,the%20two%20penalties%2C%20shall%20be

Egypt. (2013). *Law No.107 for 2013 for organizing the right to peaceful public meetings, processions and protests.* Retrieved April 5, 2024, from http://www.Constitutionnet.Org/Sites/Default/Files/Protest_law_issued_nov_24.Pdf

Egypt: News Websites and Alternative Voices. (Article 19: London, 2014), p. 12. November 26, 2014. Retrieved April 5, 2024, from https://www.article19.org/data/files/medialibrary/37780/Egypt-Report-forWeb.pdf

Egyptian Initiative for Personal Rights. (2022). May 16 session scheduled for ruling on appeal by Marco Gerges against his five-year prison sentence for blasphemy. Online at: https://eipr.org/en/press/2022/03/may-16-session-scheduled-ruling-appeal-marco-gerges-against-his-fiveyear-prison

El-Din, E. G., & El-Mahdawy, H. (2016, December 3). Egypt's supreme constitutional court deems article 10 of protest law 'unconstitutional'. *Ahram Online.* Online at: https://english.ahram.org.eg/NewsContent/1/64/251238/Egypt/Politics-/Egypt%E2%80%99s-HigherConstitutional-Court-deems-Article-.aspx

El-Morr, D. A. M., Nossier, J. A. E. R., & Sherif, A. O. (1996). The supreme constitutional court and its role in the Egyptian judicial system. In K. Boyle & A. O. Sherif (Eds.), *Human rights and democracy: The role of supreme constitutional court in Egypt* (pp. 37–60). Kluwer Law International.

El-Naggar, M. (2022, January 16). A ban on 19 singers in Egypt tests the old guard's power. *The New York Times.* Online at: https://www.nytimes.com/2022/01/16/world/middleeast/egypt-mahraganat-music.html

Fahmi, K. (2012). *Huriyat Alraay Waltaebir Fi Daw' Alaitifaqiat Alduwaliih Wa, ltashrieat Alwataniuh Wa, lsharieuh Alaslamyh Wa, jarayim Alray Waltaebir* (2nd ed.). Dar alfikr aljamiei.

Fathy, N. (2018). Freedom of expression in the digital age: Enhanced or undermined? The case of Egypt. *Journal of Cyber Policy, 3*(1), 102.

Frankfort, H. (1978). *Kingship and the gods: A study of ancient Near Eastern religion as the integration of society and nature*. The University of Chicago Press.

Freedom House. (2010). Policing belief: The impact of blasphemy laws on human rights. Retrieved April 5, 2024, from https://www.freedomhouse.org/sites/default/files/PolicingBelief_Egypt.pdf

Gordon, J. (2017). *Nasser's blessed movement: Egypt's Free Officers and the July Revolution with a new introduction*. American University in Cairo Press.

Hamad, M. (2012). The constitutional challenges in post-Mubarak Egypt. *Insight Turkey, 14*(1), 51–69.

Hamzawy, A. (2016, November 24). Egypt's anti protest law: Legalising authoritarianism. *Carnegie Endowment for International Peace*. https://carnegieendowment.org/2016/11/24/egypt-s-anti-protest-lawlegalising-authoritarianism-pub-66274

Information and Decision Support Center-IDSC). (2008). *Egyptian blogs: A new social cyberspace*. Informatics Reports. IDSC.

Jumet, K. D. (2017). *Contesting the repressive state: Why ordinary Egyptians protested during the Arab Spring*. Oxford University Press.

Kamali, M. H. (2012). *Maqasid al-shari'ah, ijtihad and civilisational renewal*. Herndon: International Institute of Islamic Thought.

Kameel, M. (2016). *Madaa kafalat haqi al'iinsan fi altaebir bayn alfaqih al'iislamii walqanun alwadeii*. Munsha'at almaearif, Alexandria.

Lombardi, C. B. (2008). Egypt's supreme constitutional court: Managing constitutional conflict in an authoritarian, aspirationally Islamic state. *Journal of Comparative Law, 3*(234), 234–253. Retrieved April 5, 2024, from https://digitalcommons.law.uw.edu/faculty-articles/719

Lombardi, C. B., & Brown, N. J. (2005). Do "Constitutions Requiring Adherence to Shari'a Threaten Human Rights-How Egypt's Constitutional Court Reconciles Islamic Law with the Liberal Rule of Law. *American University International Law Review, 21*, 379.

Mazzanti, M. (2013). From state sovereignty to responsibility to protect. *Political Science. Institut d'études Politiques de Paris - Sciences Po*. Retrieved April 5, 2024, from https://sciencespo.hal.science/tel03657509/document

MEE staff. (2021, September 29). Egypt detains prominent professor critical of pro-government media. *Middle East Eye*. Retrieved April 5, 2024, https://www.middleeasteye.net/news/egypt-detains-professorcritical-government-media.

MEE staff. (2022, April 18). Egyptian TikTok star sentenced to three years in jail for 'human trafficking'. *Middle East Eye*. Retrieved April 5, 2024, from https://www.middleeasteye.net/news/egypt-tiktok-star-threeyears-jail-human-trafficking.

Michaelson, R. (2018, July 27). Fake news becomes tool of repression after Egypt passes new law. *The Guardian*. Retrieved April 5, 2024, from https://www.theguardian.com/globaldevelopment/2018/jul/27/fake-news-becomes-tool-of-repression-after-egypt-passes-new-law.

Mohd Sani, M. A. (2008). Media freedom and legislation in Malaysia. *REKAYASA: Journal of Ethics, Legal and Governance, 4*, 69–86.

Mohie, M. (2016, December 4). Down 1 article, the protest law survives. *Mada Masr*. Retrieved April 5, 2024, from https://www.madamasr.com/en/2016/12/04/feature/politics/down-1-article-the-protest-lawsurvives/

Morsy, L. A. (1995). American support for the 1952 Egyptian coup: Why? *Middle Eastern Studies, 31*(2), 307–316.

Osman, T. (2011). *Egypt on the brink from the rise of Nasser to the fall of Mubarak*. Yale University Press.

Reid, D. M. (2002). *Whose pharaohs? Archaeology, museums, and Egyptian national identity from Napoleon to World War I*. University of California Press.

Reuters Staff. (2018, July 18). Egypt targets social media with new law. Retrieved April, 5, 2024, from https://www.reuters.com/article/us-egypt-politics/egypt-targets-social-media-with-new-lawidUSKBN1K722C.

Salam, R. (2017). *Egypt: Freedom of expression between emergency and suppression*. Eahro Books.

Smet, S. (2011). Freedom of expression and the right to reputation: Human rights in conflict. *American University International Law Review, 26*(1), 184–236.

Smith, A. (2022, April 27). Egyptian women's rights defender Rasha Azab found not guilty, but the persecution of women continues. *Middle East Monitor*. https://www.middleeastmonitor.com/20220427egyptian-womens-rights-defender-rasha-azab-found-not-guilty-but-the-persecution-of-women-continues/

State Information Service. (2022, February 3). Egypt and human rights. Retrieved April 5, 2024, from https://www.sis.gov.eg/Story/162236/Egypt-and-Human-Rights?lang=en-us

Sugita, H. (2023). Mustafa kamil al-shams al-mushriqa (The Rising Sun)(1904). In S. Saeki & T. Haga (Eds.), *Masterpieces on Japan by foreign authors: From Goncharov to Pinguet* (pp. 75–79). Springer.

Suliman, A., & Francis, E. (2022, November 5). What is COP27? What you need to know about the U.N. climate summit. *The Washington Post*. https://www.washingtonpost.com/climateenvironment/2022/11/05/cop27-egypt-climate-summit-sharm-el-sheikh/

Supreme Constitutional Court of Egypt Case No. 44 of Judicial Year 7, May 7, 1988. Retrieved April 5, 2024 from http://hrlibrary.umn.edu/arabic/Egypt-SCC-SC/Egypt-SCC-44-Y7.html

Supreme Constitutional Court, Case No 195 of Judical Year 19 (2 June 2001). Retrieved April 5, 2024, from http://hrlibrary.umn.edu/arabic/Egypt-SCC-SC/Egypt-SCC-195-Y19.html

Supreme Constitutional Court, Case No 232 of Judicial Year 36 (decided on 7 May 2017). Retrieved April 5, 2024, http://www.cc.gov.eg/Images/L/379200.pdf

Supreme Constitutional Court, Case No 37 of Judicial Year 11 (6 Feb 1993). Retrieved April 5, 2024, http://hrlibrary.umn.edu/arabic/Egypt-SCC-SC/Egypt-SCC-37-Y11.html

Supreme Constitutional Court, Case No 7 of Judicial Year 8 (15 May 1993). Retrieved April 5, 2024, from http://hrlibrary.umn.edu/arabic/Egypt-SCC-SC/Egypt-SCC-7-Y8.html

Supreme Constitutional Court, Case No 86 of Judicial Year 18 (6 Dec 1997). Retrieved April 5, 2024, from http://hrlibrary.umn.edu/arabic/Egypt-SCC-SC/Egypt-SCC-86-Y18.html

Taylor, P. M. (2020). *A commentary on the International Covenant on Civil and Political Rights: The UN Human Rights Committee's monitoring of ICCPR rights*. Cambridge University Press.

The Constitution of Egypt. (1971). Retrieved April 5, 2024, from http://www.palatauruscentrostudi.eu/doc/EGY_Constitution_1971_EN.pdf

The Constitution of Egypt. (2014). Retrieved April 5, 2024, from https://www.constituteproject.org/constitution/Egypt_2014.pdf

Tignor, R. L. (1976). The Egyptian revolution of 1919: New directions in the Egyptian economy. *Middle Eastern Studies, 12*(3), 41–67.

United Nations Human Rights: Office of the High Commissioner. (2020, April 9). *Egypt's updated terrorism law opens the door to more rights abuses, says UN expert*. Retrieved April 5, 2024, from https://www.ohchr.org/en/press-releases/2020/04/egypts-updated-terrorism-law-opens-door-more-rightsabuses-says-un-expert

Weinbaum, M. G. (1985). Egypt's "Infitah" and the politics of US economic assistance. *Middle Eastern Studies, 21*(2), 206–222.

Winter, M. (1982). *Society and religion in early Ottoman Egypt: Studies in the writings of Abd al-Wahhab al-Sharani*. New Brunswick.

Youssef, N. (2012, November 30). Egypt's draft constitution translated. Retrieved April 10, 2024, from https://www.ilo.org/dyn/natlex/docs/ELECTRONIC/91655/106411/F-196699313/Egypt.pdf

CHAPTER 5

Democratic Discourse in Context: Malaysia's Approach to Freedom of Expression

5.1 Introduction

In democratic societies, the vital essence of freedom lies in the unrestrained exercise of speech and expression by its citizens. This pivotal liberty not only empowers individuals to actively participate in the democratic machinery but also upholds the core tenets of governance—where authority is derived from the collective will of the people and operates with their best interests at heart. A democracy loses its intrinsic value when it fails to foster an environment conducive to the free exchange of ideas on matters encompassing the political and social landscapes. In essence, the vibrancy of democracy hinges on the unimpeded expression of diverse perspectives. The significance of freedom of expression extends beyond a mere democratic privilege; it serves as the linchpin for individuals to make well-informed decisions, thereby grounding the democratic process in a conscientious and informed citizenry. To curtail this freedom is to undermine the very essence of democracy, rendering it unsustainable and disconnected from the foundational principles it purports to uphold.

Within the Malaysian context, there exists a sense of national pride in the practice of parliamentary democracy. Since attaining independence in 1957, the nation has consistently upheld the mandate of free general elections, a constitutional imperative that underscores its commitment to democratic governance. This democratic framework, characterised by

A. Mohiuddin, *Human Rights Law in Egypt and Malaysia: Freedom of Religion and Expression, Volume 1*, Political Economy of Islam,
https://doi.org/10.1007/978-3-031-63859-6_5

the unfettered expression of the people's will, has been instrumental in propelling Malaysia from the status of an underdeveloped nation to a dynamic player in the league of developing countries. The symbiotic relationship between democratic values and the exercise of freedom of speech and expression has not only shaped Malaysia's political trajectory but has also been instrumental in fostering socio-economic growth and progress (Dziyauddin, 2006). The thriving of democracy hinges on affording individuals the opportunity to actively engage within the system. Malaysia's ascent as a rapidly growing economic force in the Asian region is, in part, attributed to the democratic principles that have guided its progress. Nevertheless, a contentious issue arises: in an advancing nation like Malaysia, why should any matter of public concern be stifled? If the aim is for society to mature into a developed entity, it is imperative that people are allowed to form informed opinions on issues impacting their well-being without undue constraints. Turning this aspiration into reality requires more than a mere acknowledgment of freedom of expression; it demands a pragmatic exercise of this freedom in practice, transcending its proclamation in written form. As a democratic nation, Malaysia fervently champions the right to freedom of speech and expression, as explicitly outlined in Article 10(1) of the Federal Constitution. This constitutional provision serves as the bedrock empowering citizens to voice their opinions on a myriad of subjects (Mia et al., 2021, p. 49). However, the acknowledgment of the importance of freedom of speech and expression does not imply an absolute, unrestricted right. Across democratic states, even in countries that affirm this right as a positive entitlement, such as the United States, certain limitations exist. The variations between these jurisdictions often hinge on the degree and scope of these restrictions. In the realm of freedom of speech, Malaysia has consistently employed a range of laws capable of constraining the unfettered expression of ideas.

The objective of this chapter is to conduct a comprehensive examination of freedom of speech and expression in Malaysia, grounded in the constitutional framework outlined in Article 10(1). It aims to highlight the fundamental significance of this right in a democratic context while recognizing its inherent non-absolute nature, and it draws parallels to restrictions present in other democratic jurisdictions. The chapter explores the historical development of Malaysia's legal landscape, scrutinising laws that may impose limitations on free expression. Through the cultivation of a nuanced perspective, the goal is to elucidate the intricate equilibrium between unrestricted speech and valid societal considerations.

Ultimately, this contributes to a thorough comprehension of the intricate dynamics involved in the practical exercise of this fundamental right within the Malaysian context.

5.2 Freedom of Speech in Malaysia's Complex History

The epoch of British colonial dominion, spanning the latter decades of the nineteenth century until Malaysia's triumphant attainment of independence in 1957, reflects an entrenched atmosphere of rigorous control exerted by the British administration over the domain of freedom of speech and expression (Leow, 2016). During this colonial phase, the paramount objective of the British authorities resided in the preservation of their sovereign dominion and the safeguarding of vested colonial interests, a pursuit that prompted the imposition of confinements on the exercise of political liberties and the meticulous regulation of public discourse. Such manifestations of state power manifested in the calculated manipulation and orchestration of media outlets to serve as conduits for disseminating information tailored to advance the interests and perspectives of the colonial administration. The institutionalisation of censorship mechanisms ensued as a central facet of the colonial regime's strategies, rendering newspapers, publications, and other forms of media subject to stringent scrutiny, rendering dissenting opinions or expressions that dared to challenge the established colonial policies targets for relentless suppression. By means of this carefully crafted regime of information control, the colonial authorities effectively engineered a narrative that epitomized a portrayal of British rule as favorable, thereby consolidating their dominance and perpetuating their influence over the colonized populace.

During the colonial period, the terrain of public discourse found itself ensnared within the constricting web of stringent regulations, ingeniously contrived to safeguard colonial authority against any perceived challenge. Acts of political dissension were met with unyielding severity, with punitive measures, such as incarcerations and curtailment of political activities, deployed as deterrents. The colonial administration remained steadfastly vigilant, determined to preclude the burgeoning of nationalist sentiments or the emergence of movements that could pose a plausible threat to its dominion over the territorial expanse. Moreover, the equitable extension of freedom of speech and expression to all ethnic and social factions within the colony remained an elusive aspiration. The British colonial apparatus, in the implementation of policies, selectively favored certain ethnic and social strata while concurrently relegating others to the periphery, giving rise to a landscape of uneven access to media outlets and public fora, serving as conduits for the articulation of opinions and ideas.

The British colonial regime methodically enforced a series of laws and regulations to administer tight control over the press and monitor the circulation of information deemed potentially critical or antithetical to colonial rule. Preeminent among these measures were the Straits Settlements Press Ordinance of 1907 and the Newspaper Ordinance of 1928, astutely crafted to oversee the content disseminated through newspapers and publications. Such regulations endowed the government with the prerogative to exercise censorship over materials deemed inimical to British interests or disruptive to public order (Abraham, 2002, p. 11). In conjunction with press regulations, the mantle of suppression was fortified through the instrumentality of the Sedition Act, formally promulgated in 1948, which functioned as a legal armament to quell political opposition and subdue the exercise of freedom of speech. Criminalizing any speech, writing, or action that bore a "seditious tendency," this legislative tool served as an effective mechanism to target dissent and subjugate political activism under the aegis of colonial control.

The curtailment of freedom of speech and expression during the colonial period wielded a momentous influence in shaping the trajectory of the nationalist and independence movements in Malaysia. As the shackles of political restrictions and the heavy yoke of censorship became conspicuous, the resistance against colonial hegemony attained an escalating fervor, engendering the ascendancy of ardent nationalist leaders and formidable groups, fervently advocating for the realization of self-determination and the abatement of colonial domination. Emboldened by their shared vision of a sovereign nation enshrining fundamental rights, notably the sanctity of freedom of speech and expression, these stalwart advocates galvanized a formidable struggle for independence.

The post-independence era in Malaysia marked a transformative phase, epitomizing the nation's aspiration to crystallize democratic values amidst the backdrop of entrenched political tensions (Algappa, 2013). The Federal Constitution of 1957 fortuitously served as a bastion for fundamental liberties, placing particular emphasis on the imperatives of open public discourse and unfettered freedom for all citizens. Illuminated by the visionary leadership of Prime Minister Tunku Abdul Rahman, the importance of democratic principles and the pursuit of an inclusive approach to governance were ardently espoused. Nevertheless, Malaysia confronted its own set of challenges, catalyzed by the intricacies of political fissures rooted along ethnic and religious lines. The coalescence of a Malay-Muslim majority and the ethnically diverse Chinese and Indian communities mandated adroit navigation to reconcile disparate interests while steadfastly upholding the tenets of freedom of speech and expression.

The complex interplay between facilitating open dialogues and mitigating the potential for arousing communal strife significantly influenced the government's modus operandi in regulating public discourse. The paramount objective of fostering national cohesion and ensuring social stability compelled the administration to exercise caution, occasionally leading to restrictions on freedom of speech, especially in contexts encompassing sensitive topics of ethnic or religious nature. While the underlying intention was to safeguard harmonious societal coexistence, apprehensions arose concerning the implications of potential encroachments upon individual liberties. A pivotal undertaking in nation-building, the endorsement of a "national language" policy, with Bahasa Malaysia as the official language, sought to engender a shared national identity and surmount linguistic barriers; nonetheless, it also engendered concerns regarding the usage of alternative languages, particularly in official domains and educational spheres. Striking an equitable equilibrium between fostering national unity and preserving linguistic pluralism presented an enduring quandary (Haa et al., 2013, p. 59).

During this time period, media freedom encountered challenges, with government-controlled or government-aligned outlets overwhelmingly dominating the media landscape. Independent media outlets faced arduous challenges in acquiring licenses and confronted the specter of censorship, culminating in a paucity of diverse perspectives and engendering self-censorship among journalists. The pervasive governmental influence on media content raised profound questions concerning the veracity of journalistic independence. The legal framework governing media freedom and public discourse underwent significant transformation through the enactment of various laws and regulations. Notably, the Printing Presses and Publications Act (PPPA) and the Official Secrets Act (OSA) conferred substantial authority upon authorities, bestowing them with formidable control over media content and access to information (Anuar, 2012, p. 254). These legal provisions were regarded with apprehension, given their potential for hampering critical reporting and investigative journalism.

Nevertheless, civil society organisations and opposition parties, including the Democratic Action Party (DAP) and the Pan-Malaysian Islamic Party (PAS), assumed pivotal roles as advocates for democratic reforms and the expansion of freedom of expression. Their concerted efforts aimed to foster political accountability, transparency, and democratic values, thereby challenging the restrictive policies and heralding the advent of a more open and inclusive societal framework. From 1969 to 1981, Malaysia confronted a confluence of pressing tensions and challenges that left an indelible impact on freedom of speech and expression. Foremost among these was the May 13 incident in 1969, a tumultuous event characterized by racial riots between ethnic communities, precipitating substantial loss of life and property devastation. In the wake of this cataclysm, the government instituted the National Operations Council (NOC) to restore order and stability (Show, 2021, p. 214). The aftermath of the May 13 incident spurred the government to implement measures aimed at preserving social equilibrium and controlling the trajectory of public discourse. Notable among these measures was the introduction of the Internal Security Act (ISA), authorising detention without trial. The ISA was invoked to suppress dissent and perceived threats to national security, engendering trenchant criticism for its potential for abuse and its deleterious impact on freedom of speech and expression. Detentions without trial gave rise to palpable concerns regarding due process and the preservation of individuals' rights to express divergent opinions without apprehension of arbitrary detention.

Throughout the eventful and transformative decades spanning the 1970s and 1980s, Malaysia found itself grappling with the implementation of a diverse array of laws and regulations that, contrary to bolstering the ideals of freedom of speech and expression, ushered in an era characterized by heightened constraints. Chief among these legislative instruments were the Official Secrets Act (OSA) and the Printing Presses and Publications Act (PPPA), whose farreaching implications cast an imposing shadow over the landscape of media freedom in the nation (Haas, 2016). These laws, rather than fostering an environment conducive to open public discourse and a vibrant plurality of viewpoints, contributed to an atmosphere marked by controlled narratives and limited access to diverse and independent reporting. The OSA vested authorities with sweeping powers to govern access to information deemed sensitive or classified, effectively curbing transparency and impeding the autonomy of independent journalism. Correspondingly, the PPPA accorded the government the prerogative to manipulate media content by conferring them the authority to bestow or withdraw publishing licenses, thereby fostering an environment of limited diversity in perspectives and self-censorship among media practitioners. The cumulative impact of these laws and regulations evoked apprehensions surrounding the flourishing of media freedom and the availability of pluralistic viewpoints. As a corollary, media outlets with affiliations to the government retained ascendancy in the media domain, engendering a dearth of diverse perspectives and fostering an atmosphere conducive to self-imposed journalistic restraint.

The culmination of restrictive legal instruments and governmental control in this era reverberated throughout the broader domain of freedom of speech and expression in Malaysia. The ambit of public discourse faced profound constraints, while the government's dominion over media content engendered qualms regarding the autonomy of journalism and the public's access to a wide spectrum of viewpoints. Despite the manifold challenges confronting the realm of freedom of expression, civil society organizations and opposition parties persisted in their unwavering endeavors to champion democratic reforms and advocate for a more unfettered exchange of ideas. Their concerted initiatives aimed to contest the entrenched restrictive policies, foster a culture of political accountability, and foster the advancement of democratic values.

Since the 1980s, Malaysia has borne witness to an escalating emphasis on Islamisation, wherein Islamic principles have taken on an increasingly conspicuous role in matters of governance and public life. This transformative trajectory has been impelled by a confluence of factors, encompassing the aspiration to fortify Malaysia's identity as an Islamic nation, resonate with the Muslim-majority populace, and fortify cultural and religious values. Echoes of Islamization policies resonate across various societal domains, permeating realms such as education, jurisprudence, and public administration. The government has diligently endeavored to propagate Islamic education, amplify the prominence of *sharīʿah* law, and imbue public policies and institutions with Islamic values. While these endeavors have sought to engender a more robust religious identity and cultural unity, they have also engendered misgivings about potential instances of discrimination and unequal treatment encountered by non-Muslim citizens. In pursuit of upholding social order and fostering harmonious coexistence, the government has resorted to the utilization of restrictive legal measures to oversee the realm of public discourse and restrict the dissemination of dissenting opinions. One notable instrument in this endeavor is the Sedition Act, which criminalizes the expression of speech, writing, or actions that demonstrate "seditious tendencies," thereby affording authorities the capacity to target individuals disseminating views deemed critical or menacing to the government or sensitive to the intricacies of ethnic and religious sentiments. Moreover, the Communications and Multimedia Act (CMA) and the Security Offences (Special Measures) Act (SOSMA) have been harnessed as additional tools to suppress dissent and control the critique of governmental policies (Hamid & Anwar, 2018). The CMA furnishes authorities with expansive powers to regulate online content, thereby enabling the censorship of digital expressions perceived as critical of the government or engendering controversy. In stark contrast, SOSMA permits the detention of individuals without trial in cases deemed to possess implications for national security, engendering concerns about the potential for arbitrary arrests and consequent curtailment of freedom of expression.

Detractors contend that these legislative measures have been wielded inappropriately to quell political opposition and stifle dissenting voices, thereby impeding the free flow of political discourse and undermining democratic tenets. Alarming apprehensions persist about how such measures encumber the capacity of individuals and collectives to openly express their viewpoints and engage in peaceful opposition, thereby encroaching upon the democratic fabric of the nation. The employment of these restrictive laws has garnered domestic and international censure, prompting inquiries into the government's steadfastness in upholding human rights and safeguarding freedom of expression. In recent times, mounting disquiet has arisen concerning the burgeoning control exerted by the Malaysian government over media outlets and online content. Numerous mainstream media establishments find themselves under the ownership or sway of government-affiliated entities, thereby engendering a scarcity of diverse perspectives and fostering potential self-censorship among journalists. The consolidation of media ownership in government friendly hands gives rise to disquietudes concerning journalistic autonomy and the capacity to report critically on contentious subjects. Furthermore, the government stands accused of exercising its grip over social media platforms and digital content. Instances of censorship and the deletion of content deemed critical of the government or sensitive to particular issues have come to light. Consequently, a climate of trepidation and self-censorship pervades content creators and individuals endeavoring to articulate opinions online, as they apprehensively anticipate potential repercussions for their outspokenness.

The regulation of media outlets and online content elicits apprehensions regarding the unhindered dissemination of information and the populace's access to diverse perspectives, which is crucial for fostering an environment of open public discourse. Scholars contend that such stringent control poses impediments to the democratic process, constraining the arena for critical debates and alternative narratives, thereby curtailing the vibrancy of democratic deliberations. These complexities have garnered the attention of both national and international stakeholders, with human rights organizations and foreign governments expressing reservations about the state of press freedom and freedom of expression within Malaysia. The atmosphere characterised by media control and online censorship prompts inquiries into the government's dedication to upholding democratic tenets and honoring the citizenry's inalienable right to express their opinions freely, bereft of fear or repercussions (Wok & Mohamed, 2017, p. 46).

The repercussions arising from these suppressive measures extend beyond the immediate purview of civil society organisations and activists, permeating the broader public. The ambiance of surveillance and intimidation may discourage ordinary citizens from partaking in peaceful protests or participating in deliberations on sensitive matters. Fear of retribution for expressing dissenting opinions may culminate in self-censorship among individuals, thereby limiting the multiplicity of perspectives and stifling open public discourse. International human rights organizations and foreign governments have increasingly voiced reservations concerning the constricted space for civil society within Malaysia. The encumbrances imposed on civil society organizations and activists have sparked scrutiny of the prevailing state of human rights and democratic principles in the nation. Malaysia's approach to the realm of freedom of speech and expression has garnered significant international attention and meticulous scrutiny, prompting close monitoring by human rights organizations and foreign governments. The focal point of concern revolves around the implementation of constraining legal measures and the measures undertaken against journalists, activists, and dissenting individuals. Of paramount significance among the entities taking a leading role in this discourse are Amnesty International and Human Rights Watch, whose persistent engagement has articulated profound apprehensions concerning the state of democracy and human rights within the Malaysian context. Both organizations have explicitly censured the purported misuse of legislative instruments, most notably the Sedition Act, the Communications and Multimedia Act (CMA), and the Security Offences (Special Measures) Act (SOSMA), which have ostensibly been wielded as tools to stifle political opposition and quell expressions of critical dissent. Furthermore, these organizations have expressed profound disquietude over the detrimental ramifications of these laws on the panorama of freedom of speech and expression, encompassing impediments to open political discourse and encroachments on individuals' entitlement to peaceably enunciate their perspectives (Wok & Mohamed, 2017, p. 47).

Foreign governments and international bodies have been attuned to Malaysia's stance on freedom of expression, with considerable focus directed towards the handling of arrests and legal actions targeting journalists and activists. This scrutiny has raised pivotal questions about the government's steadfastness in upholding democratic principles and safeguarding human rights. The treatment of civil society organisations and activists, perceived as a gauge of Malaysia's commitment to human rights, has spurred foreign governments to advocate for the protection of these individuals and groups that advocate for human rights, political reform, and social justice. The ramifications of international scrutiny extend to Malaysia's global standing, as the nation's democratic reputation, along with its adherence to fundamental freedoms, becomes subject to evaluation by foreign states, international organizations, and potential investors. The government's approach to journalists, activists, and civil society organizations carries significant implications for international relations, trade agreements, diplomatic ties, and foreign investments (Wok & Mohamed, 2017, p. 48).

Malaysia's response to international scrutiny varies, presenting a range of engagements. While some instances showcase dialogues and cooperation with international human rights entities, other occasions reveal discord and differing perspectives. The government justifies its actions as essential for upholding social order and stability, asserting that certain limitations on freedom of expression are indispensable to safeguard national security and prevent potential social unrest. To conclude, Malaysia's approach to freedom of speech and expression has aroused substantial international interest and appraisal. The utilization of restrictive legal measures and actions taken against journalists, activists, and dissenting voices has generated concerns about the state of democracy and human rights within the nation. Upholding essential liberties and ensuring the unhampered expression of opinions by individuals and groups without fear of reprisals emerge as imperative imperatives to maintain Malaysia's democratic reputation and foster an inclusive and vibrant society.

5.3 Constitutional Framework of Freedom of Speech and Expression in Malaysia

Within the foundational edifice of Malaysia's Federal Constitution lies an overarching and supreme legal framework, endowing its populace with an inherent and paramount entitlement—the fundamental right to freedom of speech and expression—an explicit edict embodied in Article 10(1)(a) (Yatim, 1995). Nonetheless, this constitutional guarantee is not bereft of prudent qualifications, as elucidated in Article 10(2)(a), conferring upon the government the authority to impose legitimate restrictions in pursuit of safeguarding vital interests. This encompassing ambit comprises the safeguarding of national security, nurturing harmonious diplomatic relations, upholding public order, preserving moral standards, safeguarding parliamentary privilege, countering contempt of court, curbing defamation, and quelling the incitement of offenses. This complex legal framework skillfully maintains a delicate balance, harmonising individual liberties with the need to uphold the integrity and welfare of the nation. Decisive judicial rulings have upheld the constitutionality of such restrictions, with significant cases like Madhavan Nair v. Public Prosecutor [1975] 1 LNS 94; [1975] 2 MLJ 264 emphasising that any restrictions on freedom of speech must firmly align with the parameters of Article 10 clauses (2), (3), and (4) of the Federal Constitution to be considered valid and justifiable (Mohd Noor, 2020, p. 286).

Similarly, the legal precedent established in Lau Dak Kee v. Public Prosecutor [1976] 1 LNS 54; [1976] 2 MLJ 229 reinforces the notion that while the Federal Constitution affords citizens the rights to freely express their thoughts, assemble peaceably and form associations, these constitutional privileges remain subject to reasonable and proportionate legislative measures formulated by the Parliament. Consequently, the practical implementation of such censorship measures inevitably curtails the scope of freedom of speech within the territorial boundaries of the state. The interplay between constitutionally safeguarded liberties and government-imposed limitations underscores the complex intricacies of maintaining a delicate equilibrium between individual freedoms and the collective interests of the nation.

Within the framework of the Federal Constitution of Malaysia lie Articles 149 and 150, which serve as crucial mechanisms imposing constraints on the domain of freedom of speech and expression. Article 149 proclaims the validity of any legislative enactment crafted to counteract pernicious actions initiated or threatened by substantial assemblages, both within and beyond the nation's borders (Naz & Sabaruddin, 2016, p. 60). This provision thus confers substantive authority upon the government to promulgate measures that seek to forestall potential disturbances to public order and the nation's security. Concomitantly, Article 150 grants the Yang di-Pertuan Agong the authority to declare a state of emergency, a powerful tool utilised to address situations posing a threat to the nation's security. Notably, this constitutional grant bestows upon the Yang di-Pertuan Agong the power to promulgate proclamations and Ordinances, endowing the executive with legislative potency even in the absence of parliamentary sittings, emblematic of the extraordinary nature of constitutional governance (Faruqi, 2021).

The spectrum of freedoms encapsulated within the broader realm of freedom of speech and expression is undoubtedly multifaceted. Scholars have contended that to fathom the true essence of this right, it must be perceived in conjunction with other fundamental liberties, particularly the rights to peaceful assembly and association. The fusion of these rights synergistically shapes the landscape of civil liberties, granting citizens a collective platform to influence public opinion on a myriad of profound issues. The Malaysian Federal Constitution, while acknowledging the significance of these interrelated freedoms, is not confined solely to the realm of public meetings as an expression of free speech. Indeed, the expanse of freedom of speech extends far beyond oral discourse, encompassing a spectrum of expressions in various forms. Nevertheless, it is essential to acknowledge that Article 10(2) of the Federal Constitution bestows upon the government the prerogative to impose legitimate restrictions in the interests of safeguarding national security, fostering diplomatic relations, preserving public order, upholding moral standards, safeguarding parliamentary privileges, curbing contempt of court, mitigating defamation and quelling the incitement of offenses. Thus, at this juncture, a semblance of censorship on freedom of speech emerges, sanctioned by the Malaysian Federal Constitution (Faruqi, 2021).

The Federal Constitution of Malaysia guarantees its citizens the fundamental right to freedom of speech and expression, a core principle firmly delineated within Article 10(1)(a). However, this constitutional protection is not boundless, as evidenced by Article 10(2)(a), which empowers the government to impose restrictions in order to safeguard critical interests such as national security, diplomatic relations, public order, moral standards, parliamentary privilege, contempt of court, defamation and the incitement of offenses. Within this framework, freedom of assembly plays a crucial role, providing citizens with the avenue to express their views through public gatherings and peaceful protests—a fundamental expression of democratic engagement. Embodying democratic ideals, Article 10(1)(b) of the Federal Constitution assures every citizen the right to assemble peaceably and without arms. Yet, there are contrasting aspects to consider. Article 10(2)(b) empowers Parliament to impose restrictions when national security or public order is at stake. Requiring police permission for public gatherings and processions raises concerns about potential censorship on the essential right to assemble, prompting contemplation on how to balance individual expression with maintaining societal order (Mia et al., 2021, p. 51).

Likewise, the freedom of association adds another complex hue to the constitutional framework, enabling individuals to join together and espouse their beliefs to the public. Article 10(1)(c) recognises the right of all citizens to form associations, underscoring the importance of this participatory element in democratic dialogue. However, contrasting provisions are found in Article 10(2)(c), which grants Parliament the authority to impose restrictions deemed necessary to maintain national security, public order, or morality. The delicate interplay between individual liberties and societal welfare in this realm poses questions about the boundaries of permissible expression and the specter of potential censorship. The constitution of Malaysia presents a rich and vibrant picture of rights and limitations. To understand this composition, we must strike a delicate balance between preserving freedom of expression and upholding the welfare of the nation—a dynamic process that shapes Malaysia's constitutional order.

The intrinsic interplay between freedom of speech and expression and freedom of religion manifests as two fundamental facets of individual rights. The notion of freedom of religion emerges as an innate demand of human nature, as individuals seek beliefs and values to navigate their lives. Throughout history, the acknowledgment of the significance of preserving the freedom of religion has culminated in the establishment of laws with the noble objective of nurturing societal concordance. In the context of Malaysia, the Federal Constitution in Article 11(1) recognises and upholds the right to freedom of religion, thereby empowering individuals to exercise their volition in practicing and avowing their chosen beliefs. However, an important provision arises in Article 12(4), granting parents the authority to determine the religion of their children under the age of 18. Legal cases such as Teoh Eng Huat and Lina Joy illustrate the judiciary's role in adjudicating disputes concerning religious conversion and adherence (Siladass, 2016). Furthermore, Article 11(4) of the Federal Constitution allows State and Federal laws to regulate or restrict the propagation of religious beliefs among individuals professing Islam. Consequently, several state legislatures have enacted laws to address this aspect of religious freedom. These legal provisions and their interpretation reflect the delicate balance between individual rights and the broader welfare of Malaysian society.

Within the legal framework of the Federal Constitution of Malaysia, Article 11(5) looms as a critical and judiciously crafted provision that imparts profound implications for the right to religious freedom. Elucidating its profound significance, Article 11(5) deftly underscores that the constitutional guarantee of freedom of religion, enshrined in Article 11, does not confer an unrestrained and unqualified license to engage in religious practices that run counter to the broader tenets of general laws pertaining to public order, public health, or morality. The framers of the constitution deftly reconcile the paramountcy of religious autonomy with the indispensable requirements of maintaining societal stability, safeguarding public welfare and upholding the collective moral fabric (Thomas, 2004, p. 18).

As Article 11(5) assumes its role in shaping the contours of religious liberty, the Parliament wields the levers of authority to temper religious expressions and conduct, guided by the considerations of public order, health and morality. The constitution acknowledges the exigencies of maintaining social cohesion, safeguarding communal harmony and averting any undue disruptions to the broader societal equilibrium. The ruling in the seminal case of Minister of Home Affairs, Malaysia v. Jamaluddin bin Othman [1989] stands as an exegesis affirming the harmonious consonance between the liberty of religious practices and the legitimate ambit of stateimposed limitations, thus accentuating the foundational imperative to safeguard public order, preserve public health, and fortify the moral compass of the nation (Abdullah & Li Hua, 2007, p. 265).

Moreover, the delicate interplay between freedom of speech and freedom of information resonates with the profound dynamics of democratic expression. Article 10(1)(a) of the Federal Constitution of Malaysia resoundingly heralds the entitlement of 'Every citizen' to the right of freedom of speech and expression, even as the measured contours of this freedom find elucidation in Article 10(2), (3) and (4), thus manifesting the concomitant necessity for judicious curtailments. Intriguingly paralleling this constitutional construct, Article 19(1) and (2) of the International Covenant on Civil and Political Rights (ICCPR) espouse the right to freedom of information, akin to a lifeblood nourishing an informed citizenry (Islam, 2019, p. 18).

The notion of harmonious freedom of information encounters a nuanced counterpoint in Article 19(3) of the ICCPR, which establishes a normative framework enabling states to exercise judicious restrictions, aligning with imperatives such as national security, public order, public health and public morality. This legal framework strengthens the fabric of freedom of information, navigating complex pathways of regulatory requirements and legal limitations. In doing so, it unveils situations where measures resembling censorship may be utilized to align with the broader and compelling interests of the nation.

5.4 Legal Landscape in Malaysia: Balancing Freedom of Expression

Malaysian courts consistently show a thoughtful approach to cases involving freedom of speech, finding a careful balance between protecting this right and recognising valid limitations. The Malaysian Federal Constitution, particularly Article 4(1), establishes its supreme authority, making any legislation conflicting with it null and void. To emphasise the commitment to fundamental freedoms, the Malaysian Human Rights Commission Act 1999, Section 2, outlines 'human rights,' echoing the core principles in Part II of the Federal Constitution. This legal support reflects Malaysia's strong commitment to safeguarding and promoting the rights outlined in this crucial constitutional part, especially the vital right to freedom of speech and expression (Venugopal & Hassan, 2012, p. 1455). The Malaysian Federal Constitution declares its paramount status as the supreme law of the nation under Article 4(1). This provision renders null and void any legislation enacted after Independence Day that contradicts its principles. Demonstrating an a commitment to upholding fundamental freedoms, subsequent sections of the Constitution, particularly the Malaysian Human Rights Commission Act 1999, Section 2, comprehensively outline 'human rights.' This endorsement solidifies Malaysia's dedication to protecting and championing the rights outlined in this constitutional segment, with a particular emphasis on the right to freedom of speech and expression (Venugopal & Hassan, 2012, p. 1457).

The legal system emphasises the importance of certain rights, especially the valuable right to freedom of speech and expression (Bari, 2004). Article 10(1)(a) of the Constitution gives every citizen the right to speak and express themselves in many different ways, like talking, creating art, using digital media, and being creative. People use their freedom of expression to express opinions about things like clothing or other harmless actions (Faruqi, 2018). But even though this right is really important, it's not unlimited. The Constitution acknowledges the need for some rules to balance individual freedoms with what's good for society. Malaysian courts carefully consider these issues to protect and support freedom of speech under the Constitution.

In the domain of Malaysian legal jurisprudence, the lacuna in the country's ratification of several international treaties and conventions pertaining to freedom of expression, media and information is a reality, prompting the imperative for rectification. Scholars like Faruqi, have advocated for recalibration, urging due caution in accepting 'universal standards' that may encroach upon Malaysia's deeply ingrained and rigorously upheld principles of propriety and quality (UiHua, 2017). The notion of constitutional freedom, enshrined in Article 9 of the Federal Constitution as the freedom of movement, serves as a pertinent illustration of the constitution's immanent limitations. While the Constitution grants individuals the right to traverse freely, it does not extend this privilege to trespassers who enter private premises and assert protection under Article 9, thereby accentuating the duality of liberties. Likewise, in the realm of digital expression, individuals may exercise their freedom to write and share content on the internet, but they also bear the full burden of accountability for the ensuing repercussions. These consequences encompass potential criminal charges, such as those enshrined in Section 499 of the Criminal Code, or civil actions arising from the expressions made.

Moreover, the scope of responsibility extends beyond the primary author to include individuals who share the content (UiHua, 2017). Thus, a mere collective act of sharing, however unwittingly, may draw the entirety of sharers, including the original writer, into the purview of legal proceedings. This multifaceted range of consequences encompasses various dimensions, notably false or misleading statements, defamatory content, and expressions that carry a tone of threat or harassment.

To navigate this terrain of freedom, expression and responsibility, the Communications and Multimedia Content Forum of Malaysia (CMCF) prescribes self-discipline as a commendable approach. This recourse invokes a sense of autonomy, directing individuals to exercise prudent judgment and critical discernment in their digital expressions to evade legal quagmires. Eminent legal scholars have posited a discernible paradox concerning the compression of freedom of expression, freedom of association and freedom of assembly when contrasted with other equally crucial liberties delineated in Part II of the Constitution. Scholars posit that governmental official and administrative authorities have displayed a proclivity for constraining these particular freedoms more acutely. Notwithstanding the congruence shared with the provisions of Article 10, paragraphs 2, 3, and 4, various freedoms, such as the freedom from detention without trial and protection from double jeopardy, are seemingly impaired by the very constitutional provisions found in Article 10 (Mia et al., 2021, p. 51). Consequently, the full realisation of these liberties necessitates a judicious reevaluation and repudiation of the relevant constitutional tenets.

In contemplation of the overarching ambit of Article 10, it is imperative to emphasise that Malaysians, as beneficiaries of this constitutional safeguard, indeed enjoy the privileges and agency to freely articulate and express their thoughts. The constitutional construct outlined in Article 10 primarily serves as a prescriptive framework, governing the standards, criteria and bounds that underpin Malaysians' ability to engage in uninhibited free speech, assembly and association. The collection of rights in this document protects individuals' natural right to freely express their opinions and form connections. However, Article 10, paragraph 2 (a)(b)(c), gives authority to the legislature to impose limits on these freedoms within important boundaries such as public safety, order, moral values, and societal well-being, as stated in Article 10(2). So, constitutional freedom is subject to these significant conditions and considerations (Mia et al., 2021, p. 53).

Central to the constitutional landscape is the contemplation of pertinent issues that lie beyond the remit of constitutional scrutiny. The constitutional delineation concerning the status of the national language, the privileged position of Malays, the status of Islam as the official religion, and other cognate matters stands outside the domain of public discourse. This exclusion, as codified in the Federal Constitution, demarcates a sphere that remains impervious to unfettered expression, safeguarding the nation's cherished principles and integral values. Thus, Malaysians retain the privilege to express any content of their choosing, guided by a prudent circumspection that aligns with prevailing guidelines, assiduously avoiding the transgression of public norms and the concomitant instigation of public disturbances or disorder. The dynamic milieu of freedom of speech and expression in Malaysia thus remains characterised by the interplay of liberties and limitations, carefully calibrated to preserve the delicate balance of societal harmony and the integrity of constitutional ideals (Islam et al., 2020, p. 10893).

The Malaysian Human Rights Commission (Suhakam) has astutely foregrounded a pressing and disconcerting concern, unmasking the unsettling employment of Article 233 of the Communications and Multimedia Act (CMA) and its concomitant legal instruments, including the Sedition Act of 1948, the Peaceful Assembly Act of 2012 and sections 504 and 505 of the Penal Code, as potent instruments of control, intimidation, and encumbrance that egregiously infringe upon the expansive realm of expression and free speech (Malay Mail, 2020). Suhakam's incisive critique illuminates a profound and exigent disjuncture, as these restrictive laws not only contradict the very essence of universal freedom standards that are robustly enshrined in Article 19 of the Universal Declaration of Human Rights (UDHR) but also flout the principles articulated in Article 10 of the Federal Constitution of Malaysia. These laws are supposed to create a fertile environment for sharing ideas and expressing different viewpoints freely. But sometimes, strict laws can make it hard for people to exercise these fundamental rights. This can hinder the growth of a lively and open society that values diverse voices.

The government needs to pay attention to Suhakam's advice and fulfill its duties according to Article 10 of Malaysia's Constitution. This article guarantees not only the right to free speech but also the freedoms of assembly and association. These rights aim to create a lively public space for exchanging ideas and maintaining national dialogue. By protecting these constitutional principles, the government shows its commitment to individual freedoms and building a diverse and progressive society with various perspectives. With Suhakam's watchful eye, Malaysia should consider updating its laws to align with human rights values and uphold democratic ideals. By prioritising free expression and inclusivity in legal reforms, Malaysia can become a shining example of democratic principles and a leader in global human rights, showcasing a nation where diverse voices harmoniously contribute to collective progress.

5.5 Preserving Freedom of Expression Through Legal Safeguards

The Federal Constitution of Malaysia stands as the paramount legal instrument that underpins the nation's governance. The evolution of the contemporary Federal Constitution of Malaysia can be attributed to the arduous efforts of the Reid Commission, led by Lord William Reid, tasked with crafting a constitution to pave the way for a fully self-governing and autonomous Malayan Federation. Embracing the currents of burgeoning Malay nationalism, this constitutional development was infused with selectively assimilated ideas, birthing a unique legislative framework that diverged from the traditional Western country model. Notably, the Malaysian constitution deviates markedly from the British constitution, which espouses an absolute freedom of service. This deviation can largely be attributed to the tenacious opposition mounted by the multi-ethnic society and the prevalent socialist sentiments of the time, which engendered a pragmatic approach to balancing the delicate interplay between individual liberties and societal exigencies. As such, the Malaysian constitution refrains from endowing absolute liberty and instead, opt for circumscribing freedoms to accommodate the diverse and sometimes competing demands of its populace. In contradistinction to the British model, characterised by an uncompromising embrace of unbridled freedom, the Malaysian constitutional landscape demands a judicious consideration of contextual complexities and the exigencies of its multi-ethnic society (Islam, 2019, p. cxlvii). This approach to freedom operates within the ambit of measured constraints to uphold public order and societal harmony. In this vein, it becomes imperative to expound upon the specific freedoms enshrined in the Federal Constitution that pertain to the domains of speech and expression, representing vital facets of a democratic society that nurture the free flow of ideas and open discourse.

5.6 The Right to Peaceful Assembly and State Imperatives

The Malaysian Federal Constitution is the foundation of the country's legal system, providing fundamental rights to its citizens. Article 10(1) of this constitution guarantees three essential rights: freedom of speech, the right to peaceful assembly, and the privilege of association. The right to peaceful assembly is significant, allowing Malaysian residents to gather peacefully without weapons (The Federal Constitution of Malaysia, 1957). However, this right is not absolute and Parliament has the authority to regulate gatherings, especially for reasons like national security and public order. When assessing the constitutionality of these regulations, it's crucial to consider proportionality. Regardless of the restrictions imposed, state authorities must ensure that they align with justifications, protecting constitutional rights and avoiding undue infringements on individual liberties (Johan, 2016). Recent years have witnessed laudable strides in the realm of freedom of assembly in Malaysia, with authorities evincing a greater disposition to facilitate and accommodate peaceful gatherings. This paradigm shift towards fostering an´ environment conducive to peaceful assemblies reflects a growing recognition of the pivotal role that public participation plays in buttressing the foundations of a vibrant democracy. Nevertheless, the journey towards safeguarding and promoting the exercise of this fundamental right remains an ongoing endeavour, necessitating further efforts to ensure that citizens can peacefully articulate their grievances, aspirations, and ideas, devoid of unwarranted restrictions, provocation, or intimidation.

The Peaceful Assembly Act of 2012 is the main law that governs how public gatherings are conducted and managed in Malaysia. It is essential to underscore that this law is tailored to engender orderly and non-violent assemblies, thereby distinguishing such peaceful gatherings from those tainted by the specter of violence, riots, or any form of disruptive conduct. Consequently, when an activist engages in conduct that threatens the safety of an individual or property, the very character of the assembly undergoes a transformation, as it relinquishes its peaceful essence and may thus be deemed a criminal offense under the ambit of the Criminal Code (Johan, 2016). As Malaysia traverses the labyrinthine trajectory of nation-building and democratic consolidation, the evolving interplay between the right to peaceful assembly and the state's interests in preserving public order and national security will continue to shape the contours of constitutional jurisprudence. In this unceasing endeavour, vigilant scrutiny and thoughtful legal reforms assume paramount significance, charting a course that safeguards the inherent dignity and rights of the citizenry while adroitly reconciling the manifold demands of a democratic society and the exigencies of governance.

5.7 Freedom of Association

In the Malaysian Federal Constitution, Article 10(1)(c) grants citizens the valuable right of freedom of association. However, this right is not absolute and can be subject to federal laws, particularly in areas like national security, public order, and morality. This careful balance ensures that freedom is protected while considering the well-being of society as a whole. The government has shown a commendable willingness to align with the Sanctions Act, demonstrating a connection between the proposed legislation and the right of association outlined in Article 10(1)(c) (Islam, 2019, p. cxlvii). The envisioned sanction, aiming to restrict assembly, aligns with the broader spirit of freedom of association, emphasizing Malaysians' prerogative to form and participate in associations with a sense of liberty. This commitment to freedom is further emphasized in legal cases like Kelantan State Assembly v Nordin Salleh, which serves as a crucial reference in legal discussions (Rashid, 2018).

5.8 Religious Harmony and Constitutional Realities

Within the sociopolitical landscape of Malaysia, characterised by a mosaic of ethnic diversities and deeply ingrained religious beliefs, the potent force of social sensitivity looms large as a formidable restraint on the unbridled exercise of freedom. In this terrain, a discerning approach is indispensable to preclude inadvertent transgressions upon the sensibilities of disparate constituencies. Of paramount significance is the primacy accorded to Islam as the state religion, imbuing the nation with a concomitant responsibility to exercise utmost caution in disseminating comments that might engender embarrassment, provoke acrimony, or betray neglectful dispositions towards the sacred tenets of Islam or its adherents. The Malaysian government is cautious in promoting ethnic harmony in its diverse society. This protection is embedded in various aspects, including press freedom, religious practices, trust committees, and dress codes. Unlike Western views of religious freedom, Malaysia's Constitution, particularly Article 3(1), specifically names Islam as the nation's religion, emphasizing the coexistence of various faiths. While Islamic law can address individual Muslim legal matters, Article 3(1) clarifies that it doesn't hold supreme status. Scholars like Ahmad Ibrahim and Shad Faruqi have delved into the intention behind Islam being the state religion, highlighting its ceremonial aspects, promotion of Islamic teachings for Muslims, and the establishment of Islamic institutions and courts within constitutional boundaries (Faruqi, 2018).

Religious freedom in Malaysia has certain limits to ensure it aligns with essential religious practices. Article 11(5) is a key example, prioritising public order, health and morality. Any religious expressions conflicting with these considerations are not protected by Article 11(Masum, 2009, p. 3). These limitations aim to protect Muslims from international missions that may disrupt social harmony. Religious freedom, as per Article 3(1), should be exercised peacefully, avoiding actions that might cause discord. Additionally, for Muslim citizens, Schedule 9 of the constitution allows state legislatures to create laws penalizing offenses against Islamic principles, including adultery, apostasy, gambling, and alcohol consumption (Masum, 2009, p. 3).

5.9 Academic Freedom

In the context of Malaysia's academic landscape, the evolution towards enhanced academic freedom is confronted with enduring hurdles, arising from deeply ingrained social norms that wield a constraining influence over the higher education milieu, effectively attenuating the capacity of Malaysian universities to ascend to the acme of intellectual eminence. At the heart of this complex predicament resides the delicate and intricate interplay between academic freedom and its farreaching implications on the broader fabric of society. The conspicuous absence of robust academic freedom portends deleterious ramifications for the nation's progress, a phenomenon exemplified by Malaysia's relative stagnation when juxtaposed against its more dynamic neighboring counterparts throughout the course of the past decade (Malay Mail, 2020).

Central to the enigma lies the pressing challenge of finding the delicate balance between protecting individual freedoms and fostering societal unity. This challenge resonates deeply within Malaysian academia, where the pursuit of academic freedom takes on significant importance. Embracing this undertaking necessitates a comprehensive reevaluation of entrenched perspectives and paradigms, underscoring the indispensable role of a progressive political culture in fostering an environment conducive to academic freedom. As the nation endeavours to propel its educational landscape towards unprecedented heights, the metamorphosis of academic pursuits assumes center stage, calling for an ecosystem that engenders scholarly excellence, ignites intellectual curiosity, and fosters a spirit of innovation. However, the effort to bring about change faces ongoing obstacles stemming from deeply ingrained societal norms. These norms have a strong hold on higher education institutions, limiting their ability to reach the heights of intellectual excellence.

A conspicuous absence of robust academic freedom portends adverse consequences for the nation's intellectual vibrancy and societal progress, as evinced by Malaysia's proclivity towards relative stasis when juxtaposed against its more dynamic neighboring counterparts over the past decade (Hunter, 2021). As articulated by Hunter, the crux of the matter lies in the recognition that academic freedom stands as an indispensable catalyst for societal progress (Hunter, 2021). The interplay between academic freedom and the broader societal landscape necessitates meticulous scrutiny, as the absence of the former inflicts deleterious repercussions upon the latter, undermining the nation's trajectory of growth and development. Inextricably entangled with deeprooted societal norms, the journey towards bolstered academic freedom entails surmounting formidable barriers that impede the ascent of Malaysian universities to the zenith of intellectual eminence. The convergence of individual liberties with the imperative of societal harmony casts academic freedom as a vital linchpin, engendering a paradigm shift in the very conception of educational pursuits. By fostering a vibrant academic ecosystem, anchored in the principles of unbridled academic freedom, Malaysia can chart a trajectory of intellectual excellence and societal advancement, transcending the constraints that have hitherto curtailed its developmental trajectory in the past decade.

5.10 Freedom of Information and Expression

Malaysia is working on making its information system more open and free. But this faces many challenges because of strong social traditions that can hold back the full potential of Malaysian universities. The process involves carefully balancing academic freedom, which means giving scholars the freedom to think and learn, with how it affects society. Without enough academic freedom, Malaysia might fall behind other countries.The way universities can be more creative and do better research is tied to the freedom of academics, but this is hard to achieve in Malaysia due to its political culture. Making this change needs a big shift in how people think, allowing Malaysian universities to be more innovative in their studies and discussions. However, cultural norms pose a challenge in fully allowing academic freedom. It is like walking a tightrope—creating an environment where scholars can do great work while being careful not to upset deeply held social beliefs (Azhari, 2017).

The key issue here is how academic freedom connects with society at large. If there is not enough academic freedom, it can affect the progress and intellectual growth of the nation. Looking at Malaysia compared to its neighbors, it is crucial to create an environment that supports academic freedom (Mia et al., 2021, p. 49). This involves a significant change and building a political culture that values academic freedom as a crucial part of creating and sharing knowledge (Birkinshaw, 1997, p. 27). Even though the Malaysian Federal Constitution does not explicitly mention freedom of information, it is still very important in the broader context of freedom of expression. The link between these rights shows how having unrestricted access to information is crucial for people to freely express themselves (Ikhsan, 2014). Even without explicit constitutional recognition, freedom of information plays a vital role in shaping a participatory democracy. This kind of democracy empowers informed citizens to make decisions, take part in public discussions, and hold authorities accountable. Considering the changing global landscape, it is essential for Malaysia to recognize the importance of freedom of information as a universal concept, leading the nation to take a comprehensive and inclusive approach to uphold this fundamental right (Ikhsan, 2014).

Freedom of the press and media assumes a prominent role within the contours of information freedom, significantly influencing the exercise of the right to freedom of opinion and expression (Bernama, 2019). Independent and unbiased media serve as the lifeblood of a vibrant democracy, acting as custodians of public interest, holding power to account and fostering an environment conducive to informed citizenry. The burgeoning media landscape in Malaysia signifies a positive trend towards a more free and autonomous press, as evidenced by their increasingly objective and impartial reporting, encompassing both accolades and concerns regarding the government's performance (Bernama, 2019).

5.11 Freedom of Press

Amid the dynamic and rapidly evolving landscape of social media, the paradigms of freedom of expression and press freedom confront persistent challenges, with the digital domain witnessing a proliferation of objectionable content and the propagation of violent narratives. The expansive reach and ubiquitous use of social media platforms have engendered the need for the government to deftly navigate a fine balance, effectively regulating freedom of expression while preserving the sacrosanctity of free speech (Priesner, 2019). Malaysia has recently experienced a notable upswing in the emergence of freer and increasingly autonomous media outlets, reflecting heightened objectivity and impartiality in both traditional and digital media presentations. Presently, diverse news sources are broadening their scope of reporting, encompassing not only the government's positive aspects but also candidly addressing the multifaceted challenges confronting the nation.

Undoubtedly, an autonomous and uninhibited media landscape constitutes a fundamental pillar in realizing and upholding the right to freedom of opinion and expression, constituting a pivotal underpinning for the sustenance of a robust democracy and providing the bedrock for Malaysia's ambitious pursuit of comprehensive institutional reform (Bernama, 2019). Recognising the salience of media reform, the United Nations commends the Malaysian government's proactive endeavours in revisiting pertinent legislative frameworks, including the 1948 Incitement Act, the 1984 Printing and Publishing Act, the 1972 Official Secrets Act and the 2002 Film Censorship Act. Particularly laudable is the government's commitment to reforming Section 233 of the Communications and Multimedia Act of 1998, indicative of a genuine intent to fortify press freedom.

The pivotal role of a vibrant and independent press extends beyond the mere dissemination of information; it catalyses the exchange and proliferation of ideas, fostering critical dialogues on public concerns, and empowering individuals with impactful perspectives. Freedom of speech, as enshrined within press freedom, is not the exclusive domain of journalists alone but extends to all citizens, facilitating informed and engaged participation in the collective realm (Paulsen, 2019a). While Malaysia's historical standing in the global press freedom landscape may not have garnered accolades, as evidenced in its rankings in the 2019 Press Freedom Index by Reporters Without Borders (RSF), recent developments bear the seeds of progress and promise. The RSF index evaluates and ranks 180 countries based on media autonomy, diversity, the nature of authoritative systems, the prevalence of self-censorship, and the safety of journalists (Paulsen, 2019a).

While the strides achieved in fostering a more liberal media environment warrant applause, the approach to World Press Freedom Day beckons a dual call—to celebrate the progress made and to remain resolute in addressing the unfinished agenda. Cultivating an open media landscape, propelling positive political initiatives, and fostering attitudinal shifts must be seamlessly integrated with comprehensive legal reforms (Paulsen, 2019a). The onus lies on the government to seize this opportune moment, staying true to the course of disentangling from repressive laws, thereby consolidating freedom of expression and augmenting democratic obligations. Concededly, change is not a serendipitous phenomenon; and as all ASEAN nations strive for media freedom, Malaysia is primed to ascend to the vanguard of this transformative trajectory.

5.12 Examining Limitations on Freedom of Speech

In the context of Malaysia, a substantive shift is imperative to project academic freedom as the cornerstone for knowledge creation and dissemination. This transformative endeavour encounters enduring challenges stemming from deeply entrenched social norms that impede Malaysian universities from realising their full intellectual potential and achieving eminence. The crux of this challenge lies in the interplay between academic freedom and its broader societal implications, with the absence of the former significantly impeding progress, as evident in Malaysia's comparative stagnation relative to neighbouring nations over the past decade (Mia et al., 2021, p. 57).

Notwithstanding the Malaysian Federal Constitution's omission of freedom of information, the significance of this aspect within the broader realm of freedom of expression remains undeniable. The interwoven nature of these rights postulates that unrestricted access to information serves as a pivotal facilitator for the exercise of freedom of speech and expression. Consequently, delineating the contours of freedom of information necessitates a deft balancing act between enabling information accessibility and instituting requisite restrictions. The words of John Locke serve as a poignant reminder that circumscribing individual rights can be justified for the greater good of humanity (Koetsier, 2004). Thus, the power and influence of freedom of information as an instrument for social change assumes potent efficacy in holding ruling powers accountable and instigating a conscientious discharge of duties (Birkinshaw, 1997, p. 27).

Within the Malaysian milieu, an intriguing lacuna emerges as the explicit statutory entitlement to access government data remains conspicuously absent within the contours of both the Constitution and national laws. Delving into Article 10, paragraph 1, of the Federal Constitution, one discerns the proclamation of the privilege of freedom of speech and expression, seemingly circumscribed to the exclusive purview of Malaysian residents, leaving non-residents bereft of the protective mantle conferred by this constitutional provision. However, a departure from this conventional perspective reveals a compelling and multifaceted prism wherein freedom of information emerges as an inseparable and indispensable facet. The importance of unfettered access to relevant data assumes primacy, as it engenders empowerment, empowering citizens to meaningfully and purposefully exercise their right to freedom of expression (Ikhsan, 2014). This multifaceted interplay accentuates the dire need for acknowledging the indivisibility of information freedom from the wider spectrum of expression rights, thereby mandating a comprehensive and holistic approach to fortify democratic ideals and meticulously nurture a resilient culture of unbridled expression within the Malaysian polity. Consequently, the onus lies on the government to diligently contemplate enacting sweeping legislation that would ambitiously extend this pivotal privilege to all residents, transcending geographical boundaries and ensuring that this fundamental freedom finds universal resonance. Freedom of information embodies an indispensable pillar for nurturing a vibrant participatory democracy. Consequently, Malaysia cannot remain indifferent to the incontrovertible global significance of freedom of information. Yet, the dearth of constitutional and statutory provisions delineating a coherent framework for its realization presents a conspicuous lacuna (Ikhsan, 2014). Evidently, the Constitution warrants a thorough reevaluation in relation to freedom of information. Concurrently, the Malaysian government's commendable steps towards reviewing relevant laws, such as the 1948 Incite Act, the 1984 Printing and Publishing Act, the 1972 Official Secrets Act and the 2002 Film Censorship Act, deserve praise (Bernama, 2019). This commitment is exemplified by the Government's endeavour to reform section 233 of the Communications and Multimedia Act of 1998. While laudable, progress should not overshadow the uncompleted tasks ahead, as the foundation of an informed media milieu, positive political initiatives, and attitudinal transformations must converge with legislative amendments to fortify freedom of expression and democratic obligations (Paulsen, 2019b).

The pivotal role of an independent and unrestricted media in realising the right to freedom of opinion and expression cannot be overstated. An autonomous media landscape is vital in fostering a fully functional democracy and establishing the bedrock for the comprehensive institutional reform to which Malaysia is earnestly committed (Mia et al., 2021, p. 59). The United Nations, recognising Malaysia's efforts in reviewing laws, acknowledges the government's strides in promoting media autonomy and diversity (Mia et al., 2021, p. 60). However, the Malaysian press freedom rankings in the 2019 Press Freedom Index by Reporters Without Borders (RSF) underscore the need for continued efforts in this domain (Mia et al., 2021, p. 61). Emphasising media autonomy, diversity, governmental structures, self-regulation and journalists' safety, the RSF index classifies Malaysia in a noteworthy context, encouraging further strides to lead Southeast Asia in the pursuit of a free press.

5.13 Government Practices and Freedom of Expression in Malaysia

In the context of the nation's constitution, freedom of expression faces restrictions, justified by reasons such as national security, public order, protection of ethnic Malays and preserving international relations. These limitations impact the public, media and civil society, with a particular focus on curbing freedom of the press. Freedom of expression comes under the lens of the law, as sedition and public commentary on sensitive topics, including religious and racial matters or criticism of the monarchy, are prohibited. Speech intending to hurt religious sentiments is also restricted. Activist artist Fahmi Reza faced charges in February for posting content deemed annoying. The charges arose from an image

Fahmi shared on social media, depicting beer cans with a political party's logo, in response to the government's COVID-19 measures. The case was eventually discharged. In another instance, Fahmi faced charges for an alleged "obscene" social media post, referring to a former minister, but those charges were later dropped. Opposition Member of Parliament Maria Chin Abdullah was sentenced to seven days in jail for her statement on the discriminatory nature of *sharīʿah* laws against women. This came after a prominent businessman's former wife served a jail sentence for rescheduling visitation dates. Throughout the year, police arrested 46 individuals for defamatory and insulting statements against the country's royalty, reinforcing the notion that freedom of speech has limits (Yen, 2022).

5.14 Press Freedom and Censorship

The media landscape in Malaysia has been marked by challenges to press freedom and the government's control over news content. Journalists have faced harassment and intimidation, creating a hostile environment for the media. For instance, in May, two journalists from The Vibes news portal were confronted and their equipment seized by a security guard while conducting interviews at the Immigration Department in Kuala Lumpur (National Union of Journalists Peninsular Malaysia and Gerakan Media Merdeka). The government's tight control over media content has led to censorship and restrictions on circulation. Publications deemed as threats to public order, morality, or national security have been banned, limited, or restricted. To own a printing press, a permit is required, leading to printers' reluctance to produce critical publications due to fears of reprisals. This environment has stifled independent and investigative journalism and fostered self-censorship in the print and broadcast media sectors. Although online media outlets enjoy more freedom, they are still vulnerable to legal actions and harassment. The government has also occasionally turned to the practice of censoring foreign periodicals, newspapers, and newscasts, focusing in especially on those seen to have graphic or sexually provocative material. In light of these challenges, the media landscape in Malaysia remains a complex terrain where journalists, media outlets, and freedom of expression face significant obstacles (Country Reports on Human Rights Practices-Malaysia, 2022).

5.15 Media Restrictions and National Security

Government officials frequently employed national security regulations to limit the dissemination of media content that voiced dissent against state policies and officials. In the opening month of the year, law enforcement officials summoned journalist Sean Augustin from Free Malaysia Today, in connection to his article that highlighted the armed forces' swift rescue efforts during a December 2021 flood without seeking prior authorisation from the disaster management agency. Advocates of specific political and religious beliefs endeavoured to curtail the scope of free expression by publicly denouncing any form of speech they deemed perilous or by filing criminal complaints against individuals for their allegedly seditious utterances. During the month of July, a self-proclaimed royal supporter lodged a formal complaint with the police against graphic designer Fahmi Reza for his satirical depiction of the Pahang State's regent. The regent himself, however, dismissed the necessity of the police report in response to the incident.

5.16 Internet Freedoms

Amid the vast digital expanse of Malaysia's cyber realm, a complex network of governmental measures has emerged, seeking to control the narrative around sensitive topics like race, religion and royalty. In this context, access to certain online content has become restricted, leading to a complex interplay between internet freedom and state authority. To quell dissent and maintain the facade of public security, authorities have deployed various tactics, such as website blocking and meticulous monitoring of internet activities, scrutinizing messages and blog posts that challenge the established order. As a result, the free flow of information for netizens has been hampered, and content creators find themselves navigating a maze of limitations on their expressive freedoms (Ahmad et al., 2018, p. 835). Across the digital landscape, the government's cautious warnings echo, serving as a reminder to internet users to steer clear of offensive or sensitive content related to matters of faith and ethnicity. Within this context, those who dare to voice criticisms of Islam, the monarchy, or political figures tread on precarious ground, potentially facing legal repercussions. Originally crafted to oversee the vast world of communications and multimedia, the Communications and Multimedia Act (CMA) has evolved into a tool used to legitimize the suppression of content considered undesirable. Sections 211 and 233 of the CMA confer authority to the Malaysian Communications and Multimedia Commission (MCMC), empowering them to block websites that delve into sensitive subjects, spanning from political blogs to adult content and gambling sites.

Through the digital lens of the Open Observatory of Network Interference (OONI), a mosaic of blocked websites comes into focus—encompassing issues of human rights, gambling, news outlets, adult content and religious matters (Sinar Project, 2023). Interestingly, the number of blocked websites has decreased, suggesting a more nuanced approach to internet controls. In the context of digital constraints, the challenges to Malaysia's internet freedom form a multidimensional puzzle. Striking a delicate balance between security concerns and the preservation of individual liberties remains an ongoing enigma. To safeguard democracy and fundamental freedoms, navigating this digital maze demands adroitness and wisdom. As the virtual landscape continues to evolve, addressing these complexities openly and constructively becomes essential to fostering a more inclusive and liberated digital domain for all Malaysians.

Malaysia's CMA has also been employed to hinder attempts that could challenge the status of Islam as the predominant religion in the country. The OONI dashboard data illustrates that from 2017 to 2022, the number of blocked religious websites increased but saw a decline in 2022. Selected websites critical of Islam have been targeted to prevent negative perceptions of the Muslim community from proliferating. For instance, one website called "The Religion of Peace" provides "heavy criticism "of Islam, documenting terror attacks and violence against non-Muslims globally. In 2022, most of the blocked religious websites in Malaysia feature content related to non-Muslim conversions and atheism, perceived as threats to traditional Islam. This blocking restricts users' access to diverse viewpoints on religion, limiting opportunities for open discussions outside the purview of ruling elites. Such control over online content concerning Islam curtails freedom of information and infringes upon the rights of other groups, ensuring the dominance of Islam and its adherents. Moreover, these actions infringe upon the constitutionally protected right of freedom of expression, which has implications for political dynamics and opposition parties' roles. For instance, during the 2018 elections, the MCM"'s request to block certain Malaysiakini websites raised concerns about public order. These measures impact internet freedoms negatively, influencing electoral outcomes in favor of Islamic ruling elites.

Government agencies have commonly made requests to social media platforms for the removal or restriction of online content. Throughout the years, the Malaysian Communications and Multimedia Commission (MCMC) and other governmental agencies have submitted numerous removal requests to Google, leading to the deletion of a considerable number of items from Google's products and services. Notably, YouTube underwent significant content removal in Malaysia between April and June 2022, earning the country a prominent position among those with the highest instances of removals online.

Facebook, too, faced restrictions on its content in Malaysia, with MCMC reporting 33 items that were restricted on the platform between July and December 2021 (New Straits Times, 2023). These items were found to violate various sections of the Penal Code, Common Gaming Houses Act, and pertained to blasphemy, hate speech, and obscenity. Twitter experienced similar encounters, receiving 189 legal demands from government agencies between July and December 2021. Compliance rates with these demands varied, reflecting the challenges in navigating requests related to content removal. A notable aspect of such content removal requests is the prevalence of false information, often playing a significant role in these demands. With the introduction of the anti-fake news bill, the government aims to punish those disseminating false information, yet determining what constitutes false information, especially concerning politically sensitive matters, remains contentious (Country Reports on Human Rights Practices, 2022).

Additionally, content removal has been wielded to protect the dominant status of Islam and the Muslim community in Malaysia. This was evident when Steam, a popular video-game distribution platform, faced blocking in 2017 due to the release of a fighting game called "Fight of Gods," which depicted religious figures in opposition. MCMC deemed the game a threat to religious sanctity and interracial harmony, leading Steam to withdraw the game from its Malaysian store. The government views any online content criticizing the special rights of the Bumiputera, including the Malay race and indigenous tribes, as crossing a critical boundary, just like matters related to religion and royalty. MCMC has removed such content without adhering to legal procedures and can even call upon netizens to do the same. Similarly, instances abound where authorities strive to suppress protests from non-Malay social groups, such as the Indian community, through the blocking of online content. Malaysiakini faced this in 2009 when it posted videos of Shah Alam residents protesting the relocation of a Hindu temple, with the MCMC citing Article 233 of the CMA, which targets offensive content, to justify the takedown Online content against the Malaysian monarchy has also faced removal due to social media posts and comments. For instance, in 2021, a netizen's comment on the queen's Instagram account sparked controversy, leading to the temporary deactivation of the account. Graphic artist Fahmi Reza later uploaded a Spotify playlist with songs containing the word 'jealousy,' accompanied by a photo of the monarch on his Facebook account, resulting in his arrest and the censorship of the playlist under the Sedition Act and CMA (Country Reports on Human Rights Practices, 2022).

5.17 Legal Cases and Internet Freedoms

In July 2022, an unfortunate incident unfolded involving Rizal Van Geyzel, a renowned comedian and co-founder of the Crackhouse Comedy Club. His arrest became a reality under the weight of Section 4(1) of the Sedition Act and Section 233 of the CMA. The reason behind this legal action was three social media posts he made on Facebook, TikTok and Instagram, allegedly sparking disharmony and inciting racial tensions among the populace. Pleading not guilty to all three charges, Rizal had to pay a bail of RM12000 with one surety. In addition, he had to surrender his passport and was restrained from posting anything on social media related to the case (Dzulqarnain, 2022). The impact of Rizal's case reverberates far beyond his individual plight. It underscores the growing trend of using the law to prosecute those who dare to discuss race-related topics on social media. Consequently, freedom of expression suffers a blow as the legal system is employed to muzzle dissenting voices, as evidenced in Rizal's restrictive bail conditions. These alarming developments collectively chip away at internet freedoms in Malaysia.

In a parallel scenario, individuals accused of insulting Islam online also face their day in court. In July 2022, Siti Nuramira Abdullah's comedy performance video caught widespread attention. The video was deemed offensive to Islam as it showcased Nuramira revealing her Muslim identity, disclosing her Quranic knowledge, and then discarding her hijab and baju kurung (Palani, 2022). The repercussions of such cases cast a shadow over the landscape of online expression and its potential constraints. In a series of unfortunate events, she found herself entangled in a web of accusations, facing charges of showing disrespect to Islam and violating Section 298A of the Penal Code, which pertains to fomenting discord and animosity based on religion (Rahmat, 2022). Meanwhile, her partner, Alexander Navin Vijayachandran, a freelance writer, encountered his own legal woes for sharing contentious content on Instagram and YouTube, leading to further tensions. The couple resorted to crowdfunding to secure their RM 40,000 bail, a testament to the gravity of the situation they were thrust into (Faisal, 2022).

The detention of Malaysian writer Uthaya Sankar in April 2022 sent shockwaves around the country in the midst of these troubling developments. Due to a Facebook post that was allegedly derogatory to Prophet Muhammad (PBUH), he became embroiled in legal issues and is now being prosecuted under Sections 233 of the CMA and 298A of the Penal Code (Palatino, 2022). The fact that his mobile phone and SIM card were later taken by the authorities during the arrest increased the gravity and seriousness with which similar instances are handled. These perturbing instances illuminate how Malaysia's legal landscape can undulate the discourse pertaining to race, religion, and royalty, and the far-reaching ramifications it has on the sphere of internet freedoms. Moreover, the looming specter of prosecution engenders an ambience of trepidation and apprehension, leaving an indelible impact on society's propensity to partake in open dialogue and expression.

Once Uthaya Sankar was apprehended, the director of Malaysia's Federal Commercial Crime Investigation Department took the opportunity to caution the general public on the prudent use of social media. He emphasised the importance of avoiding any digital activities that could incite public distress, as this posed a potential threat to the country's harmony. Anyone found deliberately endangering public order and safety would face uncompromising and decisive action. Another incident, concerning religion, involved the arrest of an undisclosed individual in April 2021 under Section 233 of the CMA. The arrest came after the person allegedly shared a letter on social media that condemned a Masjid and insulted the Malays. The incident was reported by SUARAM, a local human rights group (Suaram-Malaysia Human Rights Report, 2021).

In a separate case, Prajiv Lionel Proctor was charged under the CMA for making offensive remarks about Islam and the Monarch. The accused was granted bail of RM 5000 with one surety. Back in 2019, a Malaysian citizen received an exceptionally severe sentence, exceeding ten years in prison, for defaming Islam and the Prophet Muhammad on various online platforms. This sentence was deemed the harshest of its kind in the Muslim-majority nation. The unnamed individual admitted to ten counts of misusing communication networks under the CMA.

These instances underscore the recurring pattern of individuals facing prosecution for criticizing the royalty, using the law as a tool to suppress dissent. An illustrative case occurred in April 2022 when political artist Fahmi Reza was arrested and held for two days under the Sedition Act. This happened after he depicted 'Mojo Jojo' from Powerpuff Girls donning royal attire in response to a controversial painting acquired by Selangor Sultan Sharafuddin Idris Shah, which portrayed parliament members as primates and frogs (Leong, 2022). Before that, in April 2021, Fahmi was arrested again under sedition and communications laws for allegedly insulting the queen through a satirical playlist on Spotify. These examples highlight how the law has been employed to silence individuals expressing dissent or challenging authority, sparking ongoing debates about the delicate balance between freedom of expression and law enforcement in the country.

The activist's case exemplifies how individuals who criticise the monarchy on online platforms can face legal repercussions, resulting in a tightening of internet freedoms and online freedom of expression. In May 2022, Malaysian authorities, relying on the Sedition Act and the CMA, called on the public to provide information about Hussein Abd Hamid, the operator of the Steadyaku47 blog. His online article was accused of defaming the Pahang royal family (Free Malaysia Today, 2022). In February, two university students admitted guilt for posting offensive remarks against Yang di-Pertuan Agong. One of them, 22-year-old Nur Azira Azman, was fined RM 4000 (USD 920) for insulting the Yang di-Pertuan Agong and the Royal Malaysian Police (PDRM) on Twitter in 2021. Similarly, Muhammad Luqmanulhakim Mohd Aziz, another student from Negeri Sembilan, faced charges for posting offensive comments about the Yang di-Pertuan Agong and the Prime Minister on social media in 2021 (Bernama, 2022). Moreover, in January 2022, Ganesparan Nadaraja, reportedly residing in Germany, was accused of insulting Yang di-Pertuan Agong through social media, leading to legal charges against him. Prior to this, Malaysian authorities had requested the International Criminal Police Organisation (Interpol) to issue a red notice against Ganesparan for his online statements criticizing the royal institutions and the Malaysian government.

In June 2021, a member of the Sarawak PKR, Iswardy Morni, faced charges under Section 4(1)(a) of the Sedition Act due to an alleged Facebook post containing seditious remarks aimed at insulting the king. The Judge granted bail of RM 5000 (USD 1100) with one surety and imposed an additional condition prohibiting the accused from making any further seditious comments or causing social distress and public unrest through social media or any other digital or print medium (Bernama, 2022). There have been other instances of legal actions taken against individuals who criticize the monarchy. In 2016, a teenager from Johor received a one-year prison sentence under the Communication and Multimedia Act for supposedly posting a derogatory comment about the Johor royalty on the TRW Troll Story Facebook group (The Straits Times, 2016). Analysing the above cases reveals two key dynamics. Firstly, the laws from the previous BN/UMNO era are systematically utilised to investigate and prosecute those who use the internet to criticise the mainstream 3Rs (race, religion, royalty) narrative. In some cases, individuals are also legally bound not to post similar content on social media again. Secondly, the convictions serve as a clear message to others that they may also face prosecution if they make similar critical comments online.

5.18 Combating Hate Speech in Malaysia's Online Sphere

This phenomenon poses a significant challenge to the freedom of expression on the internet within the country, compelling online users to practice self-censorship and refrain from creating, sharing, or engaging with such content. While this work does not include the direct perspectives of the affected individuals, other research highlights how Malaysian youth feel restrained in expressing their thoughts. They describe an 'invisible wall' that hinders them from voicing their opinions openly (Bernama, 2022). Consequently, people become reluctant to post politically contentious content on popular platforms like Facebook or public forums, instead resorting to more encrypted platforms like Telegram out of fear.

The government has implemented additional measures to control criticism of the 3Rs. For instance, in August 2019, the MCMC introduced a WhatsApp hotline for the public to report potentially sensitive, inappropriate, or negative social media posts related to the 3Rs (Bernama, 2022). Within six weeks of its launch, the MCMC received a staggering 21,296 reports about such posts. The vast majority (80%) focused on race-related issues, while the rest (20%) pertained to religious topics (MCMC, 2019). Although those targeted by this monitoring may not undergo legal proceedings, they face immense pressure and intimidation, aiming to stifle individuals who express excessive criticism about sensitive matters. In one instance, hate speech revolved around race and religion, particularly targeting those who challenged traditional Islam and the Muslim community in Malaysia. Sisters in Islam, an organisation advocating for the rights of Muslim women, faced online violent acts and hate speech after a fatwa was issued against them in 2014. This fatwa, a formal ruling by a qualified Islamic scholar, criticised Sisters in Islam for their advocacy of religious liberalism and pluralism, branding it as a deviation from Islamic teachings. Furthermore, the fatwa prompted federal authorities to close their social media accounts (Tackling Hate, 2020).

During the COVID-19 pandemic, a Chinese woman was accused of spreading misinformation about Malacca Hospital's treatment of patients. Her video, shared on social media platforms, went viral and led to online pejorative comments targeting her nationality and race. Additionally, she was accused of violating Malaysia's Movement Control Order (MCO) (Tham & Omar, 2020). In another incident involving religious-motivated hate speech, the Malay Daily newspaper ran a front-page headline in 2011 that suggested a conspiracy between the opposition Democratic Action Party (DAP) and Christian leaders to seize control of Putrajaya and abolish Islam as the federation's official religion (Sani & Azizuddin, 2013). In response to the situation, Ibrahim Ali, the leader of a right-wing group called PERKASA, openly called for a campaign against Christians who dared to challenge the dominant position of Islam in the country. Instances of hate speech in the online realm, specifically targeting non-Malay ethnic communities, have not been uncommon, with a particular focus on individuals of Chinese and Indian descent. The constitutional recognition of Islam as the country's religion and the religion of the majority have laid the groundwork for hate speech directed at non-Malay communities, fostering an 'us' (Malay) versus 'them' (non-Malay) narrative. This classification of non-Muslims as non-Malays has been exploited and propagated in the digital domain by right-wing groups, influential Islamic preachers, and Malay politicians as a form of hate-based propaganda. In these online spaces, it is not uncommon to witness derogatory terms like '*pendatang*' (newcomers), '*kafir*' (nonbelievers/infidels), '*balik cina*' or '*balik tongsan*' (go back to China) and '*cina-babi*' (Chinese Pigs) being used to refer to members of the Chinese community (Chin, 2022). Even the main Chinese-based political party, DAP, has been labelled as 'DAPig,' with its followers often portrayed as 'anti-Islam' and part of a broader Christian conspiracy to harm Malay Muslims.

Another form of hate speech in Southeast Asia centers around foreign nationals, migrant workers, and refugees. While the Muslim-majority Malaysian society initially showed support for the Rohingya Muslim community fleeing persecution in Myanmar by Buddhist groups, sentiments shifted during the pandemic when fake news circulated, accusing refugees of bringing the coronavirus into the country (Reuters, 2020). This change in public perception paved the way for defamatory incidents. Hate speech targeting the Rohingya often revolves around the perceived privilege and superiority of the Malay community, a central theme of the 3Rs. For instance, during the COVID-19 pandemic, certain mosques in Malaysia displayed anti-Rohingya banners, along with a government announcement prohibiting non-Malaysian individuals from entering the mosques (Sukhani, 2020).

In recent times, instances of hate speech have surged in online spaces, driven by the perception among many Malays that Rohingya community members are demanding Malaysian citizenship and other rights from local politicians. A particular Facebook post falsely claiming a Rohingya leader's demand for citizenship further fuelled discontent among Malaysian citizens. Unfortunately, this led to death threats against Rohingya supporters and even Tengku Emma Zuriana Tengku Azmi, the European Rohingya Council's representative in Malaysia, faced targeting due to her objections against Malaysia's pushback of Rohingya asylum seekers (CIJ Malaysia, 2020). Months later, social media posts targeting the Rohingya community still circulated on platforms like Facebook, with pages like 'Anti Rohingya Club' and 'Foreigners Mar Malaysia's Image.' These pages were eventually taken down after being flagged by Reuters (Latiff & Ananthalakshmi, 2020). Another form of hate speech revolves around political ideology and values, aiming to incite violence against those who oppose the political establishment and seek regime change. In authoritarian regimes, this type of hate speech is often directed at activists and members of opposition parties. The Malaysian government reportedly employs non-legal means, such as cyber troops, to influence online narratives that serve as breeding grounds for hate speech and crime, significantly impacting freedom of expression and overall online freedoms (Bradshaw et al., 2021).

In the realm of digital warfare, Malaysia's cyber capabilities have been assessed as moderately robust, with organised social media manipulation being a prevalent phenomenon. Within this digital landscape, hate speech has emerged as a troubling trend, particularly centered on the sensitive issues of race, religion, and the monarchy (the 3Rs) (Perimbanayagam, 2019). Back in 2018, conservative forces, particularly Islamic political parties, fiercely opposed the government's decision to ratify the ICERD, accusing the convention and the UN of harboring 'Zionist' agendas (Asia Centre, 2020). The utilisation of cyber troopers to fabricate and disseminate misleading information to sway public opinion, as evidenced in the 2014 Teluk Intan by-election, demonstrates the manipulation of online discourse to influence political outcomes.

Moreover, hate speech takes a grim turn against women and the LGBT community, targeting them based on gender or sexual orientation. A case in point is Kow Gah Chie, a female Malaysian journalist who faced virulent online hate speech and threats following the publication of an article that implicated the Environment Minister in supporting a logging company (Palatino, 2020). For many, the Malaysian stance on LGBT rights is oppressive, as reflected in Section 377 of the Penal Code, which criminalises sodomy and carries harsh penalties, including physical abuse authorised by the state. The political exploitation of such laws, as seen in the imprisonment of Anwar Ibrahim on sodomy charges in 1998, underscores the manipulation of justice for political gain (Baume, 2020). Additionally, the legal system has imposed brutal sentences, such as ordering a beating for two women involved in a same-sex relationship in 1998. Members of the Muslim community also face the risk of capital punishment under *sharīʿah* law. These instances starkly illustrate how hate speech is undermining internet freedoms and human rights in Malaysia, necessitating a reevaluation of the digital landscape and the protection of vulnerable communities.

Sexual minorities have found themselves marginalised and facing harassment both online and offline due to their expression and social media posts. A joint study by Justice for Sisters, Diversity Malaysia, PLUHO (People Like Us Hang Out!), and Queer Lapis in 2021 confirmed that online hate speech played a pivotal role in spreading anti-LGBT narratives in Malaysia, with nearly half of the respondents (106 out of 220) reporting emotional and mental burdens from such hate speech (Justice for Sisters, 2021). The case of Nur Sajat Kamaruzzaman, a prominent Malaysian transgender figure and cosmetics entrepreneur, exemplified how hate speech can be used against individuals who defy societal norms. In 2020, Nur Sajat faced doxxing and online hate speech after sharing pictures and videos on social media showing her wearing women's attire during her pilgrimage to Mecca. Despite her identity being listed as male, she received hateful comments for donning the hijab and conducting the pilgrimage as a woman (Ishak, 2020).

During the 2022 General Election, hate speech was deployed as a digital weapon to advance the interests of right-wing groups focusing on race, religion, and royalty (the 3Rs). TikTok, a popular platform, played a significant role in influencing youth voters during GE15, featuring videos that incited hatred and division without promoting constructive conversations (Tan, 2022). One alarming viral content on TikTok warned of a potential repetition of the 1969 riot, a historical sectarian violence between the Sino-Malay communities in Kuala Lumpur. Some TikTok videos even depicted individuals brandishing weapons like knives and machetes, with messages addressing 'young Malay warriors' and threatening supporters of Anwar to 'remember the May 13 tragedy' (Latiff & Mei Chu, 2022). In response to this dangerous incitement, authorities, including the MCMC and police, issued warnings against spreading hate speech related to royalty, race, and religion. Violators faced the possibility of jail time and fines under the CMA. TikTok was also called upon to explain sponsored videos, leading to the removal of May 13-related content, with the platform claiming a 'zero tolerance' policy towards hate speech and violent extremism (Asia Centre, 2023).

5.19 Challenges to Freedom of Expression in Malaysia: Balancing Global Commitments

Malaysia's commitment to international human rights agreements, particularly the Universal Declaration of Human Rights (UDHR), serves as a concrete and undeniable testament to its deliberate dedication to upholding the foundational principles of freedom of expression and speech. These global agreements not only establish a systematic framework but also embody the intricate choreography of promoting, nurturing, and safeguarding individual liberties. This includes the unimpeded articulation, dissemination, and voicing of ideas, opinions, and perspectives while skillfully avoiding the looming threat of repression, coercion, or suppression (Ismail et al., 2011, p. 18).

An illustrative instance revolves around the Sedition Act, a legal instrument that renders verbal expressions or actions as seditious and furnishes the authorities with an extensive array of prerogatives to institute legal proceedings against individuals who articulate dissenting viewpoints or proffer criticisms directed at the governing body. This legislation has been wielded to focus on journalists, activists and political adversaries, culminating in the constriction of open political deliberation and constraining the multifarious range of perspectives that grace the landscape of public dialogue. A preeminent illustration of the Sedition Act's application transpired in 2015, during which the government apprehended and formally charged the well-known political satirist Zunar, legally identified as Zulkiflee Anwar Ulhaque (Ives, 2016). Zunar has gained recognition for his caricatures replete with political commentary, a genre that frequently casts a critical lens on governmental policies and officials. In this instance, he faced the weight of nine counts of sedition, a direct outcome of tweets disseminated through social media platforms that allegedly contained disparaging and scornful references to the judiciary, a public establishment, and the overarching governmental apparatus.

The accusations lodged against Zunar ignited a global outcry and prompted apprehensions about the misappropriation of the Sedition Act as a tool to quell voices of critique. The nebulous clauses within the Act enabled the government to construe Zunar's satirical illustrations as seditious, notwithstanding their satirical essence. This interpretation culminated in his apprehension and the looming specter of a potential imprisonment term of up to 43 years should he be found guilty on all charges. Likewise, in 2016, Malaysian human rights advocate Maria Chin Abdullah encountered arrest under the aegis of the Sedition Act due to her role in orchestrating the Bersih 5 rally—an assembly characterised by its peaceful nature, aimed at championing electoral reform and the establishment of effective governance (Nigel, 2022). Authorities levelled accusations at her for fomenting 'actions detrimental to the tenets of parliamentary democracy' and 'public order' through her involvement in the rally. This arrest acted as a catalyst for protests and accentuated further censure of the Sedition Act's deployment as a means to quash legitimate expressions of dissension and peaceful congregation.

Furthermore, the Printing Presses and Publications Act (PPPA) extends considerable influence to the government over the media landscape, entailing the authority to rescind publishing licenses. This dominion has led to the stifling of diverse viewpoints and the instigation of self-imposed censorship among journalists and media entities (Malaysia: Repeal Publications Law, 2020). The Printing Presses and Publications Act (PPPA) within Malaysia encompasses legislative provisions that bestow upon the government a pronounced dominion over the media spectrum within the nation. It furnishes the authorities with the prerogative to issue, renew, or revoke licenses for newspapers and other printed materials. This breadth of control has yielded significant repercussions for media independence and the uninhibited dissemination of expressions within Malaysia.

A prime illustration of the PPPA's influence on media autonomy emerges through the case of The Edge, a distinguished journal specialising in business and financial affairs within Malaysia. In the year 2015, The Edge undertook a publication endeavour involving an array of articles that unveiled purported financial irregularities within the 1Malaysia Development Berhad (1MDB), a state investment fund (Freedom House, 2016). This investigation laid bare potential instances of corruption and mismanagement that implicated high-ranking government officials. In reaction to the exposé unveiled by The Edge, the Malaysian government opted to suspend the newspaper's publishing license, thereby effectively terminating its operations. This suspension elicited concerns pertaining to the extent of press freedom in the nation and spotlighted the government's utilisation of the PPPA as a means to quell investigative journalism steeped in critique. In a similar vein, the governmental dominion over publishing licenses has spawned a milieu lacking in the diversity of media perspectives. Media platforms construed as being critical of the government have grappled with hurdles in procuring or renewing licenses, consequently birthing a media sphere dominated by publications sympathetic to the government or affiliated with it. This dearth of diversity impedes the fluid dissemination of information and curtails citizens' exposure to a wide array of viewpoints concerning pivotal subjects.

Furthermore, the looming specter of license annulment and potential legal ramifications has engendered self-imposed restraint among journalists and media institutions. Journalists may opt to steer clear of matters deemed sensitive or refrain from conducting critical reportage as a precaution against potential backlash from the government. This self-imposed restraint saps the foundations of an unbridled press and undermines the media's pivotal role as a vigilant overseer, an indispensably crucial facet for ensuring accountability within the echelons of power. The broadranging powers vested in the government by the PPPA have also come under scrutiny for being deployed to suppress political opposition. Newspapers or publications affiliated with the opposition have grappled with obstacles in securing or renewing licenses, further diminishing the spectrum of perspectives and the accessibility of independent journalistic coverage (Freedom House, 2016).

Moreover, the Communications and Multimedia Act (CMA) has been wielded as a tool to govern the online realm, with authorities utilizing it to bar access to websites and social media platforms critical of the government or delving into sensitive subjects (Article19, 2017). These manoeuvres have engendered apprehensions about the censorship entailed in online spheres and the transgressions against the domain of freedom of expression within the digital expanse. The ambit of the Communications and Multimedia Act (CMA) within Malaysia encompasses a comprehensive legislation encapsulating diverse facets of the communications and multimedia sector, spanning the terrain of online content and social media platforms. While this legislative entity serves multifarious legitimate intentions, its utilization as a mechanism to regulate online articulation and suppress content that critiques the government or addresses sensitive topics has prompted a disapproving response.

One glaring instance underscoring the CMA's influence on the freedom of expression in online arenas is the blocking of news-oriented websites and social media platforms. Instances have arisen where the government has exercised its prerogative to hinder access to websites engaged in governmental critique or reporting on subjects considered delicate—such as instances of corruption or human rights violations. An illustrative case can be seen in the situation of.

Malaysiakini, a well-known news portal lauded for its independent reportage and critical perspective, which has faced temporary access blocks due to the auspices of the CMA (Article19, 2017). Furthermore, social media platforms have also grappled with scrutiny and censorship under the aegis of the CMA. Authorities have capitalized on the act to pressure social media platforms into the removal of content or accounts that manifest a critical stance toward the government. This dynamic has engendered a climate of concern with regards to online censorship and the stifling of contrarian voices within the domain of the digital medium. Beyond the dimensions of website impeding and social media control, the CMA has additionally served as the impetus for legal actions against individuals due to their online engagements. The legislation integrates provisions that criminalize certain forms of online speech, encompassing actions such as disseminating "offensive content" or sharing false information. Detractors of the legislation posit that these provisions tend to be sweeping in their scope and ambiguously formulated, thus allowing for the delineation of online content as offensive or mendacious based on subjective parameters.

An illustrative example of legal measures taken under the aegis of the CMA is the case of Fahmi Reza, an artist and activist known for his graphic work. In 2016, he encountered charges under the act for uploading a satirical caricature of the Prime Minister on social media, a creation that was deemed offensive by the authorities (Article19, 2017). This incident exemplifies the apprehensions roused by the potential abuse of the CMA as a means to suppress dissent and circumscribe the contours of freedom of expression within the virtual sphere. In recent times, the government's utilisation of the Security Offences (Special Measures) Act (SOSMA) has witnessed an amplification, with its focus shifting towards the targeting of activists and individuals voicing contrarian opinions (Ganesan, 2022). The Act facilitates detentions sans trial under circumstances classified as related to national security. Such a trajectory has evoked qualms about capricious apprehensions and the curtailment of free expression, all ostensibly under the umbrella of preserving national security. The Security Offences (Special Measures) Act (SOSMA) within the sphere of Malaysia's legislative framework was initially conceived as a mechanism to combat terrorism and confront grave security threats (Ganesan, 2022). However, the contours of its application have evolved over the years, steering the government's attention toward activists and those disseminating opposing viewpoints. This transformation has elicited concerns over the possibility of misuse and infringements on the realm of free expression.

One specific instance stands out in the narrative, encapsulated in the plight of Maria Chin Abdullah. The charge levelled against her pertained to actions considered deleterious to the health of parliamentary democracy, hinging on her role in orchestrating peaceful protests (Free Malaysia Today, 2023). The reverberations of her detention, bereft of trial, resounded as a catalyst for critical inquiry, conjuring concerns of the Act's potential as an instrument to smother political activism and mute the chorus of discordant voices. In a parallel vein, the arrest and confinement of Khalid Ismath, an entrepreneur and influencer on social media platforms, constitutes another noteworthy episode. The year 2019 bore witness to his apprehension under the SOSMA banner, the trigger being his online musings critical of the government's management of specific affairs (Free Malaysia Today, 2023). This incident crystallised worries about the government's proclivity to employ the SOSMA as a mechanism to target dissenting digital voices, while simultaneously invoking questions regarding its harmony with internationally recognized standards of human rights. Additionally, the SOSMA's ambit has extended its grasp to include members of the political opposition. 2017 saw the detention of multiple constituents affiliated with the Pan-Malaysian Islamic Party (PAS), a development stemming from their involvement in a peaceful rally (Free Malaysia Today, 2023).

The coordination of these arrests raised concerns about the law being used as a tool to suppress political opposition and limit the scope of free expression and assembly. Critics argue that the broadness and ambiguity embedded in the structure of SOSMA create opportunities for arrests without justification, enabling detention without the necessary trial and lacking compelling evidence of wrongdoing. The law's predominant emphasis on national security has been interpreted expansively, providing authorities with a convenient justification to target activists, journalists, and individuals involved in political opposition that scrutinises the government's actions. These examples serve as poignant illustrations of how the government's increasing reliance on SOSMA in recent times has raised concerns about its potential for misuse and its impact on the scope of expressive freedom in Malaysia (Free Malaysia Today, 2023). The prospect of detentions without a trial, combined with arrests based on vague allegations, raises questions about the Act's alignment with internationally recognised human rights standards. Additionally, there are concerns about its potential to suppress dissent and curtail the fabric of democratic liberties.

5.20 Conclusion

The constitutional guarantee of freedom of expression implies that this right should be exercised without unjustified limitations, emphasizing its distinctiveness and the necessity for safeguarding (Dziyauddin, 2006). However, it is crucial to acknowledge that a variety of interests, whether public or private, requires protection to uphold the socio-political structure of Malaysian democratic society. While the idea of incorporating a right-based approach from Western liberal democracy into the domestic constitutional framework might seem praiseworthy, it is inappropriate due to the misalignment between the Western stress on individualism and the communitarian foundation ingrained in Malaysia's national constitutional structure. Embedded in Malaysia's constitutional principles is a prioritisation of community rights over individual rights, grounded in a communitarian ethos that highlights the well-being of society and the importance of public interest. It is essential to emphasize that this emphasis on community rights does not diminish Malaysia's dedication to upholding human rights and fundamental freedoms. From the perspective of the Malaysian constitution, the paramount objective is the protection of the public and society on a broad scale. Illustratively, the safeguarding of religious freedom under Article 11 of the Federal Constitution reflects a communitarian inclination, allowing for the simultaneous existence and practice of minority faiths like Christianity, Buddhism, and Hinduism alongside the predominant religion of Islam (Marcinkowski, 2014, p. 130).

On the flip side, majoritarianism is characterised by decisions that hinge on the rule of the majority. While ostensibly taking into account societal interests, this concept inherently places a premium on the preferences of the majority. This inclination is apparent, for instance, in the constitutional prioritisation of Bahasa Malaysia (the national language), which is predominantly spoken by the Malay majority in Malaysian society (Ying et al., 2015, p. 120). Another illustration of majoritarianism in practice is observable in the establishment of a distinct jurisdiction for Syariah courts, outlined in Article 121(1A) of the Constitution. This leads to a scenario where civil courts no longer hold jurisdiction over cases related to Islamic matters. While both communitarianism and majoritarianism prioritise societal aspects, the latter places a stronger emphasis on the numerical aggregation of individuals within society. Malaysia stands to benefit by avoiding the adoption of practices incompatible with local dynamics and steering clear of unacceptable relativism that might impede the comprehensive advancement of freedom. As Malaysia progresses economically, there is an opportunity to devote significant attention to enhancing social and political rights, including the right to privacy. Consequently, human rights could play a more prominent role in shaping the socio-political landscape of Malaysian life.

References

Abdullah, N., & Hua, C. L. (2007). Legislating faith in Malaysia. *Singapore Journal of Legal Studies*, 264–289.

Abraham, A. (2002). The transfer of the straits settlements: A revisionist approach to the study of colonial law and administration. *Journal of the Hong Kong Branch of the Royal Asiatic Society, 42*, 1–33.

Ahmad, R., Abd Aziz, A. S., & Mohd Noor, N. A. (2018). Restrictive provisions of the Communications and Multimedia Act 1998: A discussion. In A. Abdul Rahim, A. A. Rahman, H. Abdul Wahab, N. Yaacob, A. Munirah Mohamad, & A. Husna Mohd. Arshad (Eds.), *Public law remedies in government procurement: Perspective from Malaysia* (Vol. 52). *European Proceedings of Social and Behavioural Sciences* (pp. 834–840).

Alagappa, M. (2013). After GE13: Strengthening democracy in Malaysia. Carnegie Endowment for International Peace. Retrieved April 10, 2024, from https://carnegieendowment.org/2013/08/01/after-ge13-strengthening-democracy-in-malaysiapub-52639

Anuar, M. K. (2012). Reporting the environment: Human rights, development and journalism in Malaysia. *Asia Pacific Media Educator, 22*(2), 253–262.

Article 19. (2017, February). *Malaysia: The Communications and Multimedia Act 1998: Legal analysis*. Retrieved April 5 2024, from https://www.article19.org/data/files/medialibrary/38690/Malaysia-analysis-Final-December.pdf

Asia Centre. (2020). *Hate speech in Southeast Asia: New forms, Old rules*. Asia Centre. Retrieved April 5, 2024, from https://asiacentre.org/wp-content/uploads/2020/07/HateSpeech-in-Southeast-Asia-New-Forms-OldRules.pdf

Asia Centre. (2023). *Internet freedoms in Malaysia: Regulating online discourse on race, religion, and royalty*. Asia Centre. Retrieved April 6, 2024, from https://www.sis.gov.eg/Story/162236/Egypt-and-Human-Rights?lang=en-us

Azhari, A. N. A. (2017). Universities need autonomy and academic freedom. Retrieved April 5 2024, from http://www.ideas.org.my/universities-need-autonomy-and-academic-freedom/

Bari, A. A. (2004, May 27–28). The evolution of Malaysian constitution tradition in the role of law in developing Asia. In *Proceedings of the Asian Law Institute inaugural conference*. Retrieved April 5, 2024, from http://lib.perdana.org.my/PLF/Digital_Content/Journal&Papers/000001/3/The%20Evolution%20of%20Malaysian%20Constitutional%20Tradition.pdf

Baume, M. (2020). Malaysia's sodomy law, imposed by British imperialists, could soon crumble. *Them*. Retrieved April 6, 2024, from https://www.them.us/story/malaysia-couldoverturn-homophobic-anti-sodomy-law

Bernama. (2019). Has press freedom in Malaysia taken off? Retrieved April 5, 2024, from http://www.dailyexpress.com.my/news/135216/has-press-freedom-in-malaysia-taken-off-/

Bernama. (2022, December 16). Permuafakatan: Perjanjian persefahaman Kerajaan Perpaduan jamin prinsip Perlembagaan, astro Awani. Retrieved April 5 2024, from https://www.astroawani.com/berita-politik/permuafakatan-perjanjianpersefahaman-kerajaanperpaduan-jamin-prinsip-perlembagaan-397198

Bernama. (2022, February 28). Uni students plead guilty to posting offensive remarks against King. *Selangor Journal*. Retrieved April 5, 2024, from https://selangorjournal.my/2022/02/unistudents-plead-guilty-to-posting-offensive-remarks-against-king/

Birkinshaw, P. (1997). Freedom of information and open government: The European community/union dimension. *Government Information Quarterly, 14*(1), 27–49.

Bradshaw, S., Bailey, H., & Howard, P. N. (2021). *Industrialised disinformation: 2020 global inventory of organized social media manipulation*. Programme on Democracy & Technology.

Chin, J. (2022). Racism towards the Chinese minority in Malaysia: Political Islam and institutional barriers. *The Political Quarterly, 93*(3), 451–459.

CIJ Malaysia. (2020). CSOs condemn online gender-based attacks on women human rights defender Tengku Emma Zuriana. Retrieved April 10, 2024, from https://cijmalaysia.net/csoscondemn-online-gender-basedattacks-on-women-human-rights-defender-tengku-emma-zuriana/

Country Reports on Human Rights Practices: Malaysia, Bureau of Democracy, Human Rights and Labor. (2022). Retrieved April 5, 2024, from https://www.state.gov/reports/2022-countryreports-on-human-rights-practices/malaysia/

Dziyauddin, H. (2006). A comparative study of freedom of expression and right to privacy in relation to the press in Malaysia and the United Kingdom (PhD thesis). University of Newcastle Upon Tyne. Retrieved April 5, 2024, from https://core.ac.uk/download/pdf/153776225.pdf

Dzulqarnain, Q. N. (2022, July 22). Rizal van Geyzel claims trial to inciting racial tensions online. Retrieved April 5, 2024, from https://www.thevibes.com/articles/news/66513/rizal-vangeyzel-pleads-not-guilty-to-inciting-racialtensions-online

Faisal, A. (2022, July 13). Freelance writer charged with uploading insulting content. *Free Malaysia Today*. Retrieved April 5, 2024, from https://www.freemalaysiatoday.com/category/nation/2022/07/13/freelance-writer-chargedwithuploading-insulting-content/

Faruqi, S. S. (2018). Reform needed to protect free speech. Retrieved April 5, 2024, from https://www.thestar.com.my/opinion/columnists/reflecting-on-the-law/2018/09/27/reformneeded-to-protect-free-speech-we-need-an-independent-law-reform-commission-to-scrutinisethe#cJckxaGsAPQgkuM2.99

Faruqi, S. S. (2021, August 18). The monarchy and Article 150. Retrieved April 5, 2024, from https://fulcrum.sg/the-monarchy-and-article-150/

Free Malaysia Today. (2022, May 13). Cops looking for blogger steadyaku47 over 'defamatory' article'. Retrieved April 5, 2024, from https://www.freemalaysiatoday.com/category/nation/2022/05/13/cops-looking-forbloggersteadyaku47-over-defamatory-article/

Free Malaysia Today. (2023, May 12). Former activist Khalid Ismath charged with domestic violence. Retrieved April 5, 2024, from https://www.freemalaysiatoday.com/category/nation/2023/05/12/former-activist-khalid-ismathcharged-with-domestic-violence/

Freedom House. (2016, October 18). *Freedom of the Press 2016-Malaysia*. Retrieved April 5, 2024, from https://www.refworld.org/docid/582ac6c67.html

Ganesan, R. R. (2022, December 17). Explained: The controversial Sosma law. *Free Malaysia Today*. Retrieved April 5, 2024, from https://www.freemalaysiatoday.com/category/nation/2022/12/17/explained-the-controversialsosma-law/

Haa, P. L., Kho, J., & Chng, B. (2013). Nation building, English as an international language, medium of instruction, and language debate: Malaysia and possible ways forward. *Journal of International and Comparative Education*, *2*(2), 58–71.

Haas, B. (2016, November 16). Everything is an 'official secret'. DW. Retrieved April 5, 2024, from https://www.dw.com/en/in-malaysia-almost-everything-is-an-official-secret/a-36410805

Hamid, N., & Anwar, M. R. (2018, December 3). Moratorium on Draconian laws suspended on issues threatening national security, public order, race relations. NST. Retrieved April 5, 2024, from https://www.nst.com.my/news/nation/2018/12/436806/moratorium-draconian-lawssuspended-issues-threatening-national-security

Hunter, M. (2021, June 06). *Why there is no academic freedom in Malaysia*. Retrieved April 5, 2024, from https://www.malaymail.com/news/what-you-think/2015/10/05/why-there-is-noacademic-freedom-in-malaysia-murray-hunter/981899

Ikhsan, M. (2014). Legal hurdles in freedom of information in Malaysia. Retrieved April 5, 2024, from https://papers.ssrn.com/sol3/papers.cfm?abstract_id=2470291

Ishak, S. (2020). Intersex M'sian flamed for performing pilgrimage in Mecca as a woman. *Mothership*. Retrieved April 5, 2024, from https://mothership.sg/2020/02/malaysian-intersexpilgrimage/

Islam, M. Z. (2019). Contemporary debate on freedom of speech and expression concerning film censorship laws in Malaysia 1 LNS(A), cxlvii. *Legal Network Series*, 1, 1–21.

Islam, M. Z., Mokhtar, K. A. B., & Afandi NHBMB, S. M. (2020). Regulating online broadcast media in Malaysia: Legal study of compliance and regulatory enforcement in relation to freedom of speech and expression in Malaysia: Protection under the federal constitution hate speech and offensive materials. *International Journal of Psychosocial Rehabilitation, 24*(6), 10892–10898

Ismail, N. B., & Universiti Sultan Zainal Abidin. (2011). A Comparative analysis of the practice of the United Kingdom and Malaysia in respect of freedom of expression. *UUM Journal of Legal Studies, 2*, 17–38.

Ives, M. (2016, November 29). A Malaysian political cartoonist on facing his fears, and prison, for art. *The New York Times*. Retrieved April 5, 2024, from https://www.nytimes.com/2016/11/29/world/asia/malaysia-political-cartoonist-zunar-seditionnajib-razak.html

Johan, S. (2016). *The right to peaceful assembly*. Retrieved April 5, 2024, from https://www.thestar.com.my/opinion/online-exclusive/a-humble-submission/2016/11/11/theright-to-peaceful-assembly-unlike-the-police-act-before-this-the-peaceful-assembly-act-allowsas#SQuHtyH8XJ97JIFD.99

Justice for sisters, diversity Malaysia, PLUHO (People Like Us Hang Out!), & Queer Lapis. (2021). Survey findings: Impact of Covid-19 & anti-LGBT narratives on LGBTQ+ persons in Malaysia. *Queerlapis*. Retrieved April 5, 2024, from https://www.queerlapis.com/wpcontent/uploads/2021/12/311221-Survey-findings_Impact-of-Covid-19-and-anti-LGBTnarratives-on-LGBT-persons-in-Malaysia.pdf

Koetsier, L. S. (2004). *Natural law and Calvinist political theory*. Trafford Publishing.

Latiff, R., & Ananthalakshmi, A. (2020). Anti-migrant sentiment fanned on Facebook in Malaysia. *Reuters*. Retrieved April 5, 2024, from https://www.reuters.com/article/uk-facebookmalaysia-rohingya-idUKKBN26Z0BP

Latiff, R., & Chu, M. M. (2022). TikTok on 'high alert' in Malaysia as tensions rise over election wrangle. *Reuters*. Retrieved April 5, 2024, from https://www.reuters.com/world/asiapacific/tiktok-high-alert-malaysia-tensions-riseover-election-wrangle-2022-11-23/

Leong, A. (2022, April 14). Satirical artist Fahmi Reza hauled again for latest 'Mojo Jojo' satire artwork. *The Rakyat Post*. Retrieved April 5, 2024, from https://www.therakyatpost.com/news/2022/04/14/satirical-artist-fahmi-reza-hauled-againforlatest-mojo-jojo-satire-artwork/

Leow, R. (2016). *Taming Babel: Language in the making of Malaysia*. Cambridge University Press.

Malay Mail. (2020). Protection of freedom of speech and expression–Suhakam. Retrieved April 5, 2024, from https://www.malaymail.com/news/what-you-think/2020/06/23/protection-offreedom-of-speech-and-expression-suhakam/1878253

Malaysia: Federal Constitution. (1957, August 31). Retrieved April 5, 2024, from https://www.refworld.org/docid/3ae6b5e40.html

Malaysia: Repeal publications law to promote freedom of expression. (2020, February 17). Retrieved April 5, 2024, from https://www.article19.org/resources/malaysia-repeal-publicationslaw-to-promote-freedom-of-expression/

Malaysian artist held over 'insulting' Spotify Playlist. (2021, April 24). *DW.* Retrieved April 5, 2024, from https://www.dw.com/en/malaysiaartist-arrested-for-insulting-queen-with-spotifyplaylist/a-57320581

Marcinkowski, C. (2014). Religious freedom for a minority church: Impressions from Malaysia. In K. Krämer & K. Vellguth (Eds.), *Religious freedom: Foundations, reflections, models* (pp. 129–142). Claretian Publications.

Masum, A. (2009). Freedom of religion under the Malaysian federal constitution. *Current Law Journal (CLJ), 2*(1), 3.

MCMC. (2019). MCMC: Almost 22,000 reports received about insensitive '3R' social media posts in six. Retrieved April 5, 2024, from https://www.mcmc.gov.my/en/media/pressclippings/mcmc-almost-22-000-reports-receivedabout-insensit

Mia, M. T., Islam, M. Z., & Norullah, M. (2021). Freedom of speech and expression in Malaysia: Protection under the Federal Constitution. *SARJANA, 36*(2), 48–62.

Sani, M., & Azizuddin, M. (2013). Hate speech and free speech in Malaysia. *New Mandala.* Retrieved April 5, 2024, from https://www.newmandala.org/hate-speech-and-free-speech-in-malaysia/

Naz, S., & Sabaruddin, J. S. B. (2016). Malaysian preventive detention laws: Old preventive detention provisions wrapped in new packages. *Journal of Malaysian and Comparative Law, 43*(2), 59–78.

New Straits Times. (2023, May 22). MCMC working with Meta to curb Facebook activities that violate Malaysian law. Retrieved April, 5, 2024, from https://www.nst.com.my/news/nation/2023/05/912199/mcmc-working-meta-curb-facebookactivities-violate-malaysian-law

Nigel, A. W. (2022, April 26). Jail sentence for Maria Chin. *Malaysiakini.* Retrieved April, 5, 2024, from https://www.malaysiakini.com/newsletter/619261

Noor, N. F. M. (2020). Freedom of speech and the pandemic. *International Journal of Law, Government and Communication* (IJLGC), 5(21), 285–297.

Palani, T. (2022, July 13). Woman in viral 'stand-up comedy' clip charged. Retrieved April, 5, 2024, from https://theedgemalaysia.com/article/woman-viral-standup-comedy-clip-charged

Palatino, M. (2020). Malaysian journalist targeted by hate speech and racist attacks on Facebook. *Global Voice.* Retrieved April, 5, 2024, from https://globalvoices.org/2020/03/19/malaysianjournalist-targeted-by-hate-speech-andracist-attacks-on-facebook/

Palatino, M. (2022, May 2). Malaysian writer faces blasphemy probe for Facebook post. Retrieved April, 5, 2024, from https://advox.globalvoices.org/2022/05/02/malaysian-writerfaces-blasphemy-probe-for-facebook-post/

Paulsen, E. (2019a, January 6). Take freedom of speech seriously. Retrieved April, 5, 2024, from https://www.thestar.com.my/news/nation/2019/01/06/take-freedom-of-speech-seriously-wecannot-legislate-away-our-fundamental-problems-and-we-certainly#1MA7K7IitWD4px4o.99

Paulsen, E. (2019b, May 5). Press for more freedom. Retrieved April, 5, 2024, from https://www.thestar.com.my/news/nation/2019/05/05/press-for-more-freedom

Perimbanayagam, K. (2019). MCMC opens channels for offensive 'race, religion and royalty' content. *New Straits Times*. Retrieved April, 5, 2024, from https://www.nst.com.my/news/nation/2019/08/513634/mcmc-opens-channeloffensive-racereligion-and-royalty-content

Priesner, S. (2019). Freedom of Press: A cornerstone of democracy and for speaking truth to power. Retrieved April, 5, 2024, from https://www.nst.com.my/opinion/columnists/2019/05/486668/freedom-press-cornerstonedemocracy-and-speaking-truth-power

Rahmat, K. (2022, July 20). Syariah court not charging 'strip' act woman as Penal Code provides heavier sentence. *New Straits Times*. Retrieved April, 5, 2024, from https://www.nst.com.my/news/crime-courts/2022/07/815000/syariahcourt-not-charging-strip-actwoman-penal-code-provides

Rashid, H. R. A. (2018). *Proposed anti-party hopping law must consider constitutional right to freedom of association, Dewan Rakyat told*. Retrieved April, 5, 2024, from https://www.nst.com.my/news/nation/2018/10/422069/proposed-anti-party-hopping-law-mustconsider-constitutional-right

Reuters. (2020). Malaysian lawmaker calls for hate speech law after Reuters' Rohingya report. Retrieved April, 5, 2024, from https://www.reuters.com/article/us-facebook-malaysia-rohingyaidUSKBN2840LZ

Show, Y. X. (2021). Narrating the racial riots of 13 May 1969: Gender and postmemory in Malaysian literature. *South East Asia Research, 29*(2), 214–230.

Siladass, K. (2016, June 29). *The word 'parent' in Article 12(4) of the constitution*. Retrieved April, 5, 2024, from https://www.malaysiakini.com/letters/347040

Sinar Project. (2023, July 18). *Explaining the block of Malaysia now in Malaysia*. Retrieved April, 5, 2024, from https://www.malaysianow.com/opinion/2023/07/18/explaining-the-blockof-malaysianow-in-malaysia

SUARAM. (2021). *Malaysia human rights report 2021*. Retrieved April, 5, 2024, from https://www.suaram.net/human-rightsreports?pgid=kvex92wb-3a6329d5-b6ff-429b-a81d014aa2f4fba3

Sukhani, P. (2020). The shifting politics of Rohingya refugees in Malaysia. *The Diplomat*. Retrieved April, 5, 2024, from https://thediplomat.com/2020/07/the-shifting-politics-ofrohingya-refugees-in-malaysia/

Tackling Hate. (2020). Why is there double discrimination against Muslim women in Malaysia? Retrieved April 5, 2024, from https://tacklinghate.org/videos/tackling-hate-hate-against-muslimwomen-in-malaysia-interviewwith-shareena-sheriff/

Tan, N. A. (2022). Hate speech emerges on Malaysian TikTok as political uncertainty drags out. *Arab News*. Retrieved April, 5, 2024, from https://www.arabnews.com/node/2204766/media

Tham, J. V., & Omar, N. (2020). Like a virus: How racial hate speech looks like in Malaysia During the Covid-19 Pandemic. *The Centre*. Retrieved April 5, 2024, from https://www.centre.my/post/how-covid-19-influencingracial-hate-speech-malaysia

The Straits Times. (2016, June 7). Youth sentenced to 1-year jail for insulting Johor royalty on Facebook. Retrieved April 5, 2024, from https://www.straitstimes.com/asia/se-asia/youthsentenced-to-1-year-jail-for-insultingjohor-royalty-on-facebook

Thomas, T. (2004). Freedom of religion and registration of religious groups. *INSAF, XXXIII*(2), 15–37.

UiHua. (2017). *Is there freedom of speech in Malaysia if you can get arrested for Facebook posts*. Retrieved April 5, 2024, from https://asklegal.my/p/freedom-of-speech-sedition-socialmedia-facebook-whatsapp

Venugopal, A. V., & Hassan, K. H. (2012). The law of contempt of court in Malaysia: Considering reforms. *Advances in Natural and Applied Sciences, 6*(8), 1451–1465.

Wok, S., & Mohamed, S. (2017). Internet and social media in Malaysia: Development, challenges, and potentials. In B. P. Acuña (Ed.), *The evolution of media communication* (pp. 4564). Intech Open.

Yatim, R. (1995). *Freedom under executive power in Malaysia: A study of executive supremacy*. Endowment Publications.

Yen, H. K. (2022, April 25). Shariah court jails Maria Chin 7 days for 'insulting' Islamic judicial system. Retrieved April 5, 2024, from https://www.freemalaysiatoday.com/category/nation/2022/04/25/shariah-court-jails-maria-chin7-days-for-insulting-islamic-judicial-system/

Ying, S., Heng, C. S., & Abdullah, A. N. (2015). Language vitality of Malaysian languages and its relation to identity. *GEMA Online Journal of Language Studies, 15*(2), 119–136.

CHAPTER 6

Conclusion: Human Rights Protection and Challenges in Egypt and Malaysia

6.1 Introduction

The historical, cultural, and socio-political contexts in Egypt and Malaysia have significantly shaped the development of human rights regulations in these nations. Over the course of their histories, these countries have faced complex and ever-evolving situations, influenced by their unique historical backgrounds, cultural values, and societal intricacies. These factors have been instrumental in the establishment of legal frameworks aimed at ensuring the protection and advancement of fundamental individual freedoms. Through a comprehensive examination of human rights legislation, this book has thoroughly investigated the intricate aspects of human rights discourse in Egypt and Malaysia. With a specific emphasis on the progress made in the legal sphere within these regions, the publication has conducted a detailed analysis of the various laws, policies, and implementations that have impacted the human rights landscape. By delving into the intricacies of these legal structures, the text has sought to shed light on the nuanced challenges and complexities inherent in the endeavor to safeguard and promote human rights.

Throughout the earlier chapters, the recurring theme of equality and non-discrimination has surfaced as a central focus. The thorough analysis of the current legal provisions and their practical implications has emphasised the need for both Egypt and Malaysia to address the challenges and

A. Mohiuddin, *Human Rights Law in Egypt and Malaysia: Freedom of Religion and Expression, Volume 1*, Political Economy of Islam,
https://doi.org/10.1007/978-3-031-63859-6_6

deficiencies in ensuring comprehensive protection for all individuals. The book has underscored the necessity for a strong legal foundation that not only acknowledges the varied and complex nature of human rights but also actively strives to eliminate discriminatory practices and foster an environment of inclusivity and equality. By highlighting the obstacles and limitations faced by these nations, the book has advocated for a deeper comprehension of the intricacies surrounding human rights legislation. It has urged policymakers, legal experts, and civil society stakeholders to recognize the significance of ongoing reform and advancement in the domain of human rights protection. The book's exploration of the developing legal frameworks in Egypt and Malaysia has not only illuminated the current gaps but has also provided a blueprint for future efforts in the pursuit of a more fair and just society for all individuals.

This chapter offers a comprehensive analysis of the book's key findings, providing an indepth exploration of the human rights landscape in both Egypt and Malaysia. With a specific focus on the examination of constitutional provisions and the legal frameworks within these countries, the chapter attempts to shed light on the existing challenges and advancements in the realm of human rights legislation. Moreover, it puts forth a series of actionable recommendations, aiming to address the identified gaps and limitations. The emphasis is placed on the urgent necessity for the establishment of comprehensive and inclusive safeguards to ensure the protection of the rights of all individuals, regardless of their backgrounds or identities.

6.2 Legal Status and Challenges of Human Rights in Muslim-Majority Countries

Human rights laws in countries with a Muslim-majority population can exhibit notable variations, influenced by each nation's unique political, social, and cultural setting. While certain Muslim-majority countries have demonstrated substantial strides in implementing human rights safeguards, others continue to grapple with obstacles in this sphere. It is crucial to recognize that human rights possess a universal nature, being safeguarded by various international agreements and treaties, including the Universal Declaration of Human Rights and the International Covenant on Civil and Political Rights. Several Muslim-majority nations have endeavored to harmonize their domestic legislation with global human rights benchmarks, often entailing the enactment of statutes protecting fundamental human rights such as the right to life, freedom of expression, religious freedom, fair trial rights, as well as the rights of women and minority groups. Moreover, some countries have taken measures to establish institutions and mechanisms for overseeing and upholding human rights standards (Mahmoudi, 2016, p. 536).

Nevertheless, certain countries with a predominant Muslim population grapple with substantial obstacles in adequately protecting and advocating for human rights. These challenges may arise from a range of complex factors, including political instability, deficient governance structures, interpretations of religious doctrines that do not completely align with global human rights standards, and cultural traditions that may contradict human rights principles. Specific Muslim-majority nations have faced severe condemnation for their violations of human rights, which encompass restrictions on freedom of expression, inadequate provisions for safeguarding the rights of religious minorities, discrimination based on gender, and constraints on women's rights. These contentious issues have garnered considerable attention from international human rights organizations, leading to fervent calls for comprehensive reforms and intensified protection of human rights within these countries (Mahmoudi, 2016, p. 537).

While countries like Saudi Arabia place an emphasis on safeguarding human rights in line with *sharīʿah*, some constitutions directly refer to the Universal Declaration of Human Rights or the Charter of the United Nations. However, others make more general references to human rights without explicitly citing any specific instrument. Certain constitutions highlight particular human rights, either focusing on specific rights or acknowledging the complete range of rights and freedoms outlined in the 1966 UN Covenants. Despite these constitutional provisions, the practical implementation of international human rights in these Arab countries often faces diverse challenges, a circumstance not unique to these nations but widespread in many Muslim countries. A prominent challenge arises from the prevailing perspective on individuals as custodians of rights and freedoms. In some cases, constitutions prioritize the rights of God over those of human beings, suggesting that individuals inherently carry responsibilities rather than rights. This outlook can relegate rights to a secondary position, subject to limitations imposed by the state, religion, or even revolutionary ideologies (Turner et al., 2011, p. 3).

The constraints placed on rights and liberties can be explicitly outlined in the constitution or may arise from subsequent statutory regulations.

For instance, Tunisia's constitution features a general provision allowing for restrictions on the exercise of ensured rights and freedoms, as outlined by the law. In contrast, other constitutions directly include limitations, as seen in Libya's 1969 Constitution, which ensures freedom of opinion within the bounds of public interest and the principles of the Revolution. Likewise, Article 24 of the Iranian Constitution imposes restrictions on the freedom of the press (Roznai, 2013, p. 560). These limitations underscore the complex hurdles involved in the practical application of human rights within these legal frameworks, often subject to the interpretations and considerations of the state and societal interests.

An apparent obstacle observed in these constitutions is the confinement of the application of most rights solely to the citizens of the respective countries. Although limitations on fundamental political rights, such as freedom of association and the right to vote, correspond to comparable provisions in the constitutions of various Western countries, the confinement of specific rights, such as the right to equality before the law, raises notable apprehensions. Ideally, these rights should be available to all individuals, including non-citizens. Nevertheless, restricting these rights exclusively to citizens presents a potential barrier to the comprehensive safeguarding of human rights within these nations. Additionally, a critical insufficiency arises from the absence of a specific supervisory and enforcement mechanism to address reported violations of rights guaranteed by the constitution. As a result, numerous provisions concerning rights and freedoms may lack practical significance due to the lack of a monitoring body capable of overseeing the proper implementation of these rights and, if necessary, referring alleged violations to a court of law. Nevertheless, a few exceptional cases exist where certain countries' constitutions have established monitoring mechanisms. For instance, the 2005 Interim Constitution of Sudan requires the formation of a Human Rights Commission, tasked with overseeing the application of constitutionally provided rights and freedoms, as well as handling complaints related to their infringement (The Interim National Constitution of the Republic of Sudan, 2005).

Likewise, within the Constitution of Morocco, Article 19 establishes an agency tasked with countering all types of discrimination, indicating a proactive stance in protecting human rights. Similarly, the Tunisian Constitution, under Article 128, highlights the establishment of a Human Rights Commission and delineates its precise responsibilities. These instances emphasize the importance of specialized oversight institutions in guaranteeing the protection and implementation of human rights within the legal structures of these nations. Such endeavors contribute to a more efficient preservation of individual freedoms and the advancement of fair treatment for all individuals, irrespective of their status as citizens.

In countries such as Egypt and Malaysia, the constitutional approach to human rights highlights their distinct political and social dynamics. Egypt's, 2014 Constitution offers an extensive framework that encompasses various human rights categories, from civil and political rights to socioeconomic entitlements. Despite the constitutional provisions, practical constraints on these rights have been observed, particularly during periods of political instability, leading to limitations in their application (Egypt, 2010). Similarly, the Malaysian Constitution guarantees essential liberties, including freedom of expression, assembly, and religion. However, the exercise of these rights is often subject to nuanced interpretations influenced by security concerns and cultural sensitivities, which may curtail their full realization. Consequently, while both countries make efforts to safeguard human rights, the practical implementation remains a complex and delicate balance between upholding individual freedoms and addressing broader national interests. An essential query arises regarding the impact of the identified limitations and shortcomings in formulating the constitutions on the actual status of human rights in the examined countries. It becomes apparent that a thorough and clear exposition of all essential rights would simplify their invocation and safeguarding by individuals. The Interim Constitution of Sudan and the Constitution of Tunisia serve as illustrations of this strategy, as they present a comprehensive and explicit delineation of rights and freedoms, leaving no room for ambiguity that a mere reference to the Universal Declaration of Human Rights might entail. By precisely outlining each right and freedom, these constitutions make them subject to legal interpretation and enforceability.

The lucidity and exactness achieved through thorough provisions in the constitution can substantially contribute to the efficient enforcement of human rights, granting individuals a strong legal foundation for seeking remedies in the event of violations. By guaranteeing that the rights are explicitly defined and enforceable, these constitutional frameworks cultivate a climate of answerability and act as a powerful instrument for individuals to assert their claims and contest any breaches. This approach not only improves legal assurance but also establishes a sturdy basis for a more resilient and equitable human rights system within these countries.

On the flip side, the lack of comprehensive provisions or the presence of unclear and ambiguous references to human rights can create uncertainty and impede the practical enforcement of these rights. The absence of a well-defined legal framework allows for interpretation, potentially resulting in inconsistencies in the application and safeguarding of human rights. Moreover, it can pose challenges for individuals seeking legal recourse, as the ambiguity in the constitutional language might hinder their ability to effectively assert their rights. Thus, the caliber of constitutional drafting significantly influences the broader human rights landscape, impacting the accessibility and enforceability of these rights within the legal framework of the relevant countries.

The consistent and troubling accounts from different impartial and credible international bodies about systematic human rights violations in various Arab nations give rise to important queries about the effectiveness of the respective constitutions in promoting genuine respect for these fundamental rights (An-Na'im, 2001, p. 705). In spite of the solemn affirmations within these constitutional documents, the observed disparity between the constitutional assurances and the widespread human rights transgressions calls for a thorough investigation into the factors influencing the effective execution of these rights. These reports highlight the discrepancy between the constitutional principles and the tangible circumstances on the field, prompting an investigation into the reasons behind this apparent disparity between legal provisions and their actual enforcement. Furthermore, it is worth considering whether these constitutions authentically mirror the intricate intricacies of political dynamics within these countries, particularly when they assert with emphasis that sovereignty rests in the people, who are declared as the ultimate origin of all authority. The contrast between these lofty declarations and the documented breaches of human rights indicates a substantial inconsistency that merits meticulous examination. It encourages an investigation into the degree to which the political realities and power arrangements within these nations correspond with the principles advocated in their individual constitutional structures.

Understanding the complex factors contributing to the disjunction between constitutional principles and the observed human rights violations requires a meticulous analysis of various intricate elements. Delving into the influence of intricate political power dynamics, the functioning of institutional frameworks, and the deeply embedded societal values is essential. By thoroughly examining the implementation and enforcement mechanisms outlined within these constitutions, along with scrutinizing the prevailing power dynamics and decisionmaking processes within these nations, we can gain profound insights into the intricate interplay between the principles outlined in the constitution and the ground realities. This rigorous investigation is vital for identifying the gaps and deficiencies within the legal and political systems and can serve as a solid groundwork for devising more robust strategies to foster and safeguard human rights in these Arab countries (An-Na'im, 2001, p. 706).

Crafting a constitution that successfully safeguards human rights demands a profound grasp of the societal, political, and legal intricacies involved. These complexities deeply impact a country's ability to defend its citizens' rights and liberties. Furthermore, effectively implementing these constitutional principles requires a strong administrative system equipped with the requisite resources and knowledge. A well-organised and effective administrative framework is vital for ensuring that the rights outlined in the constitution are enforced and achieved. Therefore, having a competent administrative structure is crucial for transforming constitutional assurances into concrete, significant results for individuals and communities. Additionally, effectively advocating for and safeguarding human rights require not only integrating these rights into a constitution as a fundamental framework but also fostering widespread awareness among individuals about their rights and responsibilities under the law. Empowering individuals with the knowledge and comprehension of their rights is essential for nurturing a culture that respects human rights and holds both the government and fellow citizens responsible for upholding these rights. This awareness can empower individuals to request the protection of their rights and actively engage in the procedures that ensure and promote these fundamental principles. At the same time, bolstering the administrative apparatus of the state is equally crucial in guaranteeing the effective and fair implementation of human rights legislation. A strong administrative system can streamline the application of legal regulations, thereby reducing the risk of human rights abuses and enabling individuals to seek legal recourse in the event of any violation of their rights. By fortifying both the institutional structure and the public's understanding of their rights, a conducive atmosphere can be cultivated, encouraging a culture that values human rights and contributing to the comprehensive advancement and welfare of society in its entirety.

6.3 Religious Freedom: Challenges and Initiatives

The Egyptian Constitution safeguards the freedom of religion, while officially recognising Islam as the state religion. Various articles within the constitution outline the provisions for protecting the rights of religious minorities in the country. Article 2 of the Egyptian Constitution designates Islam as the official state religion and declares Islamic law, or *shari'ah*, as the primary source of legislation. This declaration significantly impacts the legal system and governance of Egypt, influencing the interpretation and application of laws in line with Islamic principles. Furthermore, Article 3 emphasises the centrality of Islamic *sharī'ah* principles as the fundamental basis of legislation. This provision underscores the significant role of Islamic law in shaping the legal framework of the country, guiding the interpretation and implementation of laws related to personal status, family law, and inheritance, among other areas (Egypt, 2014).

In Egypt, while Islam holds a prominent position as the official state religion, the Egyptian Constitution acknowledges the fundamental right to religious freedom through Article 53. This provision guarantees individuals the liberty to observe their religious customs and establish places of worship for followers of the three Abrahamic religions—Islam, Christianity, and Judaism (Agrama, 2010, p. 498). The article serves to uphold the rights of religious minorities and ensure their unrestricted practice of their faith within the boundaries of the law. Additionally, Article 64 prohibits religious-based discrimination, reinforcing the principle of equality under the law and underscoring the government's dedication to safeguarding the rights of all citizens, regardless of their religious beliefs. Despite the constitutional provisions guaranteeing freedom of religion and equality, Egypt encounters obstacles in fully materializing these rights in reality. Reports of discrimination, social conflicts, and restrictions on the construction of religious sites for minority groups emphasize the necessity for sustained endeavors to defend and protect the freedom of individuals to practice their chosen religions without the fear of discrimination or retaliation.

The Egyptian Constitution encompasses several fundamental principles pertaining to the State and its populace, incorporating the principle of citizenship. It ensures complete freedom of faith and permits adherents of celestial religions to observe religious practices and establish places of worship. These individuals can consult their respective religious laws on personal and religious matters and possess the freedom to choose their spiritual guides. The Constitution recognizes the rich and diverse civilisational, cultural and religious legacy of Egypt. The formation of the National Council for Combating Terrorism and Extremism in 2017, under the leadership of the President, seeks to utilise institutional and social resources to counteract terrorism. This initiative involves devising a comprehensive national anti-terrorism strategy, coordinating both internally and externally, and nurturing a more balanced religious discourse. Additionally, the inception of the Supreme Committee for Combating Sectarian Incidents in 2018 through a Presidential Decree focuses on crafting strategies to encourage religious tolerance, handle sectarian tensions, and execute developmental projects in regions prone to sectarian conflicts.

Additionally, the Ministry of Higher Education introduced a plan to counter extremism and takfiri ideology in Egyptian Universities during 2019–2023. This comprehensive strategy aims to monitor various manifestations of *takfiri* ideology and evaluate the strengths and weaknesses associated with combating this ideology. The Ministry of Education, in its effort to promote tolerance and civic responsibility, restructured and filtered religious curricula to remove content that promotes intolerance, while incorporating an ethics curriculum. Likewise, the Ministry of Endowments dedicated numerous Friday sermons and seminars to advocate for tolerance and denounce violence and animosity. The initiation of the 'Prophet Muhammad - Messenger of All Mankind' campaign aimed to raise awareness of Prophet Muhammad's teachings, emphasising the rejection of violence and animosity (Kohstall, 2012, p. 91).

Al-Azhar Al-Sharif collaborates with Egyptian Churches under the initiative 'The Egyptian Family House,' emphasising the significance of citizenship values, tolerance and dialogue. It produces various publications and updates educational curricula to promote human rights, citizenship principles, peaceful coexistence, and combat extremism. Additionally, *Dar Al-Iftaa* has introduced multiple research projects and initiatives to rejuvenate religious discourse, counter extremist ideologies, and conduct programs for the preparation and training of muftis and scholars globally (Periodic Report of Egypt to the African Commission on Human and Peoples Rights for 2017). Additionally, the Egyptian government implemented a program to restore various historic sites in Egypt, including Jewish temples, tombs, and religious landmarks along the Holy

Family Journey. Law No. 80 of 2016 was introduced to oversee the construction of churches, simplifying the process for obtaining permits and regularizing establishments that host Christian ceremonies. The legal status of approximately 1800 churches and structures was formalized, and the government launched initiatives to repair damaged churches and build the largest cathedral in Egypt and the Middle East in the New Administrative Capital. Law No. 190 of 2020 established endowment institutions for the Catholic and Evangelical Churches (Periodic Report of Egypt to the African Commission on Human and Peoples Rights for 2017). There is a concern about the influence of extremist ideology on some youth, leading to their involvement in violence and terrorism. Renewing the religious discourse to promote tolerance and reject extremism is seen as a crucial step. Additionally, the review of religious curricula to eliminate any content that promotes intolerance, violence, and extremism is deemed necessary. Efforts to promote a culture of human rights and respect for different beliefs are also recognized as important. Furthermore, the spread of discriminatory narratives based on religion in certain newspapers and websites is seen as a challenge.

On a contrasting landscape, the Malaysian Constitution upholds the protection of religious freedom through several key provisions, ensuring the defense of the rights of individuals from diverse faiths within the country. Article 11 of the Malaysian Federal Constitution specifically addresses the freedom of religion, highlighting every individual's entitlement to practice their religious beliefs, albeit with certain constraints related to public order, morality, or health. This provision serves as a vital safeguard to enable individuals to freely engage in their religious practices without undue intervention from authorities. Additionally, Article 3 of the Constitution designates Islam as the nation's official religion while also affirming the rights of non-Muslims to peacefully practice their own religions. This constitutional clause underscores Malaysia's commitment to preserving religious harmony and respecting the rights of religious minorities. Despite the constitutional assurance of religious freedom, certain limitations and restrictions have been implemented, leading to occasional discussions and disputes about the extent of religious freedoms in the country.

In Malaysia, issues like limitations on religious conversions, constraints on the dissemination of specific religious beliefs, and conflicts between civil and *sharīʿah* law have occasionally hindered the complete realization of religious rights for all individuals Additionally, the constitution outlines acceptable limitations, with Article 11(1) stressing the importance of religious practices not disrupting peace and harmony. Article 11(5) further specifies that no actions contradicting general laws on public order, public health, or morality can be permitted, highlighting the parliamentary control over religious conduct based on these criteria. Furthermore, there exist additional restrictions for Muslims, which grants State Assemblies the authority to impose penalties on Muslims for violating Islamic principles. This provision is commonly employed to address various activities deemed as un-Islamic, including close proximity, adultery, gambling, drinking, beauty contests and behaviors considered deviant.

There has been a growing discourse surrounding the freedom to disseminate religious beliefs among Muslims in Malaysia, as outlined in Article 11(4) of the Federal Constitution. Arguments have surfaced indicating that federal or state laws may potentially impose restrictions on this particular right. Regulations governing the propagation of religious beliefs primarily serve to shield Muslims from exposure to unorthodox religious doctrines, regardless of their origin or the identity of the individuals involved in spreading them. Some scholars suggest that the inclusion of Article 11(4) was intended to safeguard Malays from external proselytization efforts, which had gained prominence during the colonial period. Notably, the act of renouncing Islam by a Malay individual might signify a detachment from the wider Malay community, reflecting concerns encompassing ethnicity and politics alongside considerations for public order. Consequently, the dissemination of religious teachings to Muslims, whether by non-Muslims or unauthorized Muslims, is subject to regulation under state law. This regulation, primarily intended to address issues related to religious conversion, has sparked extensive debates in Malaysia, posing significant challenges to the fundamental principle of religious freedom.

In the context of conversions of minors, the Teoh Eng Huat case highlighted that children under 18 are obliged to adhere to their parents' religious choices. This decision played a significant role in diffusing potential controversies surrounding the exploitation of minors for religious purposes, a matter of considerable political sensitivity in Malaysia. The Supreme Court's decision to overturn the High Court's ruling emphasised the importance of upholding the principles of a diverse and multi-religious society in the country. The highly debated Administration of the Religion of Islam (Federal Territories) Bill 2013, allowing a child's conversion with the consent of only one parent, was withdrawn by the

Cabinet following extensive public discussions. Currently, the regulation concerning the religious rights of minors is governed by Article 12(4) of the Constitution, in conjunction with Article 160 and the Eleventh Schedule, promoting an inclusive and comprehensive approach to interpreting the law in terms of gender and pluralistic understanding. While some restrictions on religious freedom in Malaysia may seemingly contradict Article 18 of the Universal Declaration of Human Rights (UDHR), it can be argued that these limitations are justified within the framework of upholding public morality, safety, order, health, and general welfare in a democratic society, in accordance with international law. Despite the ongoing debates over these limitations, it remains imperative to uphold globally recognized human rights standards, particularly in safeguarding the rights to religious conversion and the public expression of religious beliefs.

6.4 Freedom of Speech and Expression: Constitutional Provisions and Practical Realities

Lately, the status of freedom of speech and expression in Egypt has been closely examined, characterised by a complicated interaction of legal limitations, societal pressures, and political complexities. Despite the constitutional assurance of freedom of expression, various constraints and obstacles have impeded its complete realisation. Article 65 of the Egyptian Constitution supports the right to freedom of thought and opinion, safeguarding the liberty to express one's viewpoints through different platforms, including the press, media, and other communication channels. However, this entitlement is subject to limitations specified in the law, with the aim of protecting national security, public order, and public decency. These legal regulations have been utilised to restrict freedom of expression, resulting in censorship, crackdowns on opposing views, and the prosecution of individuals for voicing opinions deemed critical of the government or conflicting with societal standards (Youssef, 2012). The Egyptian government has, in practice, employed various tactics to suppress freedom of speech and expression, resorting to stringent laws targeting defamation, blasphemy, and national security. As a consequence, journalists, activists, and individuals who have expressed dissenting views or criticized governmental policies have faced detention and legal proceedings. These actions have prompted concerns from international human rights organizations, underscoring the necessity for heightened safeguards for freedom of expression and the cultivation of an atmosphere conducive to open discussion and constructive critique. Furthermore, the digital realm has also emerged as a primary arena for constraints on freedom of expression, with the introduction of legislation governing online content and social media engagement. These measures have faced censure for their potential to inhibit online dialogue and restrict the scope for the unrestricted exchange of thoughts and information (Digital Authoritarianism in Egypt, 2015).

The Constitution ensures the right to freedom of thinking and viewpoint, granting individuals the privilege to express themselves through verbal communication, written material, visuals, and other means of transmission, encompassing diverse media platforms such as the press, as well as printed, audio, and digital publications. Additionally, the Constitution establishes autonomous institutional bodies to supervise media and press operations, assuring their unbiased and self-reliant functioning. Furthermore, the legislation safeguards the liberty of the press, media, printing, and dissemination in different formats, including newspapers, in accordance with the Constitution. It explicitly prohibits any kind of censorship, confiscation, suspension, or shutdown of newspapers and media platforms, except during limited censorship instances in times of war or national mobilization. The law also protects journalists and media professionals from legal repercussions for expressing their opinions, securing their right to access and distribute information. It prohibits the coercion of journalists to disclose their sources and forbids punitive actions that curtail the freedom of individuals for offenses committed through publication or publicity, with the exception of crimes involving incitement to violence, discrimination, or defamation of character. Egypt's media and press panorama is varied, encompassing both public and private institutions catering to different general and specialised interests (Supreme Standing Committee for Human Rights, 2021–2026). Challenges include the absence of a legal framework regulating the access to and dissemination of official information, data, and statistics, despite it being constitutionally guaranteed. In addition, the multiplicity of media platforms falls short in adequately reflecting diverse perspectives and opinions, highlighting the need for comprehensive guidelines governing all forms of media and press, ensuring the responsible exercise of freedom of expression without encroaching upon the rights of others. Furthermore, there is a pressing need to improve public awareness regarding the implementation of freedom of expression and its associated boundaries.

To achieve the desired outcomes, it is crucial to enact comprehensive legislation overseeing the accessibility of official information, data, and statistics, while fostering an inclusive environment that encourages diverse viewpoints on public matters. Efforts must also be made to safeguard the rights of media professionals and journalists, with particular attention paid to upholding constitutional provisions and relevant laws. Strengthening the practice of freedom of speech should involve the implementation of effective measures to address any infractions, ensuring alignment with both the Constitution and Egypt's international commitments through regular legislative assessments. Introducing a comprehensive ethical code for all forms of media, including digital and social media, will help ensure the responsible exercise of freedom of expression while respecting the rights of others, drawing from global best practices and in accordance with both the Constitution and international obligations. Public awareness regarding the significance of freedom of expression should be elevated through educational workshops for media practitioners, fostering a deeper understanding of the constraints associated with this freedom and potential violations.

On the other hand, in Malaysia, the domain of freedom of speech and expression has encountered a range of obstacles and limitations, reflecting a delicate balance between upholding public order, ensuring national security, and safeguarding individual rights. Although the Malaysian constitution guarantees the freedom of speech and expression, certain legal constraints and societal influences have, on occasion, restricted the complete exercise of this entitlement. Article 10 of the Malaysian Federal Constitution explicitly addresses freedom of speech and expression, allowing individuals the liberty to express their viewpoints and thoughts, with certain limitations imposed for reasons related to national security, public order, or morality. However, the interpretation and application of these limitations have, in some cases, resulted in the repression of dissenting opinions, legal prosecution for critical expressions, and the enforcement of censorship on various media formats (Digital Authoritarianism in Egypt, 2015). Additionally, legal regulations such as the Sedition Act and the Communications and Multimedia Act have been utilized to limit freedom of expression, leading to the detention and prosecution of individuals for allegedly disseminating content deemed seditious or offensive. These actions have raised concerns among human rights organizations and international observers, who have called for stronger protections for freedom of speech and expression in Malaysia. Moreover, issues concerning religious sensitivities and tensions between different ethnic groups have occasionally influenced the restrictions on freedom of speech, particularly in discussions about sensitive topics like religion, ethnicity, and the monarchy. Criticisms aimed at specific individuals or institutions have at times resulted in legal actions, fostering self-censorship and a climate of caution among journalists, activists, and individuals expressing dissenting viewpoints.

As noted by Masum, the act of expressing personal viewpoints through freedom of speech plays a pivotal role in sustaining a society built on liberty (Masum, 2009, p. 34). Nonetheless, the scope of these rights is limited due to established legal provisions within Malaysia (Wan Khairuldin, et al., 2017, p. 908). Across Articles 10, 11, 149, and 150, there are 16 acceptable constraints on freedom of expression. Faruqi points out 12 specific restrictions outlined in Article 10, including considerations of security, international relations, public order, moral values, parliamentary privileges, contempt of court, criticism, and impact on criminal activities. Moreover, any criticism regarding citizenship, the status of the Malay language, the specific stipulations of Article 153, and the rights of the Malay rulers requires parliamentary approval (Faruqi, 2018). The Parliament has implemented about 35 resolutions, utilising its constitutional authority to address issues related to freedom of speech, freedom of the press, and the right to assembly and association, which is crucial to the exercise of freedom of speech. However, these laws often involve comprehensive regulations, granting authorities extensive powers and discretion. For example, the University and University College Act prohibits politically motivated research without adhering to public requirements and other restrictions.

The handling, retention, and dissemination of government information are explicitly restricted as confidential under the Official Secrets Act of 1972, with no consideration for its relevance to disclosures or national security. Furthermore, the Printing Presses and Publishing Act of 1984 confers the minister with the meticulous authority to evaluate and make decisions on printing licenses, including granting, denying, suspending, or revoking them. Emphasizing the duties of Malaysian citizenship, the constitution underscores the responsibilities of individuals. Despite the provisions in Article 10(1) of the Constitution, opposition is faced against dissenting actions, discouraging excessive speech and hasty judgments. Within Article 10(4) of the Federal Constitution, specific constraints are outlined, allowing Parliament to enact laws prohibiting various issues, norms, and interests related to the management of matters other than its own laws and regulations. Part III delves into the examination of the application of legally determined provisions within Articles 152, 153, and 182 (Wan Khairuldin, et al., 2017, p. 910). Additionally, the suspension of the freedom of assessment in Article 149 of the Federal Constitution highlights evident inconsistencies within the Constitution, particularly in Articles 10(1) and 149.

Recognized globally as a fundamental entitlement, freedom of expression is a critical aspect of democratic societies. However, within the Malaysian legal framework, specifically under Article 10 of the Federal Constitution, this right is exclusively reserved for citizens. Despite the substantial presence of non-citizens, such as participants in the "Malaysia My Second Hometown" (MM2H) initiative, Article 10 fails to extend its protection to these individuals, creating a gap in safeguarding their freedom of speech. Consequently, nonMalaysian citizens, including long-term residents like MM2H participants, are denied this fundamental right, raising significant concerns given their sizable population in the country. The absence of non-citizens from the provisions protecting freedom of speech and expression within Malaysian law underscores the need for a more inclusive legal framework that guarantees this fundamental right for all individuals, regardless of citizenship (Mia et al., 2021, p. 51).

6.5 Recommendations

Various initiatives should be taken to raise awareness, particularly among young people, with the aim of promoting coexistence, tolerance and the acceptance of others. These programs are meant to instill values and teachings derived from celestial religions while also fostering critical thinking skills among the youth. Furthermore, youth-led projects should be launched to foster a sense of citizenship and belonging, alongside efforts to increase public awareness of religious freedoms and reinforce national identity. These endeavors also target the mitigation of intolerance and extremist ideologies. Moreover, there should be enhanced collaboration among religious institutions to implement strategies for revitalizing religious discourse, advocating for tolerance and dispelling extremist and misguided beliefs. Ongoing actions involve the continuous review of all religious educational materials, focusing on eliminating content that does not contribute to the promotion of tolerance or the rejection of violence and extremism.

New educational content should be introduced to encourage dialogue, embrace diversity, and combat various forms of hatred and intolerance (Supreme Standing Committed for Human Rights, 2021–2026). In addition to these measures, national endeavors should be undertaken to cultivate a culture of respect for human rights, reinforce the values of citizenship, raise awareness about religious freedoms, and denounce intolerance and extremist ideologies. Monitoring of media content, including online platforms and newspapers that perpetuate discrimination based on religion or incite hatred, should be carried out to facilitate appropriate legal action when necessary. Furthermore, the government and relevant authorities continue their commitment to the preservation and restoration of religious landmarks, spanning Islamic, Christian, and Jewish sites, to showcase Egypt's diverse historical heritage. Additionally, the committee tasked with regularizing the status of churches remains dedicated to extending its efforts to encompass other churches and associated structures that are yet to undergo the regularization process.

In order to enhance the promotion and protection of human rights in Malaysia, it is recommended that the country becomes a party to several international human rights instruments, including the International Covenant on Civil and Political Rights (ICCPR), the International Covenant on Economic, Social and Cultural Rights (ICESCR), the International Convention on the Elimination of All Forms of Racial Discrimination (ICERD), the Convention against Torture and Other Cruel, Inhuman, or Degrading Treatment or Punishment (CAT), the International Convention on the Protection of the Rights of All Migrant Workers and Members of Their Families (ICPMW), the International Convention for the Protection of All Persons from Enforced Disappearance (ICPPED), and other core UN human rights instruments. Additionally, it is crucial for Malaysia to uphold the commitments made to the 73rd United Nations Assembly by Prime Minister Mahathir Mohamad. The country should also reconsider its reservations to the Convention on the Elimination of all Forms of Discrimination against Women (CEDAW), the Convention on the Rights of the Child (CRC), and the Convention on the Rights of Persons with Disabilities (CRPD) to ensure alignment with the objectives of these treaties (Challenges to Freedom of Religion or Belief in Malaysia, 2019).

Furthermore, there is a pressing need to enforce the provisions of the Constitution, particularly Article 11, in accordance with the right to freedom of religion or belief as enshrined in international human rights instruments. This necessitates the removal of any constraints on proselytism and the reinforcement of safeguards for religious minorities and non-believers. The cessation of harassment, arrests, detentions, forced "rehabilitation," and selective targeting of religious minorities is crucial to enable them to exercise their freedom of religion or belief without any interference from the State. To achieve this, the application of security laws against religious minorities should be terminated. In addition, the unconditional release of individuals imprisoned solely based on charges related to the peaceful practice of their religion, as protected by international human rights law, is paramount. To foster better engagement with Islamic religious authorities, the establishment of a commission or working group aimed at preventing actions that threaten the rights of religious minorities, penalize apostasy, and impose restrictions on religious practices is recommended. Lastly, there is a need to repeal or revise legal provisions that currently allow the marriage of children under the age of 18, aligning with international standards and human rights principles.

To promote equality and protect the rights of all individuals in Egypt, it is crucial to revise the 2014 Constitution to ensure the recognition of various communities as equal citizens, guaranteeing their rights to identity, language, religion, culture, and the formation of their own associations. Additionally, discriminatory clauses, including the limitation of legal recognition to specific religions, should be eliminated, with the provision of Islamic *sharīʿah* principles in Article 2 replaced by a civic code for personal status affairs. Legislation prohibiting hate speech and incitement, comprehensive anti-discrimination laws, and the establishment of an antidiscrimination commission with effective reporting mechanisms are also essential. Specialized training for police and judicial officials on minority issues, prioritising the protection of victims of communal violence, and respecting the rights of minorities to practice their language and culture freely are crucial steps. Furthermore, ensuring the rights of all religious communities, including those not currently recognized in Egyptian law, supporting the resettlement of the Nubian population, and protecting residents of North Sinai, particularly the Bedouin, during military operations are imperative measures. Thorough investigations into allegations of official abuse, including arbitrary arrests, torture, and extra-judicial killings, are necessary to address ongoing human rights violations and historical injustices (Challenges to Freedom of Religion or Belief in Malaysia, 2019).

To ensure the protection of equality and non-discrimination in Malaysia, comprehensive constitutional and legislative measures must be implemented. This includes broadening the grounds of protection in the Federal Constitution to encompass both citizens and non-citizens, as well as defining discriminatory behaviours across all sectors. The removal of personal laws from anti-discrimination regulations and the potential elimination of preferential treatment in Islamic educational institutions should also be considered. Strengthening existing constitutional safeguards through comprehensive equality legislation is essential to eliminate all forms of discrimination and harassment. A thorough review of the Persons with Disabilities Act 2008 is necessary to align it with Malaysia's obligations under the CRPD, enabling the enforcement of rights through appropriate channels. Involving affected groups in decisionmaking processes and implementing positive action measures for marginalized groups can help overcome historical disadvantages and promote equality. By implementing these recommendations, Malaysia can fortify its legal framework, promote inclusivity, and foster a more equitable and unified society for all its citizens.

References

Agrama, H. A. (2010). Secularism, sovereignty, indeterminacy: Is Egypt a secular or a religious state? *Comparative Studies in Society and History, 52*(3), 495–523.

An-Na'im, A. A. (2001). Human rights in the Arab world: A regional perspective. *Human Rights Quarterly, 23*(3), 701–732.

Challenges to freedom of religion or belief in Malaysia: A briefing paper March 2019. Retrieved April, 7, 2024, from https://www.icj.org/wp-content/uploads/2019/03/MalaysiaFreedom-of-religion-brief-Advocacy-Analysis-brief-2019-ENG.pdf

Digital Authoritarianism in Egypt: Digital Expression Arrests 2011–2019. (2019). Retrieved April 7, 2024, from https://public.opentech.fund/documents/EgyptReportV06.pdf

Egypt. (2014). Retrieved April 7, 2024, from https://www.constituteproject.org/constitution/Egypt_2014

Faruqi, S. S. (2018). Reform needed to protect free speech. Retrieved April 7, 2024, from https://www.thestar.com.my/opinion/columnists/reflecting-on-the-law/2018/09/27/reformneeded-to-protect-free-speech-we-need-an-independent-law-reform-commission-toscrutinise-the#cJckxaGsAPQgkuM2

Kohstall, F. (2012). Free transfer, limited mobility: A decade of higher education reform in Egypt and Morocco. *Revue Des Mondes Musulmans Et De La Méditerranée, 131*, 91–109.

Mahmoudi, S. (2016). International human rights law as a framework for emerging constitutions in Arab countries. In R. Grote & T. J. Röder (Eds.), *Constitutionalism, human rights, and Islam after the Arab Spring* (pp. 535–542). Oxford University Press.

Masum, A. (2009). Freedom of speech and the internet—A case study of Malaysia. *Malayan Law Journal, 3*, 34.

Mia, M. T., Islam, M. Z., & Norullah, M. (2021). Freedom of speech and expression in Malaysia: Protection under the Federal Constitution. *SARJANA, 36*(2), 48–62.

Periodic Report of Egypt to the African Commission on Human and Peoples Rights for 2017. (2017). Retrieved April, 7, 2024, from https://hrightsstudies.sis.gov.eg/media/2004/egypt_periodic_report_eng.pdf

Roznai, Y. (2013). The theory and practice of 'Supra-Constitutional' limits on constitutional amendments. *International and Comparative Law Quarterly, 62*(3), 557–597.

Supreme Standing Committee for Human Rights. (2021). National human rights strategy, the Arab Republic of Egypt: 2021–2026. Retrieved April 7, 2024, from https://sschr.gov.eg/media/gapb5bq4/national-human-rights-strategy.pdf

The Interim National Constitution of the Republic of The Sudan. (2005). Retrieved April 7, 2024, from https://www.peaceagreements.org/viewmasterdocument/1800

Turner, B. S., Possamai, A., & Barbal, J. (2011). States, consumption and managing religions. In J. Barbalet, A. Possamai, & B. S. Turner (Eds.), *Religion and the state: A comparative sociology* (pp. 1–24). Anthem Press.

Wan Khairuldin, W. M. K. F., Embong, A. H., Nor Anas, W. N. I. W., Ibtisam Ibrahim, D. I., & Fauzi, N. (2017). Freedom of speech: A comparative study between Islam and Malaysian laws. *International Journal of Academic Research in Business and Social Sciences, 7*(2), 908–915.

Youssef, N. (2012, November 30). Egypt's draft constitution translated. *Al Masry al Youm*. Retrieved April 7, 2024, from https://www.ilo.org/dyn/natlex/docs/ELECTRONIC/91655/106411/F 196699313/Egypt.pdf

Index

A. Mohiuddin, *Human Rights Law in Egypt and Malaysia: Freedom of Religion and Expression, Volume 1*, Political Economy of Islam,
https://doi.org/10.1007/978-3-031-63859-6

J

K

L

T

U

GPSR Compliance
The European Union's (EU) General Product Safety Regulation (GPSR) is a set of rules that requires consumer products to be safe and our obligations to ensure this.

If you have any concerns about our products, you can contact us on

ProductSafety@springernature.com

In case Publisher is established outside the EU, the EU authorized representative is:

Springer Nature Customer Service Center GmbH
Europaplatz 3
69115 Heidelberg, Germany

www.ingramcontent.com/pod-product-compliance
Lightning Source LLC
Chambersburg PA
CBHW080602040725
29063CB00066BA/68
* 9 7 8 3 0 3 1 6 3 8 5 8 9 *